BOOK CRUSH

NANCY PEARL

FOR KIDS AND TEENS—RECOMMENDED READING FOR EVERY MOOD, MOMENT, AND INTEREST

SASQUATCH BOOKS
SEATTLE

12/07

Printed in the United States of America
Published by Sasquatch Books
Distributed by Publishers Group West
15 14 13 12 11 10 09 08 07   9 8 7 6 5 4 3 2 1

Cover photograph: Noel Hendrickson / Digital Vision / Getty Images
Cover design: Judith Stagnitto Abbate / Abbate Design
Author photo: Marco Prozzo
Interior design: Rowan Moore-Seifred
Interior illustrations: Sarah Plein
Interior composition: Sarah Plein

Library of Congress Cataloging-in-Publication Data is available.

ISBN 1-57061-500-4

Sasquatch Books
119 South Main Street, Suite 400
Seattle, WA 98104
(206) 467-4300
www.sasquatchbooks.com
custserv@sasquatchbooks.com

Contents

INTRODUCTION

My happiest memories of a childhood that was otherwise scarred by an anxious and raging father and a depressed and angry mother were of escaping into books. I read. I went to the Parkman branch of the Detroit Public Library after school and on Saturdays, checked out armloads of books, brought them home, and read. I climbed the apricot tree in our backyard and, wishing I had a tree house just like Suzie Green, one of the two main characters in the Best Friends series by Mary Bard, I read. I closed my bedroom door, risking my father's incomprehensible and unpredictable wrath, lay on my stomach on my bed, and read. (Looking back now, one of the things I most regret is that I didn't keep a list of those books. While my memory is pretty good, I know there are many books that I've simply forgotten.)

My parents, despite their other flaws, were readers. And though I don't have any memories of being read to, there were certainly a lot of books around. (Two I remember picking up and paging through, although I can't link either to any particular age: **The Naked and the Dead** by Norman Mailer and **Dr. Spock's Baby and Child Care**. I was struck by the fact that despite having lots of dialogue, there were no quotation marks in Mailer's book. What impressed me about the Dr. Spock book was not the advice, but the cute line drawings on many pages—those kids looked so happy.)

I was very fortunate to have a cadre of librarians, both at the public library and my elementary and high school libraries, who happily and caringly fed my reading needs.

Although I included a few books for children and teens in *Book Lust: Recommended Reading for Every Mood, Moment, and Reason* and

More Book Lust: 1,000 New Reading Recommendations for Every Mood, Moment, and Reason, I thought that it would be fun for me, and useful for parents, teachers, librarians, and other adults who lived or worked with children, to write a book devoted solely to great reads for kids and teens. And while I was mulling that thought over, teen librarian Marin Younker e-mailed me and suggested that I write a book called *Book Crush*, filled with recommendations and suggestions of good reads for children and teens.

It never occurred to me that writing *Book Crush* might be more difficult than either *Book Lust* or *More Book Lust* had been. After all, I had wanted to be a children's librarian since I was ten years old; my first job when I finished library school at the University of Michigan was as a children's librarian in the Detroit Public Library system. Even though my subsequent jobs in bookstores and libraries had been more focused on adult materials, I kept up with the field, always reading at least every year's award winners, if nothing else.

So who knew?

I realized that before I could even begin writing, I had to think through two thorny issues. The first was how the books in *Book Crush* should be arranged. With my first two books, it was easy: one alphabetically arranged list of categories, from, as in *Book Lust*, "A, My Name Is Alice" to "Zero: This Will Mean Nothing to You." But I thought that a book for children and teens wouldn't work that way, would it? Surely readers of the book—parents, teachers, grandparents, librarians—would want some indication of what age the books were intended for.

My original idea was that I could use one alphabet of topics and make creative use of fonts to designate the three broad age groupings—birth to age seven, eight- to twelve-year-olds, and teens, for example.

At first this seemed like a perfect solution. By juxtaposing the different age groupings in the same list, it would automatically expose readers to books "older" and/or "younger" than those for which they were specifically looking. For example, there are many great books for all age groups that feature strong and unquenchable young women, and I compiled them under the heading "Girls Rule." The list looked like this:

Abuela   *Pippi Longstocking*

The Cry of the Icemark   **Swamp Angel**

The Misadventures of Maude March

But then a saner voice (my own, but in its saner mode) prevailed. The fonts were extremely difficult to read; even I, who had chosen them, was having trouble remembering which font indicated which age group. Clearly, despite the fact that I believe strongly in opening up the world of books and reading through minimal labeling and divisions, I needed to come up with some way of arranging the books sans imaginative fonts.

In the end, I decided to divide the books into three broad age categories, and then come up with topics to reflect the books I chose to include. My advice is to use these categories as a first step in finding age-appropriate titles, but to keep in mind that readers of the same age can vary greatly in the books they're ready for and will enjoy. The suggested categories shouldn't be thought of as ruling out either younger or older readers.

Once I had the general arrangement of *Book Crush* figured out and was madly reading and rereading away, I had to face another issue: what to do with those titles, mostly published before 1960, that feature ethnic characters who appear to our modern eyes to be stereotypical or who are presented in a negative light. I could easily see how a young Native American child might feel both hurt and upset to read, for example, **Caddie Woodlawn, The Courage of Sarah Noble,** or **Little House in the Big Woods,** with their stereotyped, one-sided portrayals of American Indians. In lots of these otherwise perfectly wonderful books, anyone other than a Caucasian is frequently portrayed as being either stupid or evil (or sometimes both).

In many cases, I chose to include such books when I thought their overall quality justified it. While I recognize that these books can be painful to read, I think they can also be excellent conversation starters to help young readers see how our dominant culture's ideas about race and ethnicity have changed over the years. These books offer a ready-made opportunity to talk about what makes a character three-dimensional as opposed to being stereotypical, whether or not some people might still stereotype others who are different than they are, and how we might all work to overcome such destructive attitudes. I recognize that this is not a stance that will be popular with everyone, but I believe that there is an opportunity for reading and discussion to help make the world a better place.

Librarians like to say that there's something in their library to offend everyone—it wouldn't be a library, otherwise. The same is true of this book, which I like to think of as a small library catalog devoted to books for children and teens. There may be areas or subjects that you don't want your child to encounter, say fantasies or books about death and dying. If you are at all concerned about a book your child or teen might read, my best advice is to read the book first. Don't rely totally on anyone else's description or recommendation. Not even mine.

Another consideration in suggesting books for the children and teens in your life is what I call emotional readiness. Often a child or teen is able to read (understands the meaning of the words) a book well before he or she is emotionally equipped to deal with the subject matter. At one talk I gave, a mother described her eight-year-old son's reaction to reading Ursula K. Le Guin's **A Wizard of Earthsea**—he burst into tears when he finished it. While a reaction like this to a book at any age is painful, and painful to observe in a child, I can also see that it could be a valuable growth experience, even for an eight-year-old, and not one that he would regret later on (or even at the time). However, a parent's emotional support and comforting would certainly be called for, until the reader develops the tools to comfort him- or herself.

Le Guin's coming-of-age fantasy of a young boy growing into his destiny as the greatest wizard in all of Earthsea is awesome. It's intelligent, it's fast moving, it's not to be missed. (I remember when I first read it I thought that Ged's education in sorcery was the way Gandalf, in Tolkien's books, must have been trained as well.) I reread it often. Yet it contains ideas and events that are beyond the full understanding of an eight-year-old, no matter the grade level at which he or she is reading. Not that the book will harm anyone (I've never found that reading any particular book has seriously harmed any child), but he or she will miss out on many of the nuances that make the book so powerful. And the child may never go back to that book again.

I fear the same sort of situation arises with the Harry Potter books. When J. K. Rowling's **Harry Potter and the Sorcerer's Stone** was first published, millions of eight- to ten-year-olds devoured it (as did their older brothers and sisters, their parents, and their grandparents). And rightly so. It was a perfect choice for them—a three-dimensional hero near to their own age, a splendidly evoked world, and magic. Then we all waited for about two years for the second book to come out, then we waited a few years more for the third, and so on. By the time the really heavy stuff started happening (the true nature of evil being revealed, the deaths of beloved characters, a recognition that the world is not a particularly safe place), those original eight- and nine-year-old readers were in their teens, where such knowledge can be more easily assimilated and their knowledge of the ways of the world is broader. As the books grew in complexity (and length), the readers grew, too.

But what's happening now is that eight-year-olds are starting with the first Harry Potter and immediately reading all the rest in the series, so that they're confronting those terrible events with not a lot of emotional body armor. Again, it's probably not going to hurt them—they'll just miss a lot of what makes the Rowling books so great. And that would be unfortunate. I don't have an answer to this, except that I think it's important that adults suggesting reading material to young people be aware of it.

I do think that in general a sort of protective self-selection usually operates in reading (as opposed to television and film, where the material is more forced upon the viewer, rather than actively assimilated and interpreted, as it is in reading). The problem arises when children are guided to books based on their reading-level readiness rather than their emotional readiness; they simply won't appreciate all that the books have to offer. Indeed, they may then find the experience of reading books, generally, less fulfilling than it could be. In that regard, it would be interesting to examine the experience of those children who start reading the Harry Potter books at eight, and attempt to read them all straight through. Do they gradually lose interest or enthusiasm?

I am frequently asked how to encourage children to read, or read more. Here's my four-step plan: First, introduce reluctant readers to books that match their interests. Is a teen passionate about bicycling? Try Lance Armstrong's memoir, **It's Not About the Bike: My Journey Back to Life.** A ten-year-old who loves computer games? Give him Terry Pratchett's **Only You Can Save Mankind**; if he's a bit older, hand him **Snow Crash** by Neal Stephenson. Crazy about horses? Don't let her grow up without the opportunity to cry over Anna Sewell's **Black Beauty.** *Book Crush* offers some good suggestions in a large variety of subjects, and your school or public librarian can surely help, as well.

Second, it's a great idea for families to set aside half an hour, after dinner, to all sit down together and read. This can be a time when each person reads his or her own book, or it can be a time to read aloud a book the whole family might enjoy, such as John D. Fitzgerald's **The Great Brain,** Farley Mowat's **The Dog Who Wouldn't Be,** J. R. R. Tolkien's **The Hobbit,** or M. T. Anderson's **Whales on Stilts,** to name just a few. This shouldn't be a time set aside only for the children in the family; it's vital that everyone have this time every day to lose themselves in a good book.

Third, I believe that reading should never be referred to or used as a punishment—none of that "no more television until you read your book." I hate the thought that otherwise well-meaning adults are doling out books as things that are good for kids and teens rather than as sources of pure pleasure, excitement, and interesting ideas and information. Reading a book is not something to be gotten through before you go on to the really great parts of your day; it should (and can) be something that makes the day a great one.

Fourth, encourage children not to feel compelled to finish every book they start. It's silly for readers, no matter what their age, to slog through a book that they're not enjoying simply because they've been taught to finish what they start. Nine times out of ten, what determines whether or not you'll like a book is your mood at the time you're reading it. And reading moods change often. This is no less true for children and teens as it is for adult readers. The world of books is large (and growing larger even as I write this) and gorgeously diverse; there's something for everyone. There are books to enrich the senses and enlighten the mind, family stories, biographies and memoirs, science and science fiction, love stories, and gripping adventure tales. If someone finds Esther Forbes's **Johnny Tremain** slow-going today, that doesn't preclude him or her picking it up in a month or a year and trying it again, only to discover that at that later moment it's absolutely the right book at the right time.

So how much of a book should children or teens read before giving up on it? If it's a school assignment or for a book club, they ought to finish it, of course. But otherwise, have children or teens give a book three chapters. If they're enjoying it, terrific. Read on. But if not, encourage them to put the book down, return it to the library or lend it to a friend, and pick up another and try that one. There are books galore in *Book Crush* that will match any mood, interest, moment, or reason to read. My hope is that you'll find here hours and hours, days and days, of wonderful reading for the children and teens in your life.

And I'd love to hear from you and the young readers in your world. Let me know what worked, what flopped, what discoveries you've made as you interact with children, teens, and good books. My e-mail is nancy@nancypearl.com.

ACKNOWLEDGMENTS

While I was working on *Book Crush*, I had the pleasure of working with a large number of people—librarians, parents, teachers, and readers of all ages, shapes, and sizes. I took every opportunity to talk to kids about the books they loved while I was waiting at airports, at restaurants and coffee shops, and in classrooms and libraries. I talked to parents and librarians not only about the books their children read, but also about the books that they remembered reading and enjoying when they themselves were children.

During this period I had the opportunity to be part of the 2006 English Festival held by the English Department of Youngstown State University, in Ohio. For three days I met with seventh- to twelfth-grade kids and talked to them about what they were reading, how they defined a "good book," and what they would especially recommend to their peers. These kids were reading it all—Stephen King, Neil Gaiman, Robin McKinley, M. T. Anderson, Elie Wiesel, Tamora Pierce, Robin McKinley, J. K. Rowling, Dan Brown, and everything in between. I was especially pleased to learn that many of the books they loved were books I had already read, enjoyed, and have included in *Book Crush*. Not only did my visit to the English Festival provide me with *lots* of suggestions of many new titles to read, but it also renewed my faith in the future of books and reading. For information about the Festival, contact the English Department at YSU, Youngstown, Ohio.

I want to especially thank the following people who helped in one way or another with this book: Michelle Alleman; Jennifer Amerson; Karen Andring; Elinor Appel; Shelley Armstrong; Ginger

Armstrong; Anne Marie Austin; Elijah Bailey-Caffee; Jennifer Baker; Roxane Bartelt; Mary Bend; Brenda Bober; Stesha Brandon; Robyn Bryant; Peg Burington; Terry Burki; Catherine Cifelli; Jennifer Correa; Sasha Craine; Diane Darby; Kendra Doepken; Carol Edfelsen; Mary Erbe; Judy Fischetti; Linda Gau; Patty Gibbons; Gary Gisselman; Amy Gornikiewicz; Cynthia Grady; Robin Groue; Erin Hall; Lisa Hardey; Alice Hauschka and her class at The Little School; Iris Heerhold; Leigh Ann Johnson; Sue Johnson; Pat Kelly; Rebecca Kilgore; Kay Kirkpatrick; Dianna LaBate; Sandy Livingstone; Lisa Maslowe; Cheryl McKeon; Janet Miller; Anna Minard; Susan Moore; Kira Moyer-Sims; Sue Vater Olsen; Judy Ostrow; Hannah Parker; Lily Parker; Eily Pearl; Hélène Pohl; Stephanie Ponder; Carmine Rau; Julie Richards; Gayle Richardson; Hannah Ruggiero; Rebecca Schosha; Anne Schuessler; Cathy Schultis; Ruby Schultz; Molly Senechal; Venta Silins; Misha Stone; Carol Strope; Elizabeth Timmins; Loriann Tschirhart; Virginia Trujillo; Karen Vollmar; Holly Vonderohe; Betsy Voelker; Duane Wilkins; Melissa Wong; Beci Wright; Neal Wyatt; and Marin Younker.

And thanks once again to the wonderful and supportive folks at Sasquatch Books, especially Gary Luke, Sarah Hanson, Courtney Payne, and Austin Walters.

This book is for my husband, Joe, who makes everything possible, and for the most wonderful Emily Chandini Raman, the newest book lover in my life.

YOUNGEST READERS

PART I

AHH, THOSE ADORABLE ANTHROPOMORPHIC ANIMALS

I use adorable here with no bit of irony attached: this group of picture books and readers are charming, funny, and entrancing. For ease in locating particular titles, I've divided them into categories of animals:

Aardvarks

In the many books by Marc Brown about Arthur, readers can share Arthur's experiences at home, at school, and with his friends and family.

Amphibians

Froggy Gets Dressed and other amphibious tales by Jonathan London are terrific choices for reading aloud.

Dogs

Bungee, the seagoing heroine of Sally Ford's **Bungee's Voyage** and **Bungee Down Under**, undertakes a trip on her sailboat *Gypsy Rover* from her home in New Hampshire to far-flung lands on the other side of the world, down the coast of South America to the Sydney harbor, enduring a terrible storm on the Pacific along the way.

Donkeys

You have to feel sorry for Sylvester, who unknowingly—and in a moment of panic—made a wish holding what turned out to be a magic pebble and was transformed into a great big rock. But you have to feel even sorrier for his parents, who miss their son dreadfully. How they finally get him back is described in one of my favorite books ever, **Sylvester and the Magic Pebble** by William Steig.

Earthworms

Diary of a Worm by Doreen Cronin, with pictures by Harry Bliss, gives an up-close view of the daily activities of a young worm, including his observations about kids playing hopscotch ("very dangerous"), what happens when fishing season begins (dig deeper into the earth), how to do the hokey pokey, what to do with a macaroni necklace, and more. The same author and illustrator teamed up to do the equally fun **Diary of a Spider**. ("Today was my birthday. Grampa decided I was old enough to know the secret to a long, happy life: Never fall asleep in a shoe.")

Elephants

I've always felt that the very first of Jean de Brunhoff's Babar books, **The Story of Babar**, is far and away the best, but children love them all, and never fail to be interested in Babar, his wife Céleste, their children, and Babar's rise from being orphaned in the jungles of Africa to becoming crowned king of the elephants. The only problem with reading the book aloud is how to pronounce the main character's name. I've always said *Buh*-bar (first syllable stressed), but others say Bay-*bar* (second syllable stressed), so it always sounds as if we're discussing (or reading aloud) different books.

Foxes

Families with two little girls might especially delight in Laura McGee Kvasnosky's books featuring fox sisters, but they're fun for everyone else as well. The pair is introduced in **Zelda and Ivy**, and continues with **Zelda and Ivy and the Boy Next Door** and **Zelda and Ivy One Christmas**. Kvasnosky's technique of gouache resist lends itself to the brightly colored illustrations outlined in a bold black ink.

Gorillas

In Anthony Browne's **Willy the Wizard**, the young gorilla believes that he's a star player only because he wears his special soccer shoes—but on the day of the big match, he forgets them at home and has to wear a borrowed pair of shoes. Will Willy still play well?

Hamsters

What's irresistible about **I Love You So Much** by Carl Norac is not just the text, but also the tender pictures of Lola, a hamster who just loves her mother and father an awful lot.

Pigs

When Ian Falconer's **Olivia** was published, I suspect that the number of people who named their daughters Olivia increased dramatically—all in honor of this irresistible porker who's a bundle of delightful energy. Her adventures continue in **Olivia Saves the Circus**, **Olivia . . . and the Missing Toy**, and **Olivia Forms a Band**.

The eponymous Piggins is not only an impeccable butler, but—as Jane Yolen and Jane Dyer's **Piggins** shows—he's a great detective as well.

Rabbits

When Willa can't fall asleep because she's afraid of having bad dreams, her big brother Willoughby tells her about the joyful things that will happen in the morning, in **Tell Me Something Happy Before I Go to Sleep** by Joyce Dunbar, with illustrations by Debi Gliori.

Rodents

Two of my favorite and lovable picture book heroines just happen to be mice. The first is Angelina, the star of Katharine Holabird's series of books beginning with **Angelina Ballerina**, all illustrated in glorious detail by Helen Craig, and all capturing aspects of young Angelina's life.

The second is Lilly, a mousette created by Kevin Henkes. She first appeared in **Lilly's Purple Plastic Purse** and her everyday but never humdrum adventures continue in **Lilly's Big Day**. Henkes clearly has a thing for mice, at least in his picture books, as can be seen in **Sheila Rae, the Brave**; **Chester's Way** (a lovely look at how friendships can change and develop); and **A Weekend with Wendell**. (There are more Henkes mice to be found in the next section, "B Is for Babies.")

Dr. DeSoto, a mouse with a dental degree, welcomes all animals to his office, except, of course, the dangerous ones, like cats. But what should he do about a fox with an aching tooth and mischief on his mind? The answer's in **Doctor De Soto** by William Steig.

Wombats

I must say I've never actively wondered what wombats do all day, but after reading Jackie French's **Diary of a Wombat**, I now know that they live a life of ease—they sleep a lot! Or, at least, this particular wombat does.

B IS FOR BABIES

Younger brothers and sisters—their appearance in the family is often a bit traumatic for the older child. Most adults have their own stories about how they felt as children when they learned about the arrival of a new member of the family. I remember—at age three—listening unhappily on the phone when my father called from the hospital to tell me that I had a little sister and my instant negative response (not spoken, but certainly felt): nobody asked me whether I wanted a little sister! Here are some of my favorite books about babies and older siblings, all showing different ways in which children greet the newcomer (the interloper). Sometimes it's good to be honest in your reactions . . .

When her parents' attention seems to be focused entirely on baby Gloria, Frances decides to pack up a few of her possessions and run away, settling in under the dining-room table. How her parents handle Frances's unhappiness at the changes in her life can be a lesson for us all, which is why Russell Hoban's **A Baby Sister for Frances** (along with all the other Frances books), belongs on every child's must-read list.

In Anne Gutman's **Lisa's Baby Sister**, with its bright acrylic, uncluttered illustrations by Georg Hallensleben, Lisa is not so happy that her mom's pregnant, but on the upside she does have some good names for the baby (Doofus or Goofus), and she's made her best friend Gaspard promise he won't ever talk to the baby when it finally arrives. But when Lila is born, Lisa discovers that things aren't all *that* bad with a baby sister in the house.

Four other books to check out are Ed Young's **My Mei Mei**, the only book I know of about the reaction of an older child to the adoption of a younger sibling; **I Kissed the Baby!** by Mary Murphy (how different animals greet a new duckling, illustrated in black and white until the arrival of the vibrantly yellow-colored newcomer); **Julius, the Baby of the World** by Kevin Henkes (with the always entrancing Lilly in a more or less central role); and **The Perfect Friend** by Yelena Romanova, in which Archie the Dog (who wears human clothing and walks on two legs) is not overjoyed when a new baby enters his household. Boris Kulikov's humorously eerie paintings add to the pleasure of the tale.

BEDTIME STORIES

Although I have to admit that bedtime was not my favorite time to be a mother (I've always been a morning person and just wanted to go to sleep myself), it did give my daughters and me the chance to sit quietly and, depending on their ages, I would read aloud to them or we would read silently and companionably together. During those read-aloud years, I always tried to end the pre-bedtime ritual with a book that is clearly about going to bed—finally!

The classic "bedtime" book is, of course, Margaret Wise Brown and Clement Hurd's **Goodnight Moon**, but when you're tired of reading and rereading that to a baby or toddler who doesn't want to go to sleep, try Mem Fox's **Time for Bed**, with its gentle rhymes about all different animals getting ready for bed and its full-page soft watercolor pictures by Jane Dyer.

But I'm afraid that bedtime for most parents and children is far less peaceful—closer to the hilarious experiences of Mama and Papa Bear, in Stan and Jan Berenstain's **The Berenstain Bears' Bedtime Battle**, who wear out long before their children do! Mine frequently was.

Using both text and amusing detailed pictures (mostly in a palette of calming blues, greens, and grays) in **Russell the Sheep**, Rob Scotton humorously depicts a sheep who just can't fall asleep—until he tries counting guess what?

Another author/illustrator who makes good use of color is Uri Shulevitz. Right from your first glance at the cover of **So Sleepy Story**—with its yawning house and peacefully slumbering moon against a background of shades of blue—you'll know you're in for a treat in this tale about a house full of sleeping people and objects who all get awakened by music drifting in through the windows. I'm very taken with the dancing dishes.

I guess there are challenges associated with bedtime even in the animal—that is, nonhuman—world: the eponymous Baby Beebee Bird is just not ready for bed at the zoo when all the rest of the animals are. It takes some sharp thinking on the part of the other animals to get him back on the correct sleeping track, in Diane Redfield Massie's **The Baby Beebee Bird**, originally published in 1963 (now in a new edition with illustrations by Steven Kellogg).

Other bedtime stories not to be missed are **Clara and Asha** by Eric Rohmann, with stunning oil paintings of a little girl who has so many friends that it's hard to go to sleep; **What! Cried Granny: An Almost Bedtime Story** by Kate Lum; **Baby Can't Sleep** by Lisa Schroeder (a good gift, incidentally, for expectant parents); **Down in the Woods at Sleepytime** by Carole Lexa Schaefer, with pencil and watercolor illustrations by Vanessa Cabban; Barbara Helen Berger's **Grandfather Twilight**; and Audrey Woods's **The Napping House**, a tried, true, and much-loved read-aloud. (My favorite character in Woods's book has always been the very pesky—and wide-awake—flea who wreaks havoc with the nappers.)

And parents at the end of their patience at bedtime will greatly appreciate Geoffrey Kloske and Barry Blitt's **Once Upon a Time, the End (Asleep in 60 Seconds)**, although I have my doubts if kids much under five will get the humor.

BOO! HALLOWEEN BOOKS TO TREASURE (AND READ ALOUD)

When my daughters were young, Halloween was always my least favorite holiday. This was entirely due to the fact that I couldn't sew, so I was always trying to think up unusually inventive costumes that were simple to make and didn't require a sewing machine. My bible at that time of year was **Easy Costumes You Don't Have to Sew** by Goldie Taub Chernoff. While the following books won't necessarily provide costumes for your children, they'll certainly entertain them.

Two books I especially enjoy sharing with kids are Elizabeth Hatch's **Halloween Night**, which uses the old Mother Goose rhyme "This is the House that Jack Built" as the basis for a rollicking story of the experiences of a timid mouse; and **The Perfect Pumpkin Pie**, comically related by Denys Cazet. It's the story of Mr. Wilkerson, who, though not a very nice man when he was alive, did love his pumpkin pie. When he dies suddenly on Halloween night before he has a chance to eat some of his favorite dessert, he decides to make sure he gets what he wants—by haunting Jack and his grandma. How Grandma deals with the entrée of a ghost in her house is a hoot.

Try these winners as well: **The Little Old Lady Who Was Not Afraid of Anything** by Linda Williams (perfect for reading aloud all year round); **Julius's Candy Corn** by the always-worth-reading Kevin Henkes; Dav Pilkey's **Dragon's Halloween**; **It's Pumpkin Time!** by Zoe Hall; **Scary, Scary Halloween** by Eve Bunting; Rosemary Wells's **The Halloween Parade**; **The Perfectly Horrible Halloween** by Nancy Poydar; **Trick or**

Treat Countdown by Patricia Hubbard (which doubles as a counting book as well); **Gus and Grandpa and the Halloween Costume** by Claudia Mills; Elizabeth Winthrop's **Halloween Hats** (children will never want to go bare-headed again); Felicia Bond's **The Halloween Play**; **Trick or Treat, Smell My Feet** by Diane de Groat; and **Halloween Is . . .**, a sound nonfiction introduction to the holiday's history and practices by Gail Gibbons (with a book by Gibbons you are always assured of top-notch illustrations).

And there's no better time than Halloween to meet the eponymous ghostly hero of Robert Bright's **Georgie**, who has delighted readers for more than half a century.

BOOKS, BOOKS, BOOKS

What better way to introduce young children to the joys of books and reading than by sharing picture books on that very topic with them. Take a look at these:

In Deborah Bruss's **Book! Book! Book!** the whimsical illustrations by Tiphanie Beeke provide a perfect complement to this story of a group of bored animals who go to the library to check out some books to read and find it difficult to make the (human) librarian understand their wishes, until it's the hen's turn to ask. There's a chucklesome surprise at the end, too.

Alexander Stadler's **Beverly Billingsly Borrows a Book** features a plot that will be all too familiar to most adult readers—the heroine loves a book so much that she forgets to return it to the library on time. Luckily, the librarian is—of course—very understanding!

Sarah Stewart's **The Library** is one of my favorite books—it's the story of a young woman (an ancestor of the author's, in fact) who loved to read more than anything else. (I can identify with that.)

The cumulative story told in **Stella Louella's Runaway Book** by Lisa Campbell Ernst will please listeners of almost all ages, and is also a good choice for story hours and other read-aloud times.

A chimpanzee expresses his love for books of all kinds in Anthony Browne's **I Like Books**, while Meena, the main character in **The Girl Who Hated Books** by Manjusha Pawagi, has the opposite reaction, at least until she learns the delights they hold. Another non-fan of reading is Beatrice, a young shaggy basset hound, whose experience in the library is recounted in Laura Numeroff's **Beatrice Doesn't Want To**.

Suzanne Williams's **Library Lil**, as illustrated by Steven Kellogg, decides that she's going to get Bust-'em-up Bill and his fellow motorcycle gang members to start coming to the library—or else! (Beverly Cleary fans will be delighted to note that the gang members fight over being the first to check out **The Mouse and the Motorcycle**.)

And many adults as well as kids will be able to relate to Remy Charlip's slyly enchanting **Why I Will Never Ever Ever Ever Have Enough Time to Read This Book**, in which a little girl demonstrates (in great pictures by Jon J Muth) all she has to do during the day besides read.

Other bookishly wonderful titles include Judy Sierra's **Wild About Books**, with its appropriately wild illustrations by Marc Brown; Pat Mora's **Tomás and the Library Lady** (based on the life of a young migrant worker who grows up to be chancellor of the University of California at Riverside, all through his love of reading); **The Library Dragon** by Carmen Agra Deedy, with chortle-inducing illustrations by Michael P. White); **Clara and the Bookwagon** by Nancy Smiler Levinson; Marc Brown's **D. W.'s Library Card**; **Goin' Someplace Special** by Patricia C. McKissack (the time is the 1950s, and the someplace special is a library in Nashville, Tennessee); **The World That Loved Books** by Stephen Parlato, which is filled with gloriously detailed illustrations; Cari Meister's **Tiny Goes to the Library**; **The Red Book**, Barbara Lehman's wordless and magical story of the power of books; and Eileen Christelow's interesting and informative **What Do Illustrators Do?** and **What Do Authors Do?**

THE CAT'S MEOW

Cats and children's books seem to fit together in wonderful and inventive ways, as can be seen in these treasures:

One of the earliest Little Golden Books to be produced, and still popular today, is **The Color Kittens**, written by Margaret Wise Brown and charmingly illustrated by Martin and Alice Provensen. It tells the story of Brush and Hush, who create every color in the world. Brown, who surely must have been a cat lover, also wrote **A Pussycat's Christmas**, with pictures by Anne Mortimer.

There are only 220 words in Dr. Seuss's **The Cat in the Hat**, but together they make up one of the best known children's books of all.

Caramba, by Marie-Louise Gay, is a cat who—unlike all the other cats in the world—can't fly (the text and pictures describing his attempts are very funny), but he does discover that he can do something none of the other cats can . . .

The Cat Who Walked Across France by Kate Banks (with illustrations by Georg Hallensleben), a tale of a homeless cat who's trying to find a new place to live, has one of the most satisfying endings of any book I've read.

Chato is one cool East L.A. cat, and he's just thrilled to learn that his new neighbors are a family of mice. So why not invite them over for dinner—and I (and Chato) do mean *for* dinner? But the mice have a surprise of their own, as Gary Soto (with the assistance of some adorable illustrations by Susan Guevara) describes in **Chato's Kitchen**. His adventures with his best friend, Novio, continue in **Chato Goes Cruisin'**.

Millions of Cats by Wanda Gág is the delightful story of a search for the prettiest cat of all—with surprising results.

David Almond and Stephen Lambert's **Kate, the Cat and the Moon** is the haunting tale of a nighttime adventure, undertaken by the light of the moon and the stars that "glittered in the endless sky . . ."

Any book by Ezra Jack Keats is worth treasuring, and **Hi, Cat!** is no exception. Archie (who appears in Keats's **Peter's Chair** and **A Letter to Amy** as well) has a great day planned, until a stray cat decides to adopt him.

Mary Calhoun's done a whole series of books about Henry, a peripatetic Siamese cat, all with pictures by Erick Ingraham. My favorite is the first, **Hot-Air Henry**, but there's also **Henry the**

Christmas Cat, Cross-Country Cat, and **Henry the Sailor Cat** to be enjoyed.

Judith Kerr's delightfully warm stories of Mog are also well worth reading to your preschooler, beginning with **Mog the Forgetful Cat.**

Does the full moon look like a bowl of milk? Kitten, the main character in Kevin Henkes's **Kitten's First Full Moon,** certainly thinks so, and she goes to a lot of trouble to get it.

Paul Galdone does a delightful job of illustrating that familiar verse about those kittens who lost their gloves—I mean mittens—in **Three Little Kittens.** This is a good choice for story hours for the very youngest children.

A picture book that will appeal to budding Charles Addams fans is Frank Asch's **Mr. Maxwell's Mouse,** with elaborately detailed and somewhat spooky illustrations by his son, Devin Asch. It's the ultimate cat-and-mouse story, with a snooty cat getting ready to dine on his favorite dish—a rodent, who happens to possess some brains of his own. But is he smart enough to outwit Mr. Maxwell and save himself from being the main course at dinner?

Joan Sweeney's **Bijou, Bonbon and Beau: The Kittens Who Danced for Degas** combines the world of ballet and art, from the point of view of a stray cat and her kittens who wander into the theater where artist Edgar Degas is busily painting some ballerinas. Just as they make their way onto the stage (to the annoyance of the director), they'll edge their way into your child's heart, courtesy of Leslie Wu's illustrations.

Skippyjon Jones by Judy Schachner is a rollicking story of the eponymous hero, a Siamese cat convinced that he's a Chihuahua named El Skippito—a sword-fighter so extraordinaire that he's surely destined to rescue a group of Mexican Chihuahuas from an enormous bumblebeeto who's menacing them. Holy frijoles, as El Skippito would say, this is one fun book. As is the sequel, **Skippyjon Jones in the Dog-House**.

Cynthia Rylant has written a whole series of books about Mr. Putter and his cat, Tabby, that are just perfect for kids beginning to read by themselves. They can be read in any order, but I found one of the funniest to be **Mr. Putter and Tabby Feed the Fish**, in which Tabby discovers that fish (even in a fishbowl) make him go bananas, or, as Rylant puts it, "all twitchy and batty."

A British storybook series begins with **Orlando the Marmalade Cat: A Camping Holiday**, featuring Orlando, whose eyes looked like "twin green gooseberries." This oddly enthralling series by Kathleen Hale has been recently reissued.

You won't want the young children in your life to miss out on a chance to meet Kitty, the sometimes naughty, sometimes nice heroine of Nick Bruel's hilarious **Bad Kitty**. Use this as you're introducing kids to the letters of the alphabet, too, if you can stop them (and you) from giggling too much along the way.

What's a stray dog to do when he decides he wants to live in a house that's inhabited solely by cats? Why, pretend to be a feline, of course, until it becomes clear that sometimes a dog's gotta be a dog, no matter what. You'll get the engaging picture in **Widget**, written by Lyn Rossiter McFarland and illustrated by Jim McFarland.

CHAPTER ONE: GOOD BOOKS FOR THE YOUNGEST READERS

When a child is past the age of picture books and wants something a little more substantial, but still not too hard, with interesting characters, plots that move right along, and a lot of humor in the mix as well, these are great choices. They're also good for read-alouds.

I still remember when Miss Glenn, the librarian at Hally Elementary School in Detroit, Michigan, took me to the shelves and gave me a copy of **My Father's Dragon** by Ruth Stiles Gannett to read. (Actually, I still remember exactly where in the library the book was shelved—I could take you there today, more than fifty years later.) This tale of young Elmer Elevator who goes to Wild Island to free a young dragon from captivity is as enthralling today as it was when it was published in 1948.

Nate the Great by Marjorie Weinman Sharmat is the first in a perennially popular series starring an intrepid boy detective. These are prime starter books that just may lead readers to the Hardy Boys series, and then on to Arthur Conan Doyle's Sherlock Holmes, Ross Macdonald's Lew Archer, and Raymond Chandler's Philip Marlowe.

Arnold Lobel's **Small Pig** finds that there's a great difference between the mud he loves and the tar he ends up in when he runs off to the city in search of adventure.

Three children have to cope with a seemingly bad-humored, even dangerous, dog—until, much to their surprise, they learn what he's really like, in Patricia C. McKissack's **Tippy Lemmey**.

Thinking about the antics of Amelia Bedelia, a housekeeper who takes everything quite literally, still makes me laugh even now, years after I read the books with my two daughters. Read the early ones in Peggy Parish's series, beginning with **Amelia Bedelia** and **Come Back, Amelia Bedelia**.

A blue-eyed frog asking him to rescue her in the time-honored way (a kiss!) from a spell delivered by an evil wizard is not an everyday occurrence, so Davey has a lot of thinking to do before he can decide how to handle the situation, in Patricia Harrison Easton's engaging **Davey's Blue-Eyed Frog**.

Else Holmelund Minarik introduced **Little Bear** and his family in 1957, and generations of readers since have been captivated by these warmly humorous tales of family life. And with illustrations by Maurice Sendak, you simply can't go wrong.

Every day when he comes home from school, his brothers and sisters ask Charley if he got to carry the flag in school—but as Rebecca Caudill shows in her long-popular **Did You Carry the Flag Today, Charley?**, it's tough on a mischievous little boy to be good all day. Set in Appalachia, and originally published in 1966, this engaging story will appeal to both boys and girls.

Marjorie Flack's **Walter the Lazy Mouse** is a cautionary tale of a young mouse who moves ver-r-r-y slowly, is always daydreaming (both at home and at school), and is invariably late for everything. It takes a somewhat traumatic experience, three forgetful frogs (Leander, Lulu, and Percy), and a turtle to teach Walter to pay attention and be on time.

Four resourceful and orphaned brothers and sisters set out to make a home for themselves in an abandoned boxcar in order to escape from the clutches of their evil (or so they think) grandfather in **The Boxcar Children** by Gertrude Chandler Warner.

Lois Lowry's **Gooney Bird Greene** and **Gooney Bird and the Room Mother** are laugh-aloud books about a second-grader who has something to say about every subject, as well as a definite sense of fashion. She's a delight.

Ramona Quimby, the young heroine of several amusing books by Beverly Cleary, has a lot in common with Gooney Bird, except that Gooney Bird doesn't have to cope with an older sister named Beezus, and Ramona is definitely not into fashion. Do try them all: **Ramona the Pest**; **Ramona Quimby, Age 8**; **Ramona and Her Mother**; **Ramona and Her Father**; **Ramona Forever**; and **Ramona the Brave**.

Other exceptional beginning chapter books include **Holding onto Sunday** by Kathryn O. Galbraith (and her other books like **Roommates** and its sequels); Ellen Conford's **Annabel the Actress Starring in Gorilla My Dreams**; **From Slave to Soldier** by Deborah Hopkinson, based on the life of a young slave who runs away to join the Union Army during the Civil War; and **The Year of Miss Agnes** by Kirkpatrick Hill, set in 1948 in a small village in Alaska.

CHRISTMAS IS COMING!

O f course, the best-known holiday tale is Clement Moore's poem **The Night Before Christmas**, which is available in gazillions of editions (with slight variations) by various illustrators. Among my favorites are those by Mary Engelbreit, Lisbeth Zwerger, Anita Lobel, and Jan Brett.

Allen Say describes in both words and exquisitely detailed illustrations his memories of a Christmas when he was a little boy growing up in Japan, in **Tree of Cranes**.

From the moment it arrived on library and bookstore shelves, Chris Van Allsburg's **The Polar Express** had "classic" written all over it. Forget the film and check out this book.

Robert Sabuda has made a career of producing remarkable pop-up books, including **The Twelve Days of Christmas** and **The Night Before Christmas**. (But don't miss sharing with your slightly older children his **Alice's Adventures in Wonderland** and **The Wonderful Wizard of Oz**, or indeed any of the books he's done.)

In **The Twelve Days of Christmas**, Ilse Plume takes the classic carol and transforms it into an exquisite illuminated manuscript like those from the Middle Ages. (Other excellent versions of the song include those illustrated by the incomparable Brian Wildsmith, Hilary Knight, and Jan Brett; and **Twelve Lizards Leaping** by Jan Romero Stevens, illustrated by Christine Mau, which includes horned toads, tamales, and piñatas, as befits a Southwestern version of the song.)

Tomie dePaola's **Four Friends at Christmas** is the story of Mister Frog, who decides not to sleep through winter (which is what frogs usually do) in order to share the Christmas festivities with his friends.

Trina Schart Hyman beautifully illustrates Dylan Thomas's **A Child's Christmas in Wales**, his memoir of growing up in the first years of the twentieth century.

Other splendid Christmas books for this age group include **Mr. Willowby's Christmas Tree** by Robert Barry; Raymond Briggs's

Father Christmas (you'll want to check out Santa's reactions to snow, rain, fog, and other bad weather as he makes his rounds); and **Bear Noel** by Oliver Dunrea, a lovely story of animals in the north woods awaiting the arrival of Christmas and Bear Noel.

D IS FOR DINOSAURS

Jane Yolen and Mark Teague's **How Do Dinosaurs Get Well Soon?** tells the story of a dinosaur with a cold—the perfect book to read to the sneezy little Brachiosaurus fan in your house, not just because of the cheerful rhyming story, but also because each illustration features a different type of dinosaur, all depicted in miniature on the endpapers. I love the Dilophosaurus with his colorful quilt and his thermometer, the Euoplocephalus reclining in bed with a wastebasket full of used tissues next to him, and the Gallimimus with his tiny head, using the sick time to good advantage by reading a book in bed. If your child enjoys this (and what child wouldn't?) the same author and illustrator collaborated on **How Do Dinosaurs Eat Their Food?** and **How Do Dinosaurs Say Good Night?**

A little boy imagines all the exciting things that could happen if a certain group of extinct animals returns, in Bernard Most's **If the Dinosaurs Came Back**. Great fun.

In **The Dinosaurs of Waterhouse Hawkins**, Barbara Kerley tells the true story of a Victorian artist whose interest in dinosaurs led to a career creating reproductions of them for the public to enjoy.

In 1868, after achieving fame in England, Waterhouse Hawkins was invited to New York to create dinosaurs for future display at a new planned museum in Central Park. But when Hawkins ran afoul of the notorious Boss Tweed, nothing could go forward as planned. This charming and informative book, with its large and colorful illustrations by Brian Selznick, brings to light a little-known event in history.

And if your dinosaur lover wants more, try these: Carol Diggory Shields's **Saturday Night at the Dinosaur Stomp** and **Dad's Dinosaur Day** by Diane Dawson Hearn.

DEATH AND DYING

One of the hardest things a parent ever has to do (more difficult, I think, than explaining just where babies come from) is help a very young child understand the concept of death, whether the particular death has to do with a beloved family pet, a friend, or a family member. I've found these books particularly useful in meeting the challenge, and I have to say that in my own adult life I've found them to be comforting at times of sorrow, as well.

First published in 1982, Leo Buscaglia's **The Fall of Freddie the Leaf** is one of the earliest children's books to deal with this subject. It remains one of the best ways to help young readers see that death is a part of life.

Although Margaret Wise Brown is best known for **Goodnight Moon** (often the first book that parents read to their children), I've always preferred the elegiac and heartbreakingly realistic **The**

Dead Bird, the story of a group of children who find a dead bird and decide to have a funeral for it.

Writing in verse about a young boy's grief, poet Lucille Clifton describes how difficult it is for Everett when his father dies, in **Everett Anderson's Goodbye**. Ann Grifalconi's soft pencil drawings make a perfect pairing with the text.

What a lucky little boy Tommy is, to have both a grandmother (Nana Downstairs) and a great-grandmother (Nana Upstairs) to visit every Sunday with his mother and father. As Tomie dePaola shows us in **Nana Upstairs and Nana Downstairs**, Tommy appreciates it too—just take a look at the priceless picture of Tommy and Nana Upstairs eating candy and talking together. But then Nana Upstairs dies—and Tommy learns about love and loss.

"Sweet" is a much-overused adjective for describing children's books, but it so perfectly fits Cynthia Rylant's **Dog Heaven** and **Cat Heaven** that it's impossible not to use it here. Any child who's lost a much loved pet will take comfort from these.

Three other contemporary classics on this topic include Susan Varley's **Badger's Parting Gifts**, Judith Viorst's **The Tenth Good Thing About Barney**, and Hans Wilhelm's **I'll Always Love You**.

A DOG'S LIFE

Based on the number of top-notch books in this category, it's clear that publishers, artists, and authors believe that many kids (I was certainly one) want to spend much of their reading time in the company of dogs.

You won't soon forget Orville, the main (dog) character in Haven Kimmel's **Orville: A Dog Story**, who wants only to live life without a chain around his neck and with people who love him.

Is Harry a white dog with black spots, or a black dog with white spots? You'll know for sure after reading **Harry the Dirty Dog** by Gene Zion.

When a stray dog is finally adopted, he gets a new name—but what shall it be? Stephen Michael King explores the choices (which range from Radiator to Winston) in **Mutt Dog!**

The only thing that makes Officer Buckle's safety lessons bearable to the school children watching him is that police dog (and ham at heart) Gloria acts them out—to everyone's delight, in Peggy Rathmann's **Officer Buckle and Gloria**.

Marjorie Flack's **Angus Lost**, **Angus and the Ducks**, and **Angus and the Cat** are all about a Scottish terrier, who is insatiably curious about so many things. These books, originally published in the 1930s, are still a treat to read today.

There are groan-worthy puns galore in Dav Pilkey's hilarious **The Hallo-Wiener**, about a dachshund whose mother (wisely or unwisely) dresses him up for Halloween as a hot dog in a bun.

My husband's favorite Little Golden Book (one of the original dozen books published in this most-loved series) was **The Poky Little Puppy** by Janette Sebring Lowrey, in which an adventurous puppy learns there are sometimes dire consequences to being late.

Carl, the Rottweiler who stars in Alexandra Day's **Good Dog, Carl** (and its many sequels), demonstrates just how capable a babysitter he is. You can also meet Carl in **Carl's Sleepy Afternoon** and **Carl's Birthday**, among others.

In **"Let's Get a Pup!" Said Kate** by Bob Graham, after visiting an animal shelter, the family ends up with not one, but two new dogs. (I love the tattooed mom.) Another good dog adoption story is Marc Simont's **The Stray Dog**.

Using colorful illustrations and a minimum of text (making this appropriate for the very young reader) in **Whistle for Willie**, Ezra Jack Keats describes Peter's attempts to learn to whistle for his pet dog.

The adventures of the main character in **Clifford The Big Red Dog** by Norman Bridwell show that it's okay to be different, even though it's not always easy.

Cynthia Rylant must love dogs—how else could she have come up with **The Great Gracie Chase: Stop That Dog!** about a brown-and-white dog who just wants peace and quiet and (all the way back in 1987) **Henry and Mudge**, the first in a long-running easy reading series about the love between an enormous English mastiff and his little boy. (My particular favorite is **Henry and Mudge and the Great Grandpas**.)

I adore Fergus, a West Highland terrier who has a great day in David Shannon's **Good Boy, Fergus!** (We should all have his energy.)

If your child is up for quirks and kookiness, offer him or her Maira Kalman's oddball series of books about Max Stravinsky, a (dog) poet and Hollywood director, including **Ooh-la-la (Max in Love)**, **Max in Hollywood, Baby**, and **Swami on Rye: Max in India**. You'll find them delightful, too. In fact, you might enjoy them more than your child will.

In **The Sweetest Fig** by Chris Van Allsburg, a dentist is thwarted in his chance to have his dreams come true when his dog eats the second of two magical figs.

It's a well-known fact that chicken soup is good for you, but Susan Meddaugh shows us the benefits of homemade vegetable soup—at least for dogs—in **Martha Speaks**, which depicts the curious effects of eating some of Granny's alphabet soup, and **Martha Blah Blah**, which describes what happens when some letters are omitted from the soup.

EASY AS 1, 2, 3: COUNTING BOOKS

Based on their books, it seems clear to me that many illustrators love to set themselves a challenge: to come up with an inventive, attractive, and inviting counting book—putting those everyday numbers to work entertaining (and, dare we say, educating) a child (and the parent reading to him or her). Here are some of my favorites:

> Mitsumasa Anno's **Anno's Counting Book**
> Sandra Boynton's **Hippos Go Berserk!**
> Eric Carle's **1, 2, 3 to the Zoo** and **The Very Hungry Caterpillar**

Eileen Christelow's **Five Little Monkeys Jumping on the Bed**

Emma Chichester Clark's **Mimi's Book of Counting**

Lisa Campbell Ernst's **Up to Ten and Down Again**

Valorie Fisher's **How High Can a Dinosaur Count?: And Other Math Mysteries**

Mordicai Gerstein illustrates counting backwards from ten in **Roll Over!**

Paul Giganti, Jr.'s **Each Orange Had 8 Slices** (illustrated by Donald Crews)

David Kirk's **Miss Spider's Tea Party**

Satoshi Kitamura's **When Sheep Cannot Sleep**

Laurie Krebs's **We All Went on Safari: A Counting Journey Through Tanzania**, with illustrations by Julia Cairns

April Pulley Sayre and Jeff Sayre's **One Is a Snail, Ten Is a Crab: A Counting by Feet Book** (the pictures are by Randy Cecil)

FAIRY TALES (FRACTURED OR NOT)

I always found fairy tales too frightening to read when I was a child; all those Brothers Grimm stories were just, well, too grim for me. As a consequence, I didn't read very many of them to my own children when they were young. However, I think that I am (was) probably in a minority, and, in fact, if these particular books had been around all those years ago, I might have really enjoyed reading them.

What's fun about this section is that for nearly every fairy tale, there's a fractured version as well, and it's a joy to see what evident pleasure the writers and illustrators took in these new versions. I've also included here versions of fairy tales from other cultures.

Cinderella

In **The Gift of the Crocodile: A Cinderella Story**, Judy Sierra draws together bits and pieces of the classic tale from all over the world, but places her version of *Cinderella* in Indonesia. Her heroine, Damura, treats a crocodile with respect, as her mother always taught her, and reaps many benefits as a result, including the love of a handsome prince. The stepmother and stepsister are appropriately wicked, but they get their comeuppance, which will please young readers. The colorful illustrations by Reynold Ruffins beautifully reflect the Spice Islands setting of the story.

Probably the oldest version of *Cinderella* comes from China, and in Ai-Ling Louie's **Yeh Shen: A Cinderella Story from China**, with delicate and almost other-worldly pictures by Ed Young, young readers can enjoy this story of a young woman who gains all her heart desires as a result of her kindness to a magic fish. Who needs fairy godmothers, anyway?

The Frog Prince

It turns out that the frog (who had to search around a lot to find someone who would kiss him and turn him back into a man) and his princess aren't really getting along, and the prince has a feeling he might be happier back as a frog—but how can he manage that? Jon Scieszka offers an answer in **The Frog Prince Continued**.

Hansel and Gretel

Hansel and Gretel by Will Moses has gorgeous folk-art illustrations that add warmth to a classic retelling of the original Grimm Brothers' story.

Jack and the Beanstalk

The vibrant and lively illustrations (done in watercolor, acrylics, and colored inks) in Steven Kellogg's **Jack and the Beanstalk** are reason enough for stalwart kids to seek out this straightforward version of the tale—and they won't want to miss meeting the downright terrifying giant, who's a chartreuse-y sort of color.

In his delightfully contrary fashion, Raymond Briggs introduces Jim, the hero of **Jim and the Beanstalk**, and offers a post-Jack view of the giant's situation, now that he's old and unable to subsist on little boys. Lucky for him, Jim is such a good kid. Pair this with Kellogg's book for a treat for the children in your life.

Little Red Riding Hood

Carmine: A Little More Red by Melissa Sweet is both a fractured retelling of Little Red Riding Hood and a most inventive alphabet book, something I didn't even realize until I finished reading it. The illustrations are adorable—there's no other word for them—and there's even a recipe for vegetable soup included.

Kids will giggle at **Jake Gander, Storyville Detective: The Case of the Greedy Granny** by George McClements, starting with the opening line ("My name is Jake Gander. I'm a cop. My beat: Storyville, a fairy-tale town where endings aren't always happy. My job is to rewrite them."), all the way to the last picture, in which the Three Bears open his office door with another case for Jake to solve. One of my favorite cases is when Jake investigates a grandmother whose behavior is causing her granddaughter Red to become suspicious—she now has "[f]ur pajamas that never came off, really sharp teeth, and rabbit breath."

The well-known and well-regarded illustrator Trina Schart Hyman's version of **Little Red Riding Hood** was a Caledecott Honor Book in 1983, and it's easy to see why it was selected. The illustrations are richly captivating, and although both the disobedient little girl and her grandmother are devoured by the hungry wolf, they're later rescued by a kindly woodsman. Thank goodness.

Ed Young's **Lon Po Po: A Red-Riding Hood Story from China** is a powerful retelling of the Grimm tale; it was awarded the Caldecott medal in 1990. In this version, three little girls are left alone while their mother is away from home. When a sinister wolf (very scarily depicted) pretends to be their granny, it takes a smart little girl named Shang to see beneath the disguise and dispatch him to his death.

Puss in Boots

Charles Perrault's original tale has never been better illustrated than in the version of **Puss in Boots** by Fred Marcellino, which was a Caldecott Honor Book in 1991. Puss's clever plans succeed in getting his originally ungrateful owner all that he dreamed of and more, including the hand of a princess in marriage. And your children will love to see Puss dressed to the nines, tall leather boots and all.

Rapunzel

There needs to be a lifetime achievement award for artists like Paul O. Zelinsky: there's not one of his books that is not worth seeking out. He's won prizes galore for many of his books like **Hansel and Gretel** and **The Story of Mrs. Lovewright and Purrless Her Cat**, including his version of **Rapunzel** (winner of the 1998 Caldecott Medal), which he's illustrated in the style of an Italian Renaissance painting, making marvelous use of *trompe l'oeuil* to both captivate and fool the eye.

Rumpelstiltskin

Rumpelstiltskin is another triumph by Paul O. Zelinsky. Its full page illustrations in oil lend the familiar story a warmth and depth that will enthrall both children and adults.

Virginia Hamilton's **The Girl Who Spun Gold**, her West Indian version of the tale of a mysterious man who can spin straw into gold, is illustrated by Diane and Leo Dillon. Here Rumpelstiltskin is known as Lit'mahn, and his contest with Quashiba is presented in a lilting Caribbean rhythm and dialect. The pictures are simply gorgeous—textured patterns, multi-colored, and tinged everywhere with gold leaf.

Sleeping Beauty

It's not hard to tell from the title that Will and Mary Pope Osborne's **Sleeping Bobby** is a fractured retelling of the Brothers Grimm tale of a princess who sleeps for a hundred years. In the Osbornes' version, it's an 18-year-old prince who falls prey to the curse of a wicked woman and into the century-long nap, and a very perfect princess who awakens him with a kiss. Giselle Potter's humorous illustrations are a perfect complement to the text.

The Three Little Pigs

I just love David Wiesner's sense of humor, and it's at its best in **The Three Pigs**, which he begins in the old familiar way but then branches off into a wild flight of imagination that can't help but make readers of all ages chuckle in appreciation.

Eugene Trivizas's **The Three Little Wolves and the Big Bad Pig** is made special by Helen Oxenbury's amusing illustrations.

Other great renditions of this tale include **The Three Little Pigs** by James Marshall and **The True Story of the 3 Little Pigs!** as told to Jon Scieszka by Alexander T. Wolf, who was, quite simply, framed. I kid you not!

FOLK TALES

One of the best ways to get a feel for the soul of a country is to read its folk tales. There are collections of folk tales for middle-grade readers as well (see "Myths, Legends, Folk and Fairy Tales" in Part II), but the ones listed below have wonderful illustrations and are highly recommended for reading aloud, as well.

Beautiful Blackbird by Ashley Bryan (a folk tale from Zambia)

The Bossy Gallito: A Traditional Cuban Folk Tale by Lucía M. González

Crocodile and Hen: A Bakongo Folktale by Joan M. Lexau (from the French Congo)

The Faithful Friend by Robert D. San Souci, illustrated by Brian Pinkney (from the French West Indies)

Fat Cat: A Danish Folktale, retold by Margaret Read MacDonald

Fly, Eagle, Fly: An African Tale, retold by Christopher Gregorowski, with watercolor illustrations by Niki Daly (and a foreword by Archbishop Desmond Tutu) takes place in a small village in South Africa

The Flying Witch by Jane Yolen (this story of the witch Baba Yaga comes from Russia)

Frog Went A-Courtin' by John Langstaff is a retelling of a traditional American song—and you'll find yourself singing the words aloud as you share this with children

The Hatseller and the Monkeys: A West African Folktale by Baba Wagué Diakité

Head, Body, Legs: A Story from Liberia by Won-Ldy Paye and Margaret H. Lippert, illustrated by Julie Paschkis

Honey . . . Honey . . . Lion!: A Story from Africa by Jan Brett (Botswana)

Hosni the Dreamer: An Arabian Tale by Ehud Ben-Ezer, with pictures by Uri Shulevitz

The Hunter by Mary Casanova (a beautifully illustrated tale from China)

The Hunterman and the Crocodile: A West African Folktale by Baba Wagué Diakité

It Could Always Be Worse, a Yiddish folk tale by Margot Zemach

John Henry by Julius Lester, with illustrations by Jerry Pinkney (Traditional American)

The Legend of the Persian Carpet by Tomie dePaola

Mabela the Clever by Margaret Read MacDonald (Sierra Leone)

The Mitten: A Ukrainian Folktale by Jan Brett

Monkey King by Ed Young (China)

Mufaro's Beautiful Daughters: An African Tale by John Steptoe (Zimbabwe)

The Red Lion: A Tale of Ancient Persia by Diane Wolkstein (the illustrations by Ed Young resemble ancient Persian miniatures)

Seven Blind Mice by Ed Young, who uses paper collages to illustrate this retelling of the Hindu folk tale about the blind man and the elephant

The Seven Chinese Sisters by Kathy Tucker

The Six Fools by Zora Neale Hurston (Joyce Carol Thomas adapted this from one of the Gulf state folk tales collected by Hurston in the 1930s)

So Say The Little Monkeys by Nancy Van Laan (Brazil)

Something from Nothing: Adapted from a Jewish Folktale by Phoebe Gilman

Stone Soup by Marcia Brown (probably originally from France)

Strega Nona by Tomie dePaola (this Italian folk tale has been charming young readers since it was first published in 1976; there are now many sequels, and even one prequel)

The Teeny Tiny Woman: A Traditional Tale by Arthur Robins and **The Teeny-Tiny Woman** by Paul Galdone (British)

The Three Sillies by Steven Kellogg (British)

Yoshi's Feast by Kimiko Kajikawa (Japan)

GIRLS RULE

It's never too early to show impressionable young readers that girls (even if they're not human) can be the heroines of stories, and life, too.

Ludwig Bemelmans's **Madeline** grew up "in an old house in Paris, all covered with vines," with eleven other little girls, and was, as it turns out, the bravest of them all (and the only one to be rushed to the hospital in the middle of the night to have her appendix out). This is truly one of the great children's books of all time.

Think Paul Bunyan is the last word in strength and bravery? You'll think again when you read about the adventures of Angelica Longrider (who was born bigger than her mother), the heroine of Anne Isaacs's tall tale **Swamp Angel**, which describes Angelica's greatest achievement: dispatching Thundering Tarnation, a black bear bent on disturbing the lives (and stealing the food) of the pioneers far from town. The illustrations by Paul O. Zelinsky add to the enjoyment.

Cornelia Funke's amusing and instructive **The Princess Knight** provides an excellent lesson for anyone who doubts that girls can do as well (or better than) boys in most things in life. And the pictures—by Kerstin Meyer—are great fun, too. The author and illustrator also collaborated on **Pirate Girl**, in which Molly, who just wants to go visit her grandmother, is grabbed by a group of pirates, contrives her own rescue, and gives the offenders a righteous punishment.

Two little girls who know exactly what they want to wear—and wouldn't have it any other way—include **Fancy Nancy** by Jane O'Connor (with exuberant illustrations by Robin Preiss Glasser) and **Ella Sarah Gets Dressed**, written and illustrated by Margaret Chodos-Irvine.

When her seamstress mother becomes ill, Irene is asked to deliver the duchess's dress—a task that the intrepid Irene succeeds in completing, despite huge obstacles, in William Steig's **Brave Irene**.

Charlotte, the determined child who stars in Barbara McClintock's **Dahlia**, hates dolls, much preferring to climb trees and make mudpies with her dog Bruno, and she isn't happy that her Aunt Edme has sent her a particularly fussy-looking one ("Her painted mouth was prim. She was dressed in linen and lace and delicate silk ribbons. Frail hands were covered with thin gloves."). But after she includes the doll in all of her adventures (with some attendant scrapes, scratches, and more serious injuries to poor Dahlia), both doll and little girl conclude that life is better together. Set in the Victorian period, McClintock's illustrations of this lovely and timeless tale are filled with muted colors, lending to the sense of reading about a time period long long ago.

Other books featuring stalwart girls include **Tar Beach** by Faith Ringgold (based on the artist's "story quilt," displayed at the Guggenheim Museum); **Kiss the Cow!** by Phyllis Root (a marvelous selection for story hours); **Eloise** by Kay Thompson (I bet that reservations at the Plaza in New York increased a gazillionfold as a result of this book. I know that I always wanted to stay there.); **Willa and the Wind**, retold by Janice M. Del Negro from a Norwegian folk tale; **Sense Pass King: A Story from Cameroon**, retold by Katrin Tchana, with pictures by Trina Schart Hyman; **Miss Bridie Chose a Shovel** by Leslie Connor, with woodcut and watercolor illustrations by Mary Azarian; and **A Chair for My Mother** by Vera B. Williams.

GRANDMAS AND GRANDPAS

When I became a grandmother, I realized that all the truisms about being a grandparent are actually true—the time you spend with your grandchildren is an unalloyed joy (probably because you don't have to spend all your time with them). This special relationship is described in the following books, many of which are appropriate for beginning readers.

Ruddy's not very fond of his Grandmother Silk, and the prospect of spending ten days with her while his parents take a cruise doesn't thrill him at all. But when the two get snowed in during a freak Halloween storm, he learns that they have more in common than he ever realized, in Carol Fenner's **Snowed In with Grandmother Silk**.

When Grandma Ni Ni moves from Cincinnati to California, her grandson Xiao Jimmy misses visiting her every day after school, helping her make *jiao zi* and hearing her stories about growing up in China, in **The Key Collection** by Andrea Cheng.

You might be as surprised as I was to learn who the narrator is in Carol Diggory Shields's **Lucky Pennies and Hot Chocolate**, an affectionate story about a little boy and his grandfather.

A stray (and mischievous) kitten helps Rana make friends at her new school and develop a better relationship with her grandmother, in **Meow Means Mischief** by Ann Whitehead Nagda.

Trish Cooke's **Full, Full, Full of Love**, with illustrations by Paul Howard, gathers together at Grannie's house a large and loving African American family for their regular Sunday dinner.

"What if I could fly," wonders Rosalba, in **Abuela** by Arthur Dorros, as she and her grandmother, her *abuela*, take their regular trip to feed the birds in the park. And magically (I've always believed that grandmothers are capable of this), the two embark on a flying trip around Manhattan. Each landmark reminds Abuela of something from her own past, which she shares with her granddaughter. The mixed-media illustrations (watercolors, pastels, and collages) by Elisa Kleven are done in a charming folk-art style, which, combined with Dorros's use of Spanish phrases, makes this a perfect choice for a multicultural story hour.

Norton Juster's **The Hello, Goodbye Window** (with joyful and lusciously colored, almost scribble-like mixed-media illustrations by Chris Raschka) is a warm tale of the love between a young girl and her grandparents, Nanna and Poppy. One of the interesting facets of this book is that Raschka's pictures make it clear this is an interracial family—it reminded me of a picture book I read when I was a child called **Two is a Team** by Lorraine and Jerrold Beim, which depicts two little boys of different races cooperating to make a scooter. As in Juster's book, the text never mentions race at all. Because I am insatiably curious, I'd love to know who thought of presenting a mixed-race family—Juster, Raschka, or perhaps the editor? In any case, it offers a powerful, though subtle, message.

Finally, although the book itself isn't all about grandparents, there's a wonderful chapter in **Tell Me a Mitzi** by Lore Segal about a little girl who takes her younger brother for an early morning cab ride to their grandparents' house, somewhere in New York City. The grandmother also saves the day in the second chapter, when the whole family comes down with colds.

GRIN AND BEAR IT!

I couldn't bear not including this category—once you start reading the books below you'll understand why.

The Hare who lost the race to the Tortoise in **Aesop's Fables** also lost his farm to pay his debts. Now, in order to get vegetables to feed his family, he tries to trick a very tired bear, in **Tops & Bottoms**, a Caldecott Honor Book by Janet Stevens; it's a story that may go a long way in helping children love their veggies. The double-spread line-and-wash paintings add to the charm of this humor-filled tale.

The rhythmical text in Bill Martin Jr.'s **Brown Bear, Brown Bear, What Do You See?** comes to life with Eric Carle's bold and colorful illustrations. This is one of those phenomenally popular books (along with its sequels, **Polar Bear, Polar Bear, What Do**

You Hear? and **Panda Bear, Panda Bear, What Do You See?**)
that children beg to hear again and again.

Nancy White Carlstrom's series of books about Jesse Bear (with
cheerful watercolor and pen-and-ink illustrations by Bruce Degen)
are always fun to share with children, and there's the added benefit
that they remain entertaining, no matter how often you're forced
to read them aloud—start with **Jesse Bear, What Will You Wear?**
and go on to **Better Not Get Wet, Jesse Bear, How Do You Say
It Today, Jesse Bear?**, and others.

Bears can sleep through anything (or almost anything)—just take
a look at Karma Wilson's humorous **Bear Snores On**, with charming illustrations done in acrylics by Jane Chapman. (And there's
more Bear to be found in **Bear Wants More**, **Bear Stays Up for
Christmas**, and **Bear's New Friend**.)

By sharing three Zen tales with Addy, Michael, and Karl, a very
wise panda bear named Stillwater gives them new ways of thinking
about the world in **Zen Shorts** by Jon J Muth, illustrated with dark
ink drawings on pastel-colored pages.

It's amazing the lessons you can learn from a bear, especially if you're
a failed magician, as you can see in Jon Agee's **Milo's Hat Trick**.

Simple living was the mantra of nineteenth-century writer Henry
David Thoreau, and in D. B. Johnson's series of books imagining
Henry as a bear, children can easily come to see the benefits of
Thoreau's way of life, along with his love and respect for nature.
There's minimal text—the joy is in the multifaceted (color) pencil
and paint illustrations. My favorite is **Henry Hikes to Fitchburg**
(he seems to be wearing a red bathrobe and wide-brimmed hat on
his trip to the city), but try them all.

Two other bear-y good books are **Not This Bear!** by Bernice Myers (which is difficult to find but worth the hunt) and Don Freeman's now classic **Corduroy** (and sequels).

JUST FOR FUN

Sometimes reading a good book that makes you laugh out loud is just what's needed. The books in this section have always seemed to me to be equally humorous to both the listening children and the adults who are reading to them. And that's no small achievement.

Even the most dedicated bird-watcher won't find more interesting birds anywhere than in Arnold Lobel's **The Ice-Cream Cone Coot and Other Rare Birds**. Here's where you'll discover the Pincushion Piffle (who helps with the sewing) and the Jackknife Niffy (who cuts off your nose in a jiffy, if you don't watch out), the Milkbottle Midge, the Buttonbeaks, and many others. The illustrations are delightfully inventive, too.

Lobel's **Fables** (which was honored with the Caldecott Medal) is yet another example of this talented writer/illustrator's work. Here he's come up with some twists on Aesop's fables, each with its own useful moral. Read a few of these each night at bedtime—they're the perfect length and great fun besides.

Wallace Edwards's gorgeously imaginative illustrations highlight Kenyon Cox's fantastical animals (described in delightful verse) in **Mixed Beasts,** which makes this a good companion for **The Ice-Cream Cone Coot.**

Jack Prelutsky combined his wacky sense of humor with the illustrations of Peter Sís to create **Scranimals**, a guide to the most unusual fauna found on Scranimal Island.

Brock Cole has written a modern fairy tale in **Buttons**, the story of three sisters who are given the task of finding buttons to replace the ones on their (very overweight) father's britches.

As author George Shannon and illustrator Laura Dronzek show, it can be a lot of fun to have your preconceived notions of color upset; just take a look at **White Is for Blueberry** and you'll see what I mean.

The story of the Montgolfier brothers' first ride in the hot-air balloon they invented is told with tongue firmly in cheek and a strong sense of the absurd in Marjorie Priceman's **Hot Air: The (Mostly) True Story of the First Hot-Air Balloon Ride**.

Bored by Dick and Jane? Try Lane Smith's **The Happy Hocky Family** and **The Happy Hocky Family Moves to the Country!** for a delightfully satirical change of pace.

If you can find a copy of Russell Hoban's **How Tom Beat Captain Najork and His Hired Sportsmen**, you'll discover an awfully smart little boy named Tom and two aunts, Miss Fidget Wonkham-Strong and Bundlejoy Cosysweet. Guess which one Tom prefers?

How to Tame Your Dragon by Cressida Cowell is the story of Hiccup Horrendous Haddock III, puny son and heir of Haddock, Chief of the Hairy Hooligans, who has to prove his worth against his much larger and nastier peers. This over-the-top story has everything to appeal to young readers, especially those who may think that books are dull: Viking valor, adventures with dragons, suspense, and slapstick humor—all appealingly illustrated with slapdash black-and-white drawings. **HTTYD** is loosely preceded by **Hiccup the Seasick Viking** and more closely followed by **How to be a Pirate**.

The really obvious jokes and—let's be frank, here—bathroom humor that make Cowell's books so popular with little boys, especially, are also a major component in Dav Pilkey's **The Adventures of Captain Underpants**, which features George and Harold and their exploits with their awful school principal, Mr. Krupp. Great fun for all.

Young fans of the Cowell and Pilkey books will definitely enjoy reading the books about Tashi and Jack by Anna and Barbara Fienberg. This series of Australian imports by a mother and daughter team hits all the right notes as each book relates another fantastical adventure of Tashi's involving ghosts, white tigers, giants, and other fearsome creatures. My favorite is **Tashi and the Ghosts**, but you can't really go wrong with any of them.

In Mini Grey's delicious **Traction Man Is Here!** a superhero action figure who bravely guards the breakfast toast, searches in the soapy dishwater for the lost wreck of the sieve, and rescues some dolls in distress is finally almost outdone by an all-in-one green romper suit and matching bonnet that a kind grandmother knits him for Christmas. Will Traction Man prevail against the odds? Read it and laugh.

When Arnie discovers just what the fate of being a doughnut is, he realizes that he'd better try to come up with something (besides being good to eat) that he excels at, in Laurie Keller's **Arnie the Doughnut**.

A fish running away down Kearny Street toward the San Francisco Bay? Try not to laugh too much when you share Lakas's attempts to capture his pet, in **Lakas and the Manilatown Fish**, with words (in both Tagalog and English) by Anthony D. Robles and pictures by Carl Angel.

Mo Willems has a terrific sense of humor, as evidenced by **Don't Let the Pigeon Drive the Bus!**, **The Pigeon Finds a Hot Dog!**, and **Don't Let the Pigeon Stay Up Late!** Kids as young as two and three love these books.

Esphyr Slobodkina both wrote and illustrated the *cap*tivating **Caps for Sale**, in which a peddler runs into some problems with a group of monkeys who want caps of their own.

Author Jon Scieszka and illustrator Lane Smith have collaborated on a number of well-loved (and side-splittingly funny) picture books, including **Science Verse** and **Math Curse**.

The adventures of Lyle the crocodile are surefire laugh inducers. Don't miss **The House on East 88th Street**, as well as **Lyle, Lyle, Crocodile**, **Lyle Finds His Mother**, **Funny, Funny Lyle**, and **Lyle at the Office**, written and illustrated by Bernard Waber.

Don't let any child grow up without meeting Imogene, who wakes up one morning with antlers growing out of her head, in David Small's hilarious **Imogene's Antlers**.

Eugene, the hero of Jon Agee's **Terrific**, is always sure that the worst will happen, until he meets a very smart parrot named Lenny on the desert island where he's been stranded.

A group of animals learns the ins and outs of making strawberry shortcake with many laugh-aloud misunderstandings along the way, in **Cook-A-Doodle Doo!** by Janet Stevens and Susan Stevens Crummel. The group includes Big Brown Rooster, a descendant of the Little Red Hen. (Remember her? She's the one who couldn't get any of her barnyard friends to help her bake bread, but everyone wanted to eat it once it was done; you might take a look at Margot Zemach's **The Little Red Hen: An Old Story** to refresh your memory.) The recipe that Big Brown Rooster uses is included, so try it out with your preschooler.

When some Icelandic chickens start thinking that they're really middle-aged Icelandic housewives, it takes the ingenuity of real Icelandic housewives to figure out how to get the chickens back to doing what they do best—laying eggs, or at least that's the story found in **The Problem with Chickens**, a clever matching of deadpan humor in both text and illustrations, by Bruce McMillan and Gunnella, respectively.

LATKES, DREIDELS, AND LIGHTS: CHANUKAH BETWEEN THE PAGES

The main problem with finding good books about Hanukah is figuring out how to spell the name of the holiday. Does it begin with an *H*? Or a *Ch*? Does it have one *k* or two? I'd advise trying all the various spellings—these books are both entertaining and instructive, an unbeatable combination (as are latkes and applesauce—yum!). In between bites of the very special potato pancakes known as latkes, try these:

Three picture books set in Eastern European villages are **Just Enough Is Plenty: A Hanukkah Tale** by Barbara Diamond Golden, with paintings by Seymour Chwast; Nina Jaffe's **In the Month of Kislev: A Story for Hanukkah**; and Eric A. Kimmel's **Zigazak!: A Magical Hanukkah Night**.

Kimmel wrote a number of other books about Hanukkah (in fact, the selection of books on the topic would be sparse indeed without Kimmel's contributions). His best known is **Hershel and the Hanukkah Goblins**, a collaboration with illustrator Trina Schart Hyman. Among his other titles are **The Chanukkah Guest**, a hilarious story of a very unusual fan of Bubba Brayna's holiday latkes; and **The Magic Dreidels**.

Mrs. Greenberg's Messy Hanukkah by Linda Glaser describes what happens when Rachel learns that there won't be latkes on the first night of Hanukkah. Glaser also wrote a lovely, heartwarming tale of sharing the blessings of Hanukkah in **The Borrowed Hanukkah Latkes**.

A grandfather shares with his grandchildren not only the story of the first Hanukkah, but also his own Hanukkah experience in Germany during World War II in Sheldon Oberman's **By the Hanukkah Light**, illustrated by Neil Waldman.

Other Chanukah books include a retelling of the Gingerbread Man story, Leslie Kimmelman's **The Runaway Latkes**; **Inside-Out Grandma** by Joan Rothenberg (especially fun for a grandmother to read to her grandchildren); **Runaway Dreidel!** by Lesléa Newman; and David A. Adler's **Chanukah in Chelm**, which offers an invaluable introduction to the people of Chelm. (Chelm is a fictional East European village best known for its utterly foolish inhabitants. Take a look at "Noodlehead Stories" for more tales set in Chelm.)

LET ME INTRODUCE YOU TO . . .

I think that children are naturally curious about other people—the way they live, what they eat, how they dress. Lively biographies are the way to feed this curiosity. They help children realize that other people are both the same as they are, and different. Here are some of the best I've found:

Jeanette Winter wrote and illustrated **The Librarian of Basra: A True Story from Iraq**, about Alia Baker, a brave Iraqi woman who saved all 30,000 of her library's books from the ravages of war. The same story is told for middle-grade readers by Mark Alan Stamaty in **Alia's Mission: Saving the Books of Iraq**, using a graphic novel format.

The creative genius of Ben Franklin is described in energetic prose and entertaining illustrations in **How Ben Franklin Stole the Lightning** by Rosalyn Schanzer. Schanzer also wrote **How We Crossed the West: The Adventures of Lewis and Clark**, another fine example of how to bring historical figures to life for young readers.

To Fly: The Story of the Wright Brothers by Wendie Old uses a picture book format to discuss the lives of both Orville and Wilbur, who began as bike mechanics and ended up as the forefathers of the crowded planes we ride on today.

Jean Fritz wrote a number of books on famous people (many of them major figures during the Revolutionary War period) that offer a spirited introduction to their subjects. My favorite has always been **And Then What Happened, Paul Revere?**, with its homespun illustrations by Margot Tomes, but I also enjoyed **Will You Sign Here, John Hancock?** and **Where Was Patrick Henry on the 29th of May?**

Other quality biographies for young readers include **Only Passing Through: The Story of Sojourner Truth** by Anne Rockwell; Nikki Giovanni's **Rosa** (the story of Rosa Parks), with illustrations by Bryan Collier; **The Boy on Fairfield Street:**

How Ted Geisel Grew Up to Become Dr. Seuss by Kathleen Krull; **The Last Princess: The Story of Princess Ka'iulani of Hawai'i**, written by Fay Stanley with spectacular illustrations by Diane Stanley that deepen the impact of this sad tale; **Sequoyah: The Cherokee Man Who Gave His People Writing** by James Rumford; **Red Scarf Girl: A Memoir of the Cultural Revolution** by Ji-Li Jiang; **I Could Do That!: Esther Morris Gets Women the Vote** by Linda Arms White (the story of the woman who almost single-handedly made Wyoming the first state to allow women to vote and also was its first elected female politician); and Andrea Davis Pinkney's **Alvin Ailey** (illustrated by her husband Brian Pinkney), which describes the contributions to the world of dance made by the great African American choreographer.

MANY CULTURES, MANY VOICES

It's a large and diverse world we live in, and one of the greatest gifts we can give our children is a sense of that diversity. And, of course, books are one of the best tools we can use to do exactly that. These picture books do so extremely well, without being preachy or pedantic.

A little girl helps her mother shop for and cook a traditional Korean dish (recipe included) in Linda Sue Park's **Bee-bim Bop!**

In its photographs of children and adults from around the world, Ann Morris's **Shoes, Shoes, Shoes** pictures the many and varied types of footwear worn by children and adults from Colombia to

Kenya, from Sweden to Hong Kong, and beyond. As the accompanying rhyme has it: "All over the world, in lands near and far, there are shoes that are right for wherever you are." Morris uses the same format in **Bread, Bread, Bread**, **Hats, Hats, Hats**, and **Houses and Homes**.

Every family has its own traditions—in Patricia Polacco's Russian Jewish family, described in **The Keeping Quilt**, it's handing down a quilt that's been used in family celebrations for four generations.

Another book that helps children understand the passage of time, offers them a picture of historical events, and also features a quilt and its history is Jacqueline Woodson's **Show Way**, with unforgettable illustrations in a variety of media by Hudson Talbott.

Janet S. Wong's **Apple Pie 4th of July** celebrates America's birthday through the eyes of a Chinese American child, who discovers—despite her fears—that real Americans do eat Chinese food, every day of the year.

Much as they might love their adopted country of America, for many immigrants "home" will always be where they came from. In **Faraway Home**, Jane Kurtz explores this theme through the eyes of a little girl who both loves and hates to hear about her father's childhood in Ethiopia, because she worries that when he goes there for a visit, he won't come home.

Consider offering these to young readers, as well: **Crow Boy** by Taro Yashima; Allen Say's **Grandfather's Journey**, **Kamishibai Man**, and **Tea with Milk**; Riki Levinson's **Watch the Stars Come Out**, illustrated by Diane Goode; and **Mama and Papa Have a Store** by Amelia Lau Carling.

MEET MOTHER GOOSE

Mother Goose rhymes are often among the first books that parents share with their children, and rightly so—these rhythmical and rhyming tales and riddles are conveniently short (so they're easy to remember) and fun to listen to. According to Mother Goose scholars, the rhymes were handed down orally over the last five hundred years or so, and many of them perhaps originated in real events. ("Ring Around the Rosie" might refer to the ravages of the Black Plague in the fourteenth century, or it might not. You pick your scholar and make your choice.) The rhymes were first collected and printed in England in 1744 by John Newbery, who is memorialized in the children's book award named for him. There are probably as many versions of the Mother Goose rhymes as there are stars in the sky (just a slight exaggeration). It does seem as though nearly every illustrator worth his or her salt has produced a book. Here, though, are the ones I treasure, in alphabetical order by illustrator.

> Nina Crews's **The Neighborhood Mother Goose**—the neighborhood is Brooklyn, and the illustrations are photographs
> Tomie dePaola's **Mother Goose**
> Michael Hague's **Mother Goose: A Collection of Classic Nursery Rhymes**
> Arnold Lobel's **The Arnold Lobel Book of Mother Goose: A Treasury of More Than 300 Classic Nursery Rhymes**
> James Marshall's **Mother Goose**

Will Moses's **Mother Goose**, illustrated with warm oil paintings in his trademark folk art style.

Iona Opie and Rosemary Wells's **My Very First Mother Goose** and **Here Comes Mother Goose** (Opie is one of the leading scholars of folklore and children's rhymes; Wells shows her love for the subject in every line of every illustration)

Richard Scarry's **Best Mother Goose Ever**

Blanche Fish Wright's **The Real Mother Goose** (originally published in 1916 and now available in many sizes and types—get the fiftieth-anniversary edition with the wonderful introduction by children's book doyenne, May Hill Arbuthnot)

Two others that I get a kick out of are probably more appropriate for adults than children, but take a look at them and decide for yourself. Photographer William Wegman, known for using Weimaraners instead of humans in his pictures, takes on the classic rhymes in his **Mother Goose**; and the longtime *New Yorker* cartoonist makes good use of his trademark weirdness in **The Charles Addams Mother Goose**.

Janet Stevens and Susan Stevens Crummel take a familiar Mother Goose rhyme and give it a little tweak in **And the Dish Ran Away with the Spoon**. Imagine what might happen if the dish and the spoon decide they're not coming back any time soon—which means that nobody can ever read the rhyme again! Mini Grey also begins with the same rhyme, and takes it in a quirky direction, in **The Adventures of the Dish and the Spoon**, characterized by her trademark humor.

MIND YOUR P'S & Q'S

As I was writing this section, I realized that I had no idea what the title phrase meant—what are p's and q's, anyway? After several hours of research, I discovered that nobody else really knows either. The idiom did appear in the *Oxford English Dictionary* in 1779 and was used then as we use it today. Adults spend a serious amount of time trying to get their kids to be more polite—*Yes, Thank you, Please, Share, Don't hit, Don't bite, Be nice to your sister/brother*, and *Be patient* are probably among the most worn-out phrases in a parent's vocabulary. Here are some books that offer a lighter look at the topic.

Gelett Burgess's **Goops and How to be Them: A Manual of Manners for Polite Infants Inculcating Many Juvenile Virtues, etc.** was published over a century ago, but is still great fun to read—the illustrations are a delight and the verses, once read, are almost hypnotically unforgettable. Burgess covered everything from tidiness to fortitude. Here's the entry on table manners:

> The Goops they lick their fingers,
> And the Goops they lick their knives;
> They spill their broth on the tablecloth—
> Oh, they lead disgusting lives!
> The Goops they talk while eating,
> And loud and fast they chew;
> And that is why I'm glad that I
> Am not a Goop—are you?

What Do You Say, Dear? and **What Do You Do, Dear?** by Sesyle Joslin, both illustrated by a very young Maurice Sendak, are fanciful introductions to the appropriate manners for many different occasions.

How Do Dinosaurs Eat Their Food? by Jane Yolen and Mark Teague ("Do they stick green beans up their nose? . . . Do they toss their spaghetti up into the air?") will elicit a giggle from even the youngest listener.

In **Mind Your Manners!** Diane Goode drew on a primer written in 1802 to teach Americans "the advantages of good manners" as the basis of this whimsical book. While the correct behavior at a banquet in Colonial times is stated, it's immediately contradicted by the detailed and very funny watercolor illustrations.

And in **Are You Going to Be Good?** by Cari Best, poor Robert gets advice on what to do and not to do from everyone in his family.

MUSIC TO MY EARS

Music plays an important part in the creative growth of a child, and I'm pleased to tell you there are some excellent books available that give a sense of the world of music, without a note being played—and they're just waiting to be shared with a very young reader.

In **The Philharmonic Gets Dressed**, Karla Kuskin (text) and Marc Simont (pictures) offer a warm and loving picture of how the 104 musicians and one conductor of a symphony orchestra get ready for their evening's performance.

Imagine a group of farm animals setting up their own band (their specialty is "Old Macdonald Had a Farm") and rocking and rolling with the best of them at their nighttime concerts, and you just might come up with **Punk Farm**, written and amusingly illustrated by Jarrett J. Krosoczka. (This is an especially apt choice for young Wisconsin readers.)

Four terrific read-alouds that get kids' toes a-tapping and their hands a-clapping and a-snapping include Chris Raschka's **Charlie Parker Played Be-Bop** and **Mysterious Thelonious**; **Hip Cat** by Jonathan London, starring Oobie-do, an oboe-playing cat who heads for the bright lights and welcoming arms of jazz lovers in the big city; and Karen Ehrhardt's **This Jazz Man**, which gives "This Old Man" a jazz beat. (And the lighthearted illustrations by R. G. Roth add a whole new dimension to the text.) All four are marked by the strong rhythms of their texts (kids will soon be reading along with you).

Lloyd Moss's **Zin! Zin! Zin! A Violin** introduces readers to ten different orchestral instruments by means of some rollicking rhymes and Marjorie Priceman's watercolor illustrations. It also functions quite nicely as a counting book.

Kids age three and up will enjoy Peter Sís's **Play, Mozart, Play!**, a biography of the musical genius who wrote his first composition when he was five years old, and, if we can believe Sís's text and art, it's all due to his father's encouragement (not to say pushing).

NOODLEHEAD STORIES

Noodlehead stories are a subcategory of folk tales. And they're pure joy, both to read and to tell. These tales just go to show that foolishness exists in countries all over the world. There's a universality in the realization that we've all done something foolish at least once in our lives, and reading these stories gives us a chance to laugh at ourselves, too. Sometimes, as you'll see below, all the noodleheads live in a particular village, but just as often they're scattered throughout the population. Get out a world map and see how many countries are represented in these books.

A most famous town of noodleheads is Chelm, in Eastern Europe; among the many collections highlighting the escapades of these foolish men are **The Jar of Fools: Eight Hanukkah Stories from Chelm**, with text by Jeffrey A. Kimmel and illustrations by Mordicai Gerstein; three collections by Isaac Bashevis Singer, including **Zlateh the Goat and Other Stories** (with pictures by Maurice Sendak), **Stories for Children**, and **When Shlemiel Went to Warsaw and Other Stories**; and **My Grandmother's Stories: A Collection of Jewish Folk Tales** by Adèle Geras.

Epossumondas, written by Coleen Salley with delightful illustrations by Janet Stevens, is the story of a little possum who takes what's told to him very literally indeed, which leads to fun for the reader and a headache for his mother. Another book with a similar plot is **Juan Bobo Goes to Work** by Marisa Montes.

A prime collection of noodlehead tales can be found in **Noodlehead Stories: World Tales Kids Can Read and Tell** by Martha Hamilton and Mitch Weiss, and **Noodlehead Stories from Around the World** by M. A. Jagendorf, which is a good resource for adults working with children this age, but not an especially appealing book for kids.

You might also want to take a look at the "Tall Tales" category in this section.

ONE PICTURE IS WORTH A THOUSAND WORDS

S haring wordless picture books with children is an excellent way to help develop a child's imagination and language skills by making up the words to go along with the illustrations, but even better than those practical outcomes is that these books are a pleasure to pore over:

> **Anno's Journey; Anno's Italy;** and **Anno's Spain** by
> Mitsumasa Anno
>
> **A Boy, a Dog, a Frog, and a Friend; Frog on His Own;**
> **Frog Goes to Dinner;** and others by Mercer Mayer
>
> **The Boy, the Bear, the Baron, the Bard** by Gregory
> Rogers (this is a book that will work well with kids
> through the fourth grade, and it's a nice way to introduce
> the youngest readers to William Shakespeare and his life)
>
> **Breakfast for Jack** and **Jack and the Missing Piece** by
> Pat Schories (Jack's an engaging—and misunderstood—
> orange-and-white spotted terrier)
>
> **Free Fall** (a little boy's imagination runs at full speed in his
> dreams at night) and **Tuesday** (frogs explore the world
> while everyone else is sleeping) by David Wiesner
>
> **Full Moon Soup, or The Fall of the Hotel Splendide**
> by Alastair Graham (what unusual events occur when the
> chef has a bowl of soup by the light of the full moon)
>
> **The Other Side** and **Zoom** by Istvan Banyai both explore
> how the world changes depending on your angle of
> observation
>
> **Rain** by Peter Spier

Ship Ahoy! by Peter Sís

Sidewalk Circus by Peter Fleischman, with illustrations by Kevin Hawkes (almost wordless, but I couldn't resist it— and neither will young children)

Snow Day by Daniel Peddle

Sunshine by Jan Ormerod

Time Flies by Eric Rohmann (*very* strange and sure to provoke a discussion of what it's really about)

The Yellow Balloon by Charlotte Dematons (children will enjoy searching for the yellow balloon on every page as it makes its wind-driven way around the world)

You Can't Take a Balloon into the Metropolitan Museum; **You Can't Take a Balloon into the National Gallery**; and **You Can't Take a Balloon into the Museum of Fine Arts** by Jacqueline Preiss Weitzman (good books to look over before you're off on a family trip to Manhattan; Washington, D.C.; or Boston)

PICTURE PERFECT

Trust me on these—although they're done in different media, in different styles, and with very different sensibilities, the artwork in these books is simply remarkable. And best of all, you can follow these up with others illustrated by the same artists.

Animalia, written and illustrated by Graeme Base (there's a small child hidden in this intricate and detailed alphabet book)

Arrow to the Sun: A Pueblo Indian Tale by Gerald McDermott (vibrant colors radiate from every page)

Baba Yaga and Vasilisa the Brave by Marianna Mayer, with illustrations by Kinuko Y. Craft (the paintings that illustrate this Cinderella tale are reminiscent of Russian folk art)

Beauty and the Beast by Marianna Mayer, illustrated by Mercer Mayer (richly detailed pictures capture the story's emotional tone)

Canterbury Tales, retold by Barbara Cohen, with illustrations by Trina Schart Hyman (I have to believe these gorgeous pictures are exactly what Chaucer would have wanted)

The Crane Wife by Odds Bodkin (could that possibly be his real name?), with illustrations by Gennady Spirin (stunning pictures that hint at the Japanese origin of the story)

Drummer Hoff by Barbara Emberley, illustrated by Ed Emberley (lively pictures in the primary colors—good for the very youngest children)

Hailstones and Halibut Bones by Mary O'Neill, with illustrations by Leonard Weisgard (this is the original; it's been reissued with new illustrations, but this is the one I'd search for—Weisgard's graceful pictures are suffused with the colors explored in each of O'Neil's poems)

Hansel and Gretel by Rika Lesser, illustrated by Paul O. Zelinsky (colorful and extremely detailed full-page illustrations convey the haunting quality of the Brothers Grimm tale)

Joseph Had a Little Overcoat, written and illustrated by Simms Taback (detailed illustrations done in a variety of media, including gouache, watercolor, and collage, with

Taback's traditional inventive and strategic use of die cuts
to enhance the plot)

Leaf Man by Lois Ehlert (the travels of the Leaf Man, and the
Leaf Man himself, are illustrated in collages of different-
sized and -shaped leafs, in all their autumn-toned glory)

Mother Goose, adapted and illustrated by Brian Wildsmith
(whimsical interpretations of the standard nursery rhyme
denizens—I particularly love "Humpty Dumpty")

QUACK AWAY

When I was remembering the books I'd loved as a child,
or used in story hours when I was a children's librarian, or was drawn to while browsing through the picture book section of my favorite bookstore, I was struck by how
often ducks take center stage in books for young children. So drop
everything and waddle on over to the bookshelves to try these:

Probably the first two books that come to anyone's mind when
he or she thinks "ducks" are Robert McCloskey's classic, Caldecott
Medal–winning **Make Way for Ducklings** and Marjorie Flack's
The Story About Ping. Ping, the little yellow duck who's the
hero of Flack's book, learns the potentially disastrous consequences
that follow when he deliberately disobeys his owner. (But don't
worry, it all turns out fine. At least this time.)

Make Way for Ducklings is perfect to read before you take
your child to Boston's Public Garden, where you can find a statue
of Mrs. Mallard and her brood of children, Jack, Kack, Lack, Mack,
Nack, Ouack, Pack, and Quack.

Big brothers come in handy when a small duckling decides he can't walk all the way back to his mother, in Simon James's **Little One Step**.

Doreen Cronin and Betsy Lewin teamed up to write and illustrate the Caldecott Honor story of a group of typing cows, called **Click, Clack, Moo: Cows That Type**, and its sequels, featuring Duck, who busily takes their notes around to show the other animals in **Giggle, Giggle, Quack**, runs for office in **Duck for President**, and is featured in **Click, Clack, Quackity-Quack: An Alphabetical Adventure** and **Click, Clack, Splish, Splash: A Counting Adventure**.

A contest between Duck and Gander over who's the champion almost ends in disaster when Fox comes along with the idea of making the two his dinner, in **Don't Fidget a Feather** by Erica Silverman.

Young readers will be enchanted with the colorful art and the funny story of a duck and a goose who find an egg (an odd-looking egg, it's true) and argue over who is going to help hatch it, in **Duck and Goose** by Tad Hills.

Other simply ducky choices include **Gossie** (actually a gosling) by Olivier Dunrea; David Shannon's colorful **Duck on a Bike**; **Come Along, Daisy!** by Jane Simmons; **Cold Little Duck, Duck, Duck** by Lisa Westberg Peters, with pictures by Sam Williams, which is a good read-aloud about a patient and determined quacker; **Off to School, Baby Duck!** by Amy Hest, where Grampa helps his granddaughter adjust to the first day of school; **Guji Guji** by Chih-Yuan Chen, the story of a mama duck who hatches, along with her new brood of ducklings, a crocodile; **Lizette's Green Sock** by Catharina Valckx, which offers one reason not to throw anything away, not even an unmatched sock;

and you'll find a very smart mother duck in Judy Hindley's **Do Like a Duck Does!**, drawn (as being very appropriately pleased with herself) by Ivan Bates.

REALITY CHECK

The subject matter of some of my favorite picture books is those ordinary events that take place fairly frequently in the life of a child—losing a stuffed animal, troubles with toilet training, adjusting to younger siblings, being teased by family members, visiting relatives, being scared of the dark, making friends. Children will not only identify with the situations depicted in these books, but they (and the adults sharing the story with them) will often get a chuckle, too.

When Trixie loses her favorite toy (and can't quite communicate to her parents what exactly is wrong), it takes some detective work and a fast dash to the Laundromat to rescue **Knuffle Bunny**, in one of the many delightful books by Mo Willems.

Willems also wrote **Time to Pee!**, perfect to read to children just beginning toilet training. It comes complete with a success chart and stickers (such as "Nice aim!" or "Better luck next time!").

Susan Middleton Elya and G. Brian Karas combined their talents on **Oh No, Gotta Go!**, about a little girl out for a drive with her parents who realizes that she *really* needs to go to the bathroom. One of the charms of this book is that it seamlessly blends Spanish and English in its rollicking rhymes.

In **Bebé Goes Shopping**, Elya captures the common experience of parents going a little bit nuts while shopping for groceries with their toddler. Once again mixing Spanish and English in the rhyming text, Elya will make all parents laugh at a scene they've lived time and again.

When Adèle picks up her younger brother Simon from school, he starts out with his hat and gloves and scarf and sweater and coat and knapsack and books and crayons and a drawing of a cat that he did that morning. But as their walk home progresses—with slight detours at two museums and a pastry shop, a stop to watch a parade and a puppet show, acrobats and a sword swallower—gradually many of Simon's possessions disappear. How they're returned to Simon will delight young readers of Barbara McClintock's **Adèle & Simon**. There's a map from a 1907 edition of Baedeker's *Paris and Environs* on the endpapers showing the children's route home and a guide to the illustrations at the close of the book. The detailed and intricate pen-and-ink illustrations are filled in with soft watercolors, and if you look closely you'll find McClintock has introduced some familiar characters from another beloved picture book set in France in the early twentieth century in one of the pictures.

After Ramon's older brother tells Ramon that his drawings stink, it takes some wise words from his sister to reassure him that it's okay not to be perfect at what he loves to do, in **Ish** by Peter H. Reynolds. (Kids will also feel enormously comforted by the events in Reynolds's **The Dot**, in which a wise and understanding teacher shows Vashti the possibilities of art in everything he creates, even if it's just a dot of color on a white sheet of paper.)

Two of the most reassuring books I know of for children deal with the progression of time. Both Charlotte Zolotow's **The Sky Was Blue** and Kathryn O. Galbraith's **Laura Charlotte** show that the world goes on and love is passed down from generation to generation.

Sometimes kids (not unlike adults) just wake up in a bad mood, and the day gets worse and worse as it goes along—as you can see in Judith Viorst's **Alexander and the Terrible, Horrible, No Good, Very Bad Day**.

For the heroine of **Flyaway Katie** by Polly Dunbar, it's easy to get yourself out of a funk—just make yourself more colorful. Would that it were always so simple!

Jacqueline Woodson, who's written many excellent books for young people of all ages, tackles the subject of a child dealing with having a parent in prison—and going to visit him, in **Visiting Day**.

Two books from a child's-eye view about moving to America from another country are **My Diary from Here to There** by Amada Irma Pérez, the story, in both Spanish and English, of a little girl about to leave her home in Mexico for Los Angeles, where her father hopes to find a good job; and **My Name is Yoon** by Helen Recorvits, in which a little girl searches for a new name for herself in her adopted country.

Philosophically inclined children—those who wonder why the sky is blue, why this and why that—and their parents will appreciate Jon J Muth's **The Three Questions** (based on a short story by Leo Tolstoy), in which Nikolai tries to find the answer to three important questions: When is the best time to do things? Who is the most important one? and What is the right thing to do? You might be surprised by the responses he gets.

REBELS WITH A CAUSE

One of the hardest lessons for a child (or anyone, really) to learn is that being different, though not easy, is not always a bad thing. In fact, as Ferdinand (see below) makes clear, you can end up with a very happy life. Take these examples to heart:

Tacky the Penguin by Helen Lester always goes his own way, despite the advice and behavior of his friends, Angel, Lovely, Goodly, Neatly, and Perfect. Don't you love those names? Every time I remember them I have to smile.

Swimmy, written and illustrated by Leo Lionni, is a black fish who lives with a group of red fish, and discovers that he has an important part to play in their plans to fool larger predators.

What do you do with a Spanish bull who doesn't want to take part in any bullfights, and would rather sit, eat daisies, and enjoy the ambiance of the pasture in which he lives? Munro Leaf's **The Story of Ferdinand**, illustrated by Robert Lawson (who wrote some terrific children's books of his own, including **Rabbit Hill** and **The Sea Is Blue**), explores this dilemma.

In Maurice Sendak's **Where the Wild Things Are**, Max refuses to obey his mother, so he's sent to bed without his dinner—but then the fun begins, as Max is made King of the Wild Things, presiding over the Wild Rumpus. And when Max decides to go home, he finds his dinner waiting—still hot. (I was using this in a story hour once, and as I turned over the last page and started saying, "And it was still . . ." a little boy piped up and said, "too hot!" Shades of **The Three Bears**.)

I suppose the lesson of Beatrix Potter's **The Tale of Peter Rabbit** is to obey your mother and *not* go into Mr. McGregor's garden—terrible things happen if you do (they certainly did to Peter's father). However, Peter can't resist the garden's lure....

Anu Stohner's eponymous **Brave Charlotte** is a sheep who isn't particularly sheeplike—she's determined to do her own thing, much to the dismay of her fellow sheep, who run much more closely to type. Of course, like the penguin Tacky, Charlotte's independence will be the salvation of her more obedient pals.

In **Veronica** by Roger Duvoisin, a young hippopotamus is tired of blending in with all the other hippos at their favorite muddy riverbank, so she hies herself off to the city, where she discovers that while being anonymous has its problems, being a conspicuous hippopotamus is not much fun either.

While George is not so much a rebel as the others in this category, he certainly never learns it's better not to be curious, no matter how much trouble he gets into in **Curious George** (and its sequels) by H. A. Rey.

And Leo, the main character in Robert Kraus's **Leo the Late Bloomer**, is also not so much a rebel as, say, Ferdinand or Tacky. Leo just does things in his own time. Jose Aruego's illustrations add immeasurably to this tender, loving tale, which will provide comfort to parents who worry about their child's physical and intellectual development.

Mama Cat has two kittens who always do what she says, but that third kitten gets into mischief (when he's not sleeping), in **Mama Cat Has Three Kittens** by Denise Fleming.

Janell Cannon both wrote and illustrated **Stellaluna** and **Verdi**, two picture books that kids will delight in. Stellaluna is a baby bat who learns that even if your friends do things slightly differently (like not hanging upside down by their feet), it's okay, while Verdi is a young yellow snake who's determined to do everything he can not to turn green and boring.

RHYMING READ-ALOUDS FOR THE VERY YOUNG

I'm always looking for good read-alouds for the four- to seven-year-olds in my life. What I especially enjoy are those rhythmical (and often joyfully nonsensical) rhymes that flow trippingly off the tongue. I'm happy to report there are some grand selections out there in the world of picture books, as you can be see here.

One of the best is **Down the Back of the Chair**, written by Margaret Mahy and illustrated by Polly Dunbar. In this tongue-twisting tale, Dad's lost his car keys, and two-year-old Mary, the narrator's sister, suggests he look down the back of the chair for them. What they find there will elicit chuckles from everyone: "A crumb, a comb, a clown, a cap, a pirate with a treasure map, a dragon trying to take a nap, down the back of chair" is just one example. Dunbar's colorfully winsome watercolor and cut paper illustrations are a perfect complement to one's enjoyment of the story.

Other good choices include:

Margaret Wise Brown's **Where Have You Been?**
Stephanie Calmenson's **Dinner at the Panda Palace**
Remy Charlip's **Sleepytime Rhyme**
Bruce Degen's **Jamberry**
Lisa Campbell Ernst's **This Is the Van That Dad Cleaned**
Mem Fox's **The Magic Hat**

Deborah Guarino's **Is Your Mama a Llama?**

Mary Ann Hoberman's **A House Is a House for Me**

Verla Kay's **Gold Fever**

John Langstaff's **Over in the Meadow**, which has been illustrated over the years by various artists, including Ezra Jack Keats and (nearly fifty years ago) Feodor Rojankovsky

Tony Mitton's **Once Upon a Tide**

Charlotte Pomerantz's **How Many Trucks Can a Tow Truck Tow?**

Adam Rex's **Tree Ring Circus**

Linnea Riley's **Mouse Mess**

Dr. Seuss's **And to Think That I Saw It on Mulberry Street**

Nancy Shaw's **Sheep in a Jeep**

Chris Van Dusen's **If I Built a Car**

Lisa Wheeler's **Sixteen Cows**

Anna Witte's **The Parrot Tico Tango**

Audrey Wood's **Silly Sally**

SCHOOL DAZE

S chool is a big deal in a child's life—whether it's starting kindergarten, changing teachers, or simply experiencing the day-to-day newness of it, and these books explore the experience from the inside out.

Little girls especially adore the series of more than fifteen titles about Junie B. Jones by Barbara Park, which follow Junie's everyday adventures as she starts kindergarten in **Junie B. Jones and the Stupid, Smelly Bus**, and gets to first grade in the aptly titled **Junie B., First Grader (at last!)**.

The brilliant Miss Brilliant discovers the best way to help the class bully overcome his bad behavior in Aliki's **A Play's the Thing**, the closest to a graphic novel that I've seen for the preschool set.

Denys Cazet captures a busload of active first-graders' chaotic field trip to an aquarium in his hilarious—and somehow right on the mark—**Are There Any Questions?** (It's clear he must have had up close and personal experience with one or two school field trips himself.)

Harry Allard wrote and James Marshall illustrated the contemporary classic **Miss Nelson Is Missing!**, the story of what happens when a substitute teacher named Viola Swamp (supposedly based on Marshall's own least-favorite teacher) takes over her class. This book is a great example of a perfect melding of text and pictures.

Back to School Is Cool! by Jim Jinkins features Pinky Dinky Doo, heroine of **Polka Dot Pox** and **Where Are My Shoes?**, in an encore appearance. This time, Pinky Dinky tries to reassure her younger brother, Tyler, who's a little bit nervous about starting school.

Patricia Reilly Giff has written a whole series of books under the general title of The Kids of the Polk Street School. Readers get to spend a year with their friends in Ms. Rooney's class, beginning with **The Beast in Ms. Rooney's Room**.

Mean Jean—the bully of the playground—gets her comeuppance (and learns some lessons in friendship) when Katie Sue comes to school, in Alexis O'Neill's **The Recess Queen**, with exuberant illustrations by Laura Huliska-Beith.

Even nonhumans are a little nervous about going to school, and Miss Spider's first day is a real learning experience for her, in David Kirk's **Little Miss Spider at Sunny Patch School**.

Wemberly is just like an ordinary little girl, except that she's a mouse with a lot of fears. Kevin Henkes describes her anxiety about beginning nursery school in **Wemberly Worried**.

Other animals-at-school books include **Amanda Pig, Schoolgirl** by Jean Van Leeuwen; Rosemary Wells's **Yoko** (a grey kitten brings sushi to school for lunch, but everyone makes fun of her—until they take a bite); **Froggy Goes to School** by Jonathan London; and Carey Armstrong-Ellis's **Seymour Slug Starts School**.

Although her mother wants her to stay home and learn to be bad, Little Witch really wants to go to school—which she does, with her broomstick in hand, in Deborah Hautzig's **Little Witch Goes to School**.

Sarah and her rascally cat, Ralph, appear in several books by Jack Gantos, beginning with **Rotten Ralph**; in **Back to School for Rotten Ralph**, he insists on accompanying Sarah to school.

Juan Felipe Herrera tells the story—in Spanish and English—of the first time his migrant family stayed put in one place so that he could go to school, in **The Upside Down Boy** (with entertaining illustrations by Elizabeth Gómez). Very simply told, Herrera shares with readers the feelings of a child who thinks that everything he does is wrong, because he doesn't know how to behave in this new environment. (Thankfully, the book ends happily.)

Rosemary Wells's **Emily's First 100 Days of School** doubles as a counting rhyme, as each day in Miss Cribbage's class, as well as at home, Emily learns something new.

In **Countdown to Kindergarten** by Alison McGhee, with darling pictures by Harry Bliss, our heroine realizes—ten days before school starts—that she needs to learn how to tie her shoes all by herself. Just imagine what trauma (for the parents, too) follows! The two also collaborated on another school tale—**Mrs. Watson Wants Your Teeth**.

I wonder how autobiographical **Little Cliff's First Day of School** by Clifton L. Taulbert is—in this tender story, set in the South in the 1950s, he's captured the feelings of an African American boy as he faces his first day of school.

In **Marvin One Too Many** by Katherine Paterson, poor Marvin is having a difficult time getting used to his new school, being sure that his teacher doesn't like him, and worst of all, trying to learn to read.

SIMPLE AS ABC

Clearly, the attraction of alphabet books is not that they're filled with suspense—you know they're going to end with Z! And it's not that the characters are so winsome—you hardly have a chance to get to know them as the letters whirl by. What's so much fun about the best alphabet books is their inventiveness and high spirits (and seeing how the author and illustrator handle that pesky letter X). Here are some winners:

Chicka Chicka Boom Boom by Bill Martin Jr. and John Archambault, and illustrated by Lois Ehlert (herself a children's book author of note) makes a wonderful read-aloud, as you follow the adventures of the letters of the alphabet as they try to climb a coconut tree.

In **Alligator Arrived with Apples: A Potluck Alphabet Feast** by Crescent Dragonwagon, with pictures by Jose Aruego and Ariane Dewey, a Thanksgiving dinner is made infinitely more interesting by the different foods each animal brings (notice the Dragon and the Deer on a tandem bicycle, delivering diced dates).

In Joseph Slate's **Miss Bindergarten Gets Ready for Kindergarten**, each letter of the alphabet depicts an animal getting ready for the first day of school, while the teacher, Miss Bindergarten (a dog in human clothing), is readying the classroom for her new students. The humorous watercolor and gouache illustrations by Ashley Wolff capture the zest of the rhyming text perfectly.

Ashanti to Zulu: African Traditions by Margaret Musgrove introduces western readers to the culture of Africa, with lots of help from award-winning illustrators Diane and Leo Dillon.

You won't want to miss Lois Ehlert's **Eating the Alphabet: Fruits and Vegetables from A to Z**, which is illustrated in bright primary colors and whose choice for the letter X may send us all to the grocery store to purchase an unfamiliar vegetable.

Check out **Ellsworth's Extraordinary Electric Ears and Other Amazing Alphabet Anecdotes** by Valorie Fisher, in which the author uses dioramas with plastic figures to illustrate the letters, each accompanied by a tongue-twisting description of what's happening. The scene for A is an acrobat being eyed hungrily by an alligator with its mouth wide open in anticipation.

The caption reads: "Alistair had an alarming appetite for acrobats." You get the picture.

In **Alphabet Under Construction** by Denise Fleming, the lovely illustrations (which "were created by pouring colored cotton fiber through hand-cut stencils") and the buck-toothed mouse hero, who uses all sorts of action verbs as he nails, okays, unrolls, tiles, yanks, and x-rays the appropriate letters, will delight beginning readers.

STOP BUGGING ME: INSECTS GALORE

If you must know, I am not a nature kind of person—I'd prefer insects to be outside and me inside, reading a book, perhaps. But I do find that kids love these books, even if reading them too often may drive an adult a bit buggy.

Kevin O'Malley's delightful **Little Buggy** is the tale of a young ladybug determined to learn how to fly, who succeeds despite the many difficulties that continually bug him. (Don't miss the two snails who offer their opinions on the progress of Little Buggy's attempts. They're a sort of Greek chorus for the toddler set.) O'Malley is also the author of **Leo Cockroach ... Toy Tester**. Leo's the best employee of Waddatoy Toys, but unfortunately Mildred Splatt, the president and CEO of the company, doesn't realize it—so Leo is constantly in fear for his life (death by Splatt's shoe).

With Sally Hewitt's rhyming text and Chris Gilvan-Cartwright's pop-up illustrations, **Bugs Pop-Up: Creepy Crawlers Face to Face** will delight buggy-inclined youngsters.

Miss Spider's Tea Party, written and illustrated by David Kirk, describes the problems a hostess has when her invited guests are afraid to accept—for fear they'll be eaten.

The Very Hungry Caterpillar by Eric Carle is often the first book that a child bugs his or her mother (or father) to read—so it's fortunate for all adult readers that it's a good one.

Fiona's Bee by Beverly Keller is about a lonely little girl who rescues a bee from drowning and discovers in the process how to make friends. It's much less staid and stolid than it might sound. . . .

Ugh! A Bug by Mary Bono offers lots of choice ideas (in a sort of verse format) for when a child next encounters a creepy-crawly (all from the point of view of the bug, it must be said), including this bit of practical advice: "So next time you see a bug / don't make a fuss— / after all, / there's a lot more of them / than of us." Too true.

All Roberto has ever wanted to be was an architect, joining such luminaries in the field as Fleas Van Der Rohe and Hank Floyd Mite. He wants to be interviewed on television by Barbara Waterbugs, and the subject of a movie by Steven Shieldbug—but Roberto's a termite, and everyone knows that termites can't be architects—or can they? **Roberto: The Insect Architect** by Nina Laden offers the answer.

Combining an alphabet book and the antics of a busy fly make for an outstanding read-aloud in the hands of Jim Aylesworth (text) and Stephen Gammell (illustrations), in **Old Black Fly**.

Two delightful books by Richard Egielski that kids will bug you to read again and again are **Buz** (what happens when a little boy swallows a bug with his breakfast cereal and pandemonium breaks out both inside and outside his body) and **Jazper**, about an unnamed type of insect who gets a job house-sitting in Bugtown for five moths and makes good use of his employers' library (which is filled with books about magic)—think cheese doodles and pickles.

TALL TALES

The books in this category and in "Noodlehead Stories" (more than in most categories) overlap between this section, Part I: Youngest Readers, and Part II: Middle-Grade Readers. The important thing is not to overlook them, because they're all enormous fun and perfect for sharing with a class or an individual reader. Some of these tall tales evolved from the life of a real person, while others are whoppers—contrived out of whole cloth, plain and simple; often you just don't know who's real and who's invented. An added benefit to these books is that women show up as main characters almost as often as men do.

One author you don't want to miss introducing kids to is Steven Kellogg, whose contributions to this category include his books **I Was Born About 10,000 Years Ago: A Tall Tale** (based on a traditional folk song); **Mike Fink: A Tall Tale**; **Pecos Bill: A Tall Tale**; **Sally Ann Thunder Ann Whirlwind Crockett: A Tall Tale** (about Davy Crockett's energetic wife); and **Paul Bunyan: A Tall Tale**.

Just from the title you know you're in for an entertaining time reading Deborah Hopkinson's **Apples to Oregon: Being the (Slightly) True Narrative of How a Brave Pioneer Father Brought Apples, Peaches, Pears, Plums, Grapes, and Cherries (and Children) Across the Plains**; it has equally charming illustrations by Nancy Carpenter.

You'll find more indomitable women in **Doña Flor: A Tall Tale about a Giant Woman with a Great Big Heart**, by Pat Mora, which has gorgeous illustrations by Raul Colón, who uses several different artistic media, including watercolor washes, etchings, and litho pencils, all done in a Southwest desert color scheme; **Steamboat Annie and the Thousand-Pound Catfish** by Catherine Wright; **Avalanche Annie: A Not-So-Tall Tale** by Lisa Wheeler (the main character, Annie Halfpint, is only 4 foot 3, but manages to lasso an avalanche and save her neighbors); and **Thunder Rose** by Jerdine Nolan, which depicts one very talented little girl.

Davy Crockett Saves the World by Rosalyn Schanzer is one of numerous stories about the hero of the Alamo; here, he saves the world from Halley's Comet and captivates Sally Ann in the process. Another enticing Crockett tall tale is **The Narrow Escapes of Davy Crockett: From a Bear, a Boa Constrictor . . . Trees, Tornadoes, a Sinking Ship, and Niagara Falls** by Ariane Dewey.

What seems ordinary to the Bunyan family makes for tall tale pleasure, in **The Bunyans** by Audrey Wood, the only book I'm familiar with that provides Paul with companionship other than Babe the Blue Ox.

Christopher Myers adapted and illustrated some of the tall tales that author Zora Neale Hurston collected on a trip through the southern United States in 1939 in **Lies and Other Tall Tales**, told in the diction and cadence of old-timey storytellers.

There are also some not-to-be-missed non-American tall tales, including **Master Man: A Tall Tale of Nigeria** by Aaron Shepard, a Hausa tale about how thunder was introduced into the world; **Finn MacCoul and His Fearless Wife: A Giant of a Tale from Ireland**, retold and illustrated by Robert Byrd; and a good companion tale to tell—from another point of view—**Mrs. McCool and the Giant Cuhullin** by Jessica Souhami, a feminist take on the same Irish legend.

THANKS FOR THANKSGIVING

Way, way back in 1886, Lucretia P. Hale wrote a very funny book about a very silly family (or at least a family who does very silly things), called **The Peterkin Papers**. Elizabeth Spurr adapted the original chapter in **The Peterkins' Thanksgiving**, with illustrations by Wendy Anderson Halperin. (The same pair did **The Peterkins' Christmas**.)

If you've ever been asked why it is that we celebrate Thanksgiving as a national holiday, fear not—you can find the answer in **Thank You, Sarah: The Woman Who Saved Thanksgiving**, written by Laurie Halse Anderson and illustrated by Matt Faulkner.

Barbara Cohen's **Molly's Pilgrim** is both a Thanksgiving tale and a moving story about recent immigrants to the United States.

A Turkey for Thanksgiving, written by Eve Bunting and warmly illustrated by Diane de Groat, is a humorous tale (perfect for reading aloud) about Mr. Moose and his friends searching for a turkey for his wife to cook for dinner.

Can there be a different fate for a turkey other than ending up as the main dish at Thanksgiving dinner? **Thelonius Turkey Lives! (on Felicia Ferguson's Farm)**, written and illustrated by Lynn Rowe Reed, offers another—colorful and happy—alternative.

The illustrations of a family gathering for dinner in Diane Goode's **Thanksgiving Is Here!** are filled with wonderful details that both adults and children will enjoy poring over.

Dav Pilkey wrote **'Twas the Night Before Thanksgiving**, a loving parody of *The Night Before Christmas*, and clearly had a ball illustrating it, too. I especially loved the picture of the schoolchildren rescuing the turkeys from their inevitable fate.

Young readers will enjoy Anne Warren Smith's **Turkey Monster Thanksgiving**, in which fourth-grader Katie learns that there are many different ways of celebrating Thanksgiving, with or without a turkey.

Lillian Hoban's books about Silly Tilly Mole are all set around different holidays. In **Silly Tilly's Thanksgiving Dinner**, Hoban describes how Silly Tilly's holiday feast is almost ruined (but saved just in time by her friends). Others in the series include **Silly Tilly's Valentine** and **Silly Tilly and the Easter Bunny**.

TRICKSTER TALES

T rickster tales are a subgroup of folk tales, in which the main character (who's usually, but not always, an animal) outwits the other animals or people around him. It's a form of folk tale that's found in cultures all over the map, from Germany's Tyl (sometimes Till) Eulenspiegel to America's Brer Rabbit to the Anansi tales from Africa. Because they usually feature a hero who overcomes the odds to outsmart others (who are usually older and supposedly wiser), they're favorites of children and make for spirited read-alouds, too. Try these:

Many of the picture books by multiple-award-winning author/illustrator Gerald McDermott are trickster tales, including **Anansi the Spider: A Tale from the Ashanti**; **Zomo the Rabbit: A Trickster Tale from West Africa**; **Jabuti the Tortoise: A Trickster Tale from the Amazon**; **Raven: A Trickster Tale from the Pacific Northwest**; and **Coyote: A Trickster Tale from the American Southwest**.

Other goodies include Gail E. Haley's **A Story, A Story**, an African tale starring Kwaku Ananse, the Spider Man (no, this is not the basis for the film starring Tobey Maguire!); **Anansi and the Moss-Covered Rock** by Eric A. Kimmel, with illustrations by Janet Stevens; and the tale of a trickster guinea pig (yes, really!) from Peru—**Zorro and Quwi** by Rebecca Hickox.

Some entertaining trickster tales that feature humans rather than animals include **The Old Woman and the Red Pumpkin: A Bengali Folk Tale** by Betsy Bang, with illustrations by Molly Bang; Margaret Willey's **Clever Beatrice: An Upper Peninsula Conte** (illustrated by Heather Solomon), about a little girl who makes a bet with a giant—a rich giant, true, but not a particularly smart one—in order to earn enough money so that she and her mother won't starve, and its sequel, **Clever Beatrice and the Best Little Pony**, another folk tale from the French Canadians; **The Hungry Coat: A Tale from Turkey** by Demi; **Just a Minute: A Trickster Tale and Counting Book** by Yuyi Morales, in which Death (in the form of Señor Calavera, a skeleton) is outwitted by his target, Grandma Beetle, who's getting ready for her big birthday celebration; and **Please, Malese! A Trickster Tale from Haiti**, written by Amy MacDonald and illustrated by Emily Lisker.

Lapin Plays Possum: Trickster Tales from the Louisiana Bayou was adapted by Sharon Arms Doucet, with pictures by Scott Cook. Fans of Brer Rabbit will recognize some of these stories, which are especially appropriate for reading aloud.

For a solid collection of Uncle Remus stories, take a look at **The Tales of Uncle Remus: The Adventures of Brer Rabbit** as told by Julius Lester and illustrated by Jerry Pinkney.

A Ring of Tricksters: Animal Tales from America, the West Indies, and Africa is a collection of stories told by the ever-talented Virginia Hamilton, with pictures by Barry Moser. The author and illustrator also collaborated on **When Birds Could Talk and Bats Could Sing: The Adventures of Bruh Sparrow, Sis Wren, and Their Friends**, which is made up of stories originally told by African slaves in the United States.

If you're interested in using trickster tales during story hours or for slightly older children, take a look at **American Indian Trickster Tales**, selected and edited by Richard Erdoes and Alfonso Ortiz, a collection of tales (but no illustrations) from many different tribes, showing the Trickster in his different incarnations, including Coyote and Iktomi the Spider-Man, as well as tales featuring the slightly less well-known Veeho (from the Cheyenne Indians) and Glooskap, whose stomping ground was the northeastern United States and Canada.

WEATHER OR NOT

Remember the nursery rhyme, "Rain, rain, go away, come again another day"? I think even very young children wonder about the varieties of weather, since so much of what they wear or even whether or not they can go outdoors to play depends on what it's like outside. These books speak to that sense of wonderment.

First there are days and days of snow, and then days and days of heavy rain, which means, Grandma predicts, "It'll come a tide," and sure enough, the river floods—which means, Grandma says, that it's time to "make friends with a shovel" in George Ella Lyon's **Come**

a Tide, tenderly illustrated by Stephen Gammell. Wait till you see Grandma's chin—this is one determined lady!

There's lots of rain, too, in Uri Shulevitz's magical **Rain Rain Rivers**, although here the rain is presented not as a destructive force, but rather as a cause for celebration.

Trouble begins when the rain starts falling and things only right themselves when the sun—finally!—comes out, in David Shannon's **The Rain Came Down**.

William Steig's **Pete's a Pizza** gave me some chuckles and a way to entertain children on the next rainy day. You've got to give a lot of credit to Pete's dad, too.

Karen Hesse and Jon J Muth combine text and illustrations in **Come On, Rain!**, about a little girl who's looking forward to an end of the seemingly endless dry spell and heat of summer.

David Wiesner's **Hurricane** describes the adventures of two brothers when a hurricane blows in and knocks down an elm tree near their house.

It's winter and there's snow—what fun for these children, who don't seem to mind the cold: **The Snowy Day** by Ezra Jack Keats and Olivier Dunrea's **It's Snowing!** (I just love the exclamation point there—it's so indicative of the joy found in this book about a mother and her baby sharing the delights of his first snowfall.) That same joy can be found in Raymond Briggs's wordless classic, **The Snowman**, a book no child (or adult) will want to miss; **The First Day of Winter** by Denise Fleming (a rollicking cumulative tale that's great for a snowy story hour); **Snow** by Uri Shulevitz, celebrating the joy a boy and his dog find in a snowfall in the city; **Winter Friends** by Mary Quattlebaum (a collection of poems about wintertime); and Manya Stojic's **Snow**, which is all about how different animals prepare for the coming of winter.

In **Lucille's Snowsuit** by Kathryn Lasky, poor Lucille has so much trouble getting into her snowsuit that she almost misses out on playing in the snow with her older brother and sister (you can find out more about Lucille and her other exploits in **Starring Lucille** and **Lucille Camps In**).

If you've ever wondered what snowmen do when all the kids go home to dinner and sleep, you'll find the answer in Caralyn Buehner's **Snowmen at Night**; and of course no list of wonderful weather books could omit the heroics of Katy, who works throughout a huge blizzard to help out her small town, in Virginia Lee Burton's **Katy and the Big Snow**.

YOU'VE GOT A FRIEND

As these picture books show, friends come in all shapes and sizes, and the best of friends stick together through thick and thin, through good times and bad. Just look at these: Arnold Lobel's signature characters Frog and Toad are two of my favorites in all of fiction; their relationship really defines the characteristics of friendship: tolerance for the other's quirks, a little bit of sacrifice, perhaps, and a deep concern for the other's happiness. They're found in **Frog and Toad Are Friends**, **Frog and Toad Together**, and **Days with Frog and Toad**.

Kids who enjoy the Frog and Toad stories will also enjoy Kate McMullan's tales about the lovely friendship between Pearl (a bunny) and Wagner (a mouse), including **Pearl and Wagner: Two Good Friends** and **Pearl and Wagner: Three Secrets**, and the stories of a friendship between two hippopotami, in **George and Martha** and **George and Martha One Fine Day** by James Marshall. Annabelle Bernadette Clementine Dodd only comes to really appreciate her grown-up friend Bea after a potentially dreadful mishap in **The Friend**, written and illustrated by the wife and husband team of Sarah Stewart and David Small.

Rabbit is a terrible trial to his best friend, Mouse, but despite that, their friendship knows no bounds, in **My Friend Rabbit** by Eric Rohmann.

Al, a janitor, and his best friend, a dog named Eddie, learn a valuable lesson together in **Hey, Al** by Arthur Yorinks, with remarkably detailed and clever illustrations by Richard Egielski.

Other friendship books include **Andy and the Lion** by James Daugherty; Holly Keller's **Farfallina and Marcel** (a caterpillar and a gosling); **You're Not My Best Friend Anymore** by Charlotte Pomerantz; **Chicken Sunday** by Patricia Polacco; Charlotte Zolotow's **My Friend John**; **Mr. George Baker** by Amy Hest; **Metropolitan Cow** by Tim Egan (can a cow overcome his parents' disapproval and remain friends with the pig next door?); and Christopher Raschka's **Yo? Yes!** and **Ring! Yo?**

MIDDLE-GRADE READERS
AGES 8–12

PART II

ADVENTURE AHOY!

T he four classic adventure novels that no one, child or adult, should go through life without reading are, of course, Robert Louis Stevenson's **Kidnapped** and **Treasure Island**—filled as they are with pirates, treasure, heroes, and lots of derring-do—and Daniel Defoe's **Robinson Crusoe** and Jules Verne's **20,000 Leagues Under the Sea**. You can see their benign but telling influence on the contemporary adventures described here.

Airborn by Kenneth Oppel, which takes place in a world similar to, but subtly different from our own, is a rousing tale of pirates, lighter-than-air ships that sail through the sky, mysterious creatures that may or may not be dangerous, and a resourceful and ambitious cabin boy named Matt, who wants to live up to his memories of his father. It's followed up by **Skybreaker**, an equally enjoyable tale.

Pirates also play a major part of Michele Torrey's exciting **Voyage of Plunder**. Set in the early 1700s, this is the swashbuckling story of Daniel Markham, who, after his father's murder aboard their merchant ship, has no choice but to join the *Tempest Galley* and work for its captain, the pirate Josiah Black. Torrey is also the author of **Voyage of Ice**, a gripping story of a young man's adventures on a whaling boat circa 1850, and **To the Edge of the World**, in which the orphaned and penniless Mateo becomes a cabin boy on Ferdinand Magellan's great voyage of discovery.

Interestingly, Hugh Montgomery's **The Voyage of the Arctic Tern** is told in verse, which brings to mind the epic tales of old like *The Iliad* and *The Odyssey*, but it has a certain charm and definite page-turning qualities all its own. Bruno, the captain of the *Arctic Tern*, is doomed to a life of wandering, and his attempts to free himself from this curse bring him into conflict with both kings and buccaneers.

John Masefield, if he's known these days at all, is remembered as a poet, but he wrote at least one terrific book for young people. **Jim Davis**, the eponymous hero, gets involved (against his will) with smugglers during the Napoleonic era in Devon, England—an adventure that he will barely survive. Or will he?

In **The Ring of the Slave Prince**, Bjarne Reuter's hero pursues his dreams of treasure across the high seas of the pirate-ridden Caribbean.

Fifteen-year-old Gabe Rogers finds himself stranded in the Canadian wilderness of the Northwest Territories along with his classmate, Raymond Providence, in **Far North** by Will Hobbs. This is a good choice as a companion read for anyone who loved Gary Paulsen's **Hatchet**.

Other heart-pounding adventures can be found in Zizou Corder's **Lion Boy** (followed by **Lion Boy: The Chase** and **Lion Boy: The Truth**); **The Thief Lord** by Cornelia Funke; both **The Convicts** and **The Cannibals** by Iain Lawrence (lots of swashbuckling derring-do in these tales of Tom Tin, sentenced to be deported from England in the 1830s to serve a long prison term in Australia for a crime he didn't commit); and Joan Aiken's multivolumed series The Wolves Chronicles, beginning with **The Wolves of Willoughby Chase**, which is also an alternative history, positing the existence of a King James III of England. (I've actually never met a girl who didn't love this book.) Be sure to have kids read as far into the series as (or just begin with) **Cold Shoulder Road**, with its Edward Gorey cover illustration.

ALL IN THE FAMILY

Before children's literature became dominated by the fantasy genre, this category—what we used to call, somewhat quaintly, "family stories"—was exceedingly popular with eight- to twelve-year-olds. And much as I love fantasy and science fiction, I am always heartened when a kid tells me that he wants to read something with ordinary, non-magic people in it. Well, here are some great titles with which to begin:

Elizabeth Enright's **The Saturdays, The Four-Story Mistake, Then There Were Five**, and **Spiderweb for Two** are all about Mona, Rush, Randy, and Oliver Melendy. (The big question here is how to pronounce their names: I've always divided up the word into three syllables—*Mel*-en-dy—with the accent on the first, but several devoted fans of these books accent the second syllable. Whatever works for you.) The four brothers and sisters are different enough that children tend to gravitate toward (and like best) the child who's most like them. My favorite was always Randy. And be sure to check out Enright's other books, including **Gone-Away Lake** (and **Return to Gone-Away**), **Tatsinda** (a fantasy), **Thimble Summer**, and **The Sea Is All Around**.

Eleanor Estes's **The Moffats, The Middle Moffat**, and **Rufus M.**, are all about Sylvie, Joey, Janey, and Rufus, growing up in a yellow house on New Dollar Street in Cranbury, Connecticut, in the years leading up to World War I.

Sydney Taylor's autobiographical stories of life in a Jewish family just before World War I include **All-of-a-Kind Family**, **More All-of-a-Kind Family**, **All-of-a-Kind Family Uptown**, and **All-of-a-Kind Family Downtown**. Each of the five daughters, Ella, Henny, Sarah, Gertie, and Charlotte, gets to star in a chapter or two, and, as with the Elizabeth Enright books, each reader will pick her own favorite, although I think that Sarah (who I suspect is based on Taylor herself) plays the most prominent role.

I love Maud Hart Lovelace's series of autobiographical books about Betsy Ray, her family, and her friends (and all the women I know who read these books as children still adore them as much as I do). Published in the 1940s and set in a fictionalized Mankato, Minnesota (here called Deep Valley), in the first two decades of the twentieth century, we first meet Betsy and her friends when they're just beginning school and follow their everyday adventures through adolescence, love, and marriage. While the first titles in the series are just right for young readers starting on their first chapter books, the later ones, when Betsy and her friends are in high school, are perfect for ten-, eleven-, and twelve-year-old girls. The books include (in order) **Betsy-Tacy**, **Betsy-Tacy and Tib**, **Betsy and Tacy Go Over the Big Hill**, **Betsy and Tacy Go Downtown**, **Heaven to Betsy**, **Betsy in Spite of Herself**, **Betsy Was a Junior**, **Betsy and Joe**, **Betsy and the Great World**, and **Betsy's Wedding**. There are also three related titles, **Winona's Pony Cart**, **Emily of Deep Valley**, and **Carney's House Party** (which offers a terrific peek at Vassar College in the early twentieth century). Just writing these titles here makes me want to go and reread all of them.

When I first went to work as a children's librarian at the Detroit Public Library, I was surprised to find that the only Lovelace book in the library was **Emily of Deep Valley**. I investigated further and discovered that the librarians reviewing these books way back in the 1940s deemed them "too sentimental" to purchase for the collection. I'm not convinced that sentimentality is bad for children, at least in the small dosage found here. For many years the Lovelace books languished, out of print, but HarperCollins has made them all available once again for a new generation of readers. Thank goodness, because I finally got to replace my ratty old copies with new editions.

Carol Ryrie Brink is best known for her Newbery Award–winning **Caddie Woodlawn**, but you won't want to overlook two of her other books. **Family Grandstand** details the everyday adventures of Susan, George, and Dumpling Ridgeway, who live in a house with a tower overlooking the football stadium in a midwestern college town along with their professor father and their mystery-writing mother, and **Family Sabbatical**, when the Ridgeways spend a year in France and, among other events, Dumpling loses her beloved doll in a dankly ancient prison.

The Penderwicks: A Summer Tale of Four Sisters, Two Rabbits, and a Very Interesting Boy by Jeanne Birdsall is similar in tone to Brink's books and also features an awfully nice family and the joys of the quotidian life. It was awarded the 2005 National Book Award.

Other superb family stories include Jordan Sonnenblick's **Drums, Girls & Dangerous Pie**, in which Steven's younger brother is diagnosed with leukemia and the whole family's world is turned upside down; Tim Kennemore's **Circle of Doom** (a wacky, good-natured tale that's a hoot to read); **Jacob Have I Loved** by Katherine Paterson; the series of books about the Casson family, including **Saffy's Angel**, **Permanent Rose**, and **Indigo's Star** by Hilary McKay; **The Steps** by Rachel Cohn (stepsiblings try to coexist in Sydney, Australia); and Pam Muñoz Ryan's **Becoming Naomi León**.

ANIMAL TALES

These are books with an enduring appeal—not only for immediate rereading, but also to pass on from one generation to the next.

Sheila Burnford's **The Incredible Journey** is the story of how two dogs—a bull terrier and a Labrador retriever—and a Siamese cat travel on their own through the Canadian wilderness to reach their home. I'm happy to tell you in advance that, thankfully, it ends happily.

New folks are coming to live in the big house, and Georgie the Rabbit and his friends and family wait with hope (will they be garden-planters?) and trepidation (are they the sort to put out poison to kill the wild critters?) to see just what kind of folks they are, in **Rabbit Hill** by Robert Lawson. The same characters reappear in **The Tough Winter**. Other imaginative and entertaining animal stories by Lawson include **Ben and Me: An Astonishing Life of Benjamin Franklin By His Good Mouse Amos**; **Captain Kidd's Cat**; and **Mr. Revere and I** (written by Paul Revere's horse, who played a very important part in broadcasting the news that the British were on their way). A good accompaniment to this latter book is Christopher Bing's illustrated version of Henry Wadsworth Longfellow's **The Midnight Ride of Paul Revere**.

If you're an orphan pig who wants to herd sheep, you can't do better than be adopted by a kindly farmer and his very experienced sheepdog. Such is the situation in **Babe: The Gallant Pig** by Dick King-Smith, which concludes with Babe's big win at a herding competition. For fans of Babe, another enjoyable selection is King-Smith's **The Golden Goose**, which recounts what happens when the animal of the title appears on Farmer Skint's farm. The Skint family's luck starts to change from bad to good, but it's hard to keep their treasure a secret. In fact, all of King-Smith's animal stories are well loved by children, including **The Fox Busters** and **Martin's Mice**. (Hint: Martin is a wimpy cat who keeps the mice he catches as pets, rather than eat them.)

One of the first books that Miss Frances Whitehead, the children's librarian at my neighborhood library, gave to me to read was Kenneth Grahame's **The Wind in the Willows**, the unforgettable story of the adventures of Mr. Toad of Toad Hall, Ratty, Badge, and Mole. If you've never read this as an adult and only barely remember it from when you read it as a child (or maybe you missed it altogether), add it to your own must-read list as well.

Freddy Auratus spent his early life in a pet shop, along with his golden hamster brothers and sisters, but he has plans to make something of himself and his life—how he succeeds (knowing how to use a computer comes in very handy), and the adventures he has (along with Enrico and Caruso, two guinea pigs, and Sir William, a cat) are described with gusto in Dietlof Reiche's **I, Freddy**, **Freddy in Peril**, **Freddy to the Rescue**, and **The Haunting of Freddy**.

Did you ever wonder what happened to the prince-who-was-turned-into-a-frog-by-a-wicked-witch during his time as an amphibian? Donna Jo Napoli's **The Prince of the Pond** explores his life post-princehood from the point of view of the frog he marries.

Tasha Tudor's **Corgiville Fair** is a delightful book set in the imaginary village of Corgiville, which is "west of New Hampshire and east of Vermont," and populated by, among other denizens, cats, Welsh corgis, goats, and boggarts. (Boggarts? What are they doing there?!) Happily, the same cast of characters reappears in **Corgiville Christmas** and **The Great Corgiville Kidnapping**.

Other quality animal tales for this age group include **Whittington** by Alan Armstrong; Erin Hunter's Warriors series, starting with **Into the Wild**, about a group of feral cats fighting enemy clans; **Freddy the Detective** and its twenty-five sequels by Walter R. Brooks; Randall Jarrell's **The Animal Family**; **The Cricket in Times Square** (and the other tales of Chester Cricket) by George Selden; Kathryn Lasky's series about Soren the barn owl, beginning with **The Capture**; and of course, E. B. White's best-beloved **Charlotte's Web**.

AUTHOR! AUTHOR!

There are some writers that you can pretty much rely on to come up with excellent novels for middle-grade readers. Along with the author's name, I've included the book (or two) that I feel best represents a high point in his or her work—but listen, find an author here you like and then try all of his or her books:

Lloyd Alexander's Prydain Chronicles, which include **The Book of Three, The Black Cauldron, The Castle of Llyr, Taran Wanderer**, and **The High King**

Beverly Cleary's **Henry Huggins** and **Dear Mr. Henshaw**

Susan Cooper's **Over Sea, Under Stone** and sequels

Roald Dahl's **The Twits**

Doris Gates's **Blue Willow**

Deborah and James Howe's **Bunnicula**

Diana Wynne Jones's **Howl's Moving Castle, Charmed Life**, and **Dark Lord of Derkholm**

E. L. Konigsburg's **From the Mixed-Up Files of Mrs. Basil E. Frankweiler**

Madeleine L'Engle's **Meet the Austins**

Lois Lowry's **The Giver**

A. A. Milne's **Winnie-the-Pooh** and **The House at Pooh Corner**

Daniel Pinkwater's **Alan Mendelsohn, the Boy from Mars**

Jon Scieszka's **Knights of the Kitchen Table** and sequels

Kate Seredy's **The Good Master**

AUTOBIOGRAPHIES

A lot of kids are insatiably curious about the lives of real people, especially if it's someone they've heard of. Many of these autobiographies were written by well-known authors, and reading them always seems to give additional insight into their books.

Bill Peet, author of **Chester the Worldly Pig** and nearly thirty other favorite picture books, tells the story of growing up in Indianapolis and then going to work for Walt Disney, where he was instrumental in the success of such children's films as *Dumbo* and *101 Dalmatians*.

Although they're frequently shelved in the juvenile fiction section, Farley Mowat's **Owls in the Family** and **The Dog Who Wouldn't Be** are really autobiographical stories that chronicle this Canadian writer's experiences with the animals he loved when he was growing up in Ontario and Saskatchewan in the 1930s.

Artist William Kurelek also recalls—in stories and paintings—his childhood on the Canadian prairies during approximately the same period in **A Prairie Boy's Winter** and **A Prairie Boy's Summer**.

Other autobiographies not to miss include **26 Fairmount Avenue**; **Here We All Are**; **On My Way**; and **What a Year** by Tomie dePaola; **The Lost Garden** by Lawrence Yep (which is especially good at showing the relationship between Yep's life and his award-winning books); **Looking Back: A Book of Memories** by Lois Lowry; Beverly Cleary's **A Girl from Yamhill** and **My Own Two Feet**; **Homesick: My Own Story** by Jean Fritz; and **The Abracadabra Kid: A Writer's Life** by Sid Fleischman (what he really wanted to be was a magician, not a writer).

BEFORE AND AFTER HARRY
(POTTER, OF COURSE)

Although the recent huge popularity of this genre can be traced back to the impact of J. K. Rowling's **Harry Potter and the Sorcerer's Stone** and its terrific sequels, fantasy novels have always been an important part of children's publishing. Long before Harry, Ron, Hermione, Snape, et al. were even a gleam in their author's eye, writers such as J. R. R. Tolkien, E. Nesbit, C. S. Lewis (as I wrote those names, I wondered why they all chose to be known by their initials), and others were writing books that are still excellent choices for middle-grade readers.

There are basically two kinds of fantasy novels (whether for children or for adults). The first type is when the action of the novel takes place in a wholly fantastical world, peopled with dragons, princesses, witches, sorcerers, warlocks—the whole lovely magical shtick—and there's no real connection with our everyday lives. Examples of this include Rowling, of course (one of the major appeals of her novels is the splendid evocation of Hogwarts), and Tolkien (once read, who can ever forget Middle Earth?). In the second type of novel, ordinary humans somehow stumble across or into something magical, and they usually, but not always, return to their everyday life at the book's conclusion. The novels of E. Nesbit exemplify this second sort, as do the Narnia novels of C. S. Lewis, and **Alice in Wonderland** and **Through the Looking-Glass** by Lewis Carroll.

Publishing these days seems to be focused on the first type of novel, that is, writers dreaming up fully realized worlds (definitely not our own world) where magic prevails and there's often an epic struggle between good and evil. There are lots of these books that will please young fantasy readers.

The story goes that J. R. R. Tolkien wrote **The Hobbit** as a series of tales for his young children (and when they grew up he wrote **The Lord of the Rings** trilogy for them). In any case, **The Hobbit** is pretty much irresistible for any fantasy fan—it's got dragons, elves, dwarfs, and a diminutive hero who succeeds in his quest by means of a riddle game.

Someone referred to the Artemis Fowl books by Eoin Colfer "*Die Hard* with fairies" and it's so true. Start with **Artemis Fowl** and continue on through **The Arctic Incident**, **The Eternity Code**, **The Opal Deception**, and whatever's come out since *Book Crush* was published.

Other good choices include The Spiderwick Chronicles by Tony DiTerlizzi and Holly Black, beginning with **The Field Guide**; Angie Sage's **Magyk**, the first in the series featuring the magically talented seventh son of a seventh son; Jonathan Stroud's The Bartimaeus Trilogy, including **The Amulet of Samarkand**, **The Golem's Eye**, and **Ptolemy's Gate** (all dealing with a djinn named Bartimaeus and his master, Nathaniel); Jean Ferris's **Love Among the Walnuts**; Jeanne DuPrau's **The City of Ember** (where the secrets are revealed at just the right pace, and readers will want to go immediately on to the sequel, **The People of Sparks**, and the prequel, **The Prophet of Yonwood**); shape shifters are the main characters in Robin Jarvis's **Thorn Ogres of Hagwood** (and sequels); **The Wizard's Map** by Jane Yolen; Carol Kendall's **The Gammage Cup** and **The Whisper of Glocken**; Herbie Brennan's **The Faerie Wars** and its sequel, **The Purple Emperor** (which has a well-drawn, realistic hero and a possible if not exactly plausible plot—sort of).

As I mentioned, the novels of E. Nesbit and C. S. Lewis exemplify the type of novels in which children stumble into a magical world. Good examples of the former's books are **Five Children and It** and **The Phoenix and the Carpet**. When it comes to C. S. Lewis, where the children discover Narnia via a wardrobe, the question is always in what order to read the books (it's not really a question of whether or not you do read them). In terms of Narnia time, the series begins with **The Magician's Nephew**, but I would recommend beginning with the first (and best) **The Lion, the Witch and the Wardrobe**, and then going on to **Prince Caspian**, **The Voyage of the** *Dawn Treader*, **The Silver Chair**, **The Horse and His Boy**, **The Magician's Nephew**, and **The Last Battle**. I'm probably prejudiced here (and likely in the minority), but this is the order in which I read them as they were first published in the 1950s. The heavy Christian allegory with which Lewis frontloaded his books will probably go over the heads of most readers (as it did mine at that age), who will just read these for the grand adventure.

Edward Eager, who wrote in the 1950s and 1960s, was heavily influenced by Nesbit. In Eager's novels, some perfectly ordinary boys and girls have to cope with the entrance of magic into their lives. They find the magic, make sense of it, and then actually use it. Eager's books include **Half Magic, Knight's Castle, Seven-Day**

Magic (a particular favorite of bookworms), **The Time Garden**, **Magic or Not?**, **Magic by the Lake**, and **The Well-Wishers**.

Suzanne Collins's **Gregor the Overlander** and its sequels are a fine addition to fantasy literature. You'll discover that Gregor is one brave eleven-year-old, but a word of warning—don't start the last few chapters of this novel on a school night, because the suspense builds to an almost unbearable level, and you will either a) not be able to stop reading until it's far too late, or b) not be able to fall asleep when you finish because your heart is still pounding too fast to relax.

The 13th Is Magic! by Joan Howard is about Ronnie and Gillian, who live in an apartment on Central Park West on the floor above the twelfth floor, only it's called the fourteenth floor. It takes a cat called Merlin to take them to that magical missing floor.

Others not to miss are **The Enormous Egg** by Oliver Butterworth (a splendid family read-aloud); Natalie Babbitt's **Tuck Everlasting** and **The Eyes of the Amaryllis** (a superb novel that deserves a wider readership); and **The Secret of Platform 13** by Eva Ibbotson (just one of her many excellent fantasies).

BIOGRAPHICAL FICTION

Biographical fiction is a particularly good way to introduce young readers to interesting people. It's an easy leap from reading these to the whole world of nonfiction, and each of these books is practically guaranteed to start the reader off on a personalized journey of discovery with all sorts of interesting byways. For many, reading these books will begin a lifelong love affair with historical fiction (and that's not a bad thing at all). That was certainly the case for me.

Jean Lee Latham's **Carry On, Mr. Bowditch**, winner of the 1955 Newbery Medal, is the story of the self-taught, eighteenth-century genius Nathaniel Bowditch, who grew up in the sailing town of Salem, Massachusetts, and despite never achieving his life's dream of attending Harvard, revolutionized the practice of navigation through his book **The American Practical Navigator**, known familiarly as the "Sailors' Bible."

I, Juan de Pareja by Elizabeth Borton de Treviño is written in the form of a diary and tells the story of de Pareja, an African slave who becomes the assistant to the great seventeenth-century Spanish court painter Diego Velázquez, and grows up to become a great artist himself, despite having to overcome the ban on teaching slaves to paint.

While waiting for her second husband, King Henry II of England, to join her in heaven, Eleanor of Aquitaine (married to two kings—although not simultaneously!—the mother of two kings, and a not-inconsequential woman in her own right) and three of her friends look back over her long and eventful life in E. L. Konigsburg's **A Proud Taste for Miniver and Scarlet**.

What's it like to have a genius living in your house? Particularly if he's an eccentric, not to say weird, sort of guy? That's the situation presented in **Beethoven Lives Upstairs** by Barbara Nichol, as Christopher describes his feelings in a series of letters to his uncle about the strange musician boarding in his home.

BOYS WILL BE BOYS

The best thing about the books in this category is that even if you're not a boy age nine to about twelve, the chances are good that you'll enjoy reading about these appealing characters.

What if you could earn a lot of money (well, a lot of money to you) just by eating a worm a day for fifteen days? How bad could it really be? And how many ways could you find to disguise the—ugh—slithery taste of worm? Billy faces the challenge in Thomas Rockwell's hilarious and yucky **How to Eat Fried Worms**. Skip the movie and stay home and read the book.

When Zachary Beaver Came to Town by Kimberly Willis Holt is the story of an important summer in the life of thirteen-year-old Toby Wilson, when his mother leaves to pursue her dream as a country singer, his best friend's brother is off risking his life in Vietnam, and Zachary Beaver, the world's fattest boy, comes to their small Texas town as a circus freak.

Joey Pigza, the main character in Jack Gantos's **Joey Pigza Swallowed the Key**, describes himself as "messed up but lovable." Adults will recognize that Joey's problem is ADHD, and many young readers will probably see parts of themselves in this warm and human portrait of a boy who just can't control his behavior.

John D. Fitzgerald grew up at the turn of the twentieth century in Adenville, Utah, where it seemed that everyone in town—except him and his family—was a Mormon. But whatever difficulties he might have on that account are minor, because John D.'s older brother, Tom D., just happens to be the smartest person around (renowned for solving the deepest dilemmas, swindling his friends out of their prized possessions, and always confounding his little brother). Start with Fitzgerald's **The Great Brain** and go on from there, including **More Adventures of the Great Brain** and **The Great Brain at the Academy**. (It was a toss-up for me whether to put these titles in the "LOL: Laugh Out Loud" section or here.)

It's 1935, and twelve-year-old Moose Flanagan has just moved to Alcatraz Island, off the coast of northern California, where his dad is doing double duty as an electrician and a guard at the prison there (where Al Capone, once the most hunted criminal in America, is now housed behind bars). In his journal, Moose shares with us his resentment at being stuck babysitting for his sister, Natalie (whose odd and sometimes difficult behavior is often embarrassing), so that he can't take part in lots of the school activities, and the adventures that his good friend Piper, the warden's daughter, comes up with. It all adds up to the entertaining **Al Capone Does My Shirts** by Gennifer Choldenko.

Two novels in which the main character has to overcome some pretty powerful fears in order to prove his courage to himself and others are **Jungle Dogs** by Graham Salisbury, which takes place in Hawaii, and **Call It Courage** by Armstrong Sperry, set in Polynesia.

Polly Horvath's **The Vacation** has her trademark ditsy plot, outlandish characters, and snappy dialogue. When his parents go off to Africa (his mother decides she wants to be a missionary), Henry's aunts Pigg and Magnolia come to stay with him and the three take off on a wild car trip that includes Henry's being lost in a swamp in Florida, Pigg meeting the true love of her life (and changing her name to Peg), and, finally, the return of Henry's parents, who've had their own adventures in Africa. My favorite character might possibly be Henry's father, who always comes up with these great pronouncements and tidbits of advice for his son like "Son . . . many of the things you are going to buy in your life are going to be lemons. There is nothing you can do about this. Do not blame yourself. Do not blame your spouse. Try not to blame each other."

What if you found a whole lot of money and needed to spend it really fast? That's the premise of the enjoyable and engaging novel **Millions** by Frank Cottrell Boyce, which was made into an equally pleasurable film.

In **Golden and Grey (An Unremarkable Boy and a Rather Remarkable Ghost)** by Louise Arnold, the new boy in school, who's being bullied and picked on, is befriended by a ghost, who ends up helping both of them find acceptance in their respective worlds.

Joseph Bruchac's **The Heart of a Chief** is set on an Indian reservation in New Hampshire and narrated by an eleven-year-old boy. It concerns three issues facing Native Americans today: casinos, rampant alcoholism, and how to deal with high school and college sports teams whose names seem to denigrate Indian culture. It's heavy, but not overly so.

Other great "boy" books include **Leon and the Spitting Image** and **Leon and the Champion Chip** by Allen Kurzweil; Roald Dahl's **Charlie and the Chocolate Factory**; **The Phantom Tollbooth** by Norton Juster; **Tales of a Fourth Grade Nothing** by Judy Blume; Louis Sachar's **Holes** and **Small Steps**; Avi's **Nothing But the Truth: A Documentary Novel**; and **Loser** by Jerry Spinelli (with a wonderful picture of a supportive family).

COMING OF AGE

I find it interesting that most of the books I describe in this category could also just as easily fall under the heading of "fantasy." It makes me wonder if it is no longer possible to develop self-knowledge without the help of a wizard. Still, these books touch on significant themes, and, most important, are quite enjoyable reading.

In Dia Calhoun's **Aria of the Sea**, thirteen-year-old Cerinthe Gale must choose between two possible careers: becoming the dancer her mother always wanted her to be, or fulfilling her interest in, talent for, and fear of becoming a mederi, a healer.

When Robert Norel is asked by a strange old woman in a nursing home to explore the mysteries of Chance House and discover the truth about a boy who fell to his death from the upstairs flat, he discovers things about himself as well as the past, in Nicky Singer's **Feather Boy**.

I first read Ursula K. Le Guin's **A Wizard of Earthsea** when I was early in my career as a children's librarian, and I remember being simply stunned by the novel's inventiveness and theme. I've always felt, in fact, that the training the hero, Sparrowhawk, goes through to become a wizard is probably the same training that Gandalf (of J. R. R. Tolkien fame) received as a youngster. Le Guin's novel (which is followed by **The Tombs of Atuan**, **The Farthest Shore**, and **Tehanu**) functions both as a grand fantasy and a rattling good coming-of-age tale.

Fans of the Le Guin novel will also not want to miss Michael Gruber's spectacular **The Witch's Boy**, in which the most unattractive and unattractively named Lump, abandoned as an infant, is adopted by a witch (against the wishes of her familiar, a cat named Falance), who is extremely powerful at witchcraft but alas, also totally unfit for parenting. Lump's experiences growing up reflect his adopted mother's emotional coldness, and it takes many plot twists and turns for Lump to finally accept himself, learn his true name, and forgive his mother.

Paul Stewart and Chris Riddell collaborated on a madly popular and inventive series of books called The Edge Chronicles. Unlike some series, it's important to start with the first title, **Beyond the Deepwoods**, which introduces Twig, the young human hero. When Twig, who's being raised by woodtrolls in the world of the Edge, learns from his mother that he was discovered as a baby wrapped in a quilt under a tree, he sets out on a perilous journey to discover the truth about where he comes from and who he is, but not before he's threatened by a variety of evil and dangerous beings. Although each book in the series tells a separate tale, there are internal sequences that make subsequent books hard to follow unless you read them in order. Some of my favorites involve librarian Rook Barkwater, including **The Last of the Sky Pirates** and **Vox**, but in fact they're all good, complicated, suspense-filled fun.

Another top-notch coming-of-age-with-the-help-of-magic novel for this age group is Nancy Farmer's **The Sea of Trolls**. Based on Norse mythology, and notable for the excellent writing and three-dimensional characters that mark all of Farmer's novels, this tale of a young boy thrust into a world of Berserkers, bards, and trolls is just outstanding.

D@%! THE TORPEDOES, FULL STEAM AHEAD

Novels centered around war for this age group are great for getting kids to think about some very deep stuff, like courage and conquering one's fears, what it means to be a hero, the whole knotty question of good versus evil, and the consequences of our choices. So if you think your readers are up to the emotional depth of the titles in this category, try these:

Set during Napoleon's attempt to conquer Russia with his *Grand Armée* in 1812, **An Innocent Soldier** by Josef Holub tells the story of a sixteen-year-old orphan farmhand, Adam, and how he ends up fighting in the place of his master's son. This is not only an interesting story about the Napoleonic War, but also a fine introduction to the social systems and lifestyles of the early nineteenth century. Because it's translated from German, Holub's writing sounds a little different than readers may be used to but once you're used to it, the story rockets along.

I think one of the very best novels about the Revolutionary War for any age reader is **Johnny Tremain** by Esther Forbes. It's the sometimes emotionally wrenching story of a boy who is an apprentice silversmith. After a terrible accident he becomes a messenger carying secret communications between members of the Sons of Liberty during the months leading up to the American Revolution. Readers come to know many of the movers and shakers of this period, including Sam Adams and, of course, Paul Revere, all through the eyes of a young boy. (Forbes won the Pulitzer Prize for her biography of Revere and drew on her voluminous research to write this outstanding historical novel, which won the 1944 Newbery Medal.)

Other exceptional Revolutionary War novels include **My Brother Sam Is Dead** by James and Christopher Collier (Tim Meeker has to decide where his loyalties lie—with the revolutionary Americans or the Tories); **Guns for General Washington** by Seymour Reit (the story of Colonel Henry Knox and his daring plan to move 183 cannons from Fort Ticonderoga on Lake Champlain three hundred miles to Boston, Massachusetts, during the winter of 1775–76); and Howard Fast's **April Morning** (young Adam Cooper signs up to fight the British in 1775).

The Boys' War: Confederate and Union Soldiers Talk About the Civil War by Jim Murphy is based on first-person accounts of both Confederate and Union soldiers. Filled with vintage photography, it packs a real punch.

World War II provides the background for many children's novels. Be sure to put **Code Talker** by Joseph Bruchac on your list of must-reads. It tells the true story (via Ned Begay, a fictional character) of Navajo children who spent their childhoods at U.S. mission schools "erasing" all outward signs of their culture as members of the Navajo nation, only to be recruited later by the U.S. Marine Corps specifically because they were Navajos. The story starts a bit slowly but rapidly picks up pace as Ned and his fellow marines lead U.S. forces through Guam, Iwo Jima, and Okinawa.

Two others to offer to interested readers are **Snow Treasure** by Marie McSwigan, based on the true story of a group of Norwegian children who smuggle nine million dollars in gold bullion right past the Nazis to the Allies, and Robert Westall's **Time of Fire**.

In **A Boy at War** and its sequel **A Boy No More** by Harry Mazer, fourteen-year-old Adam Pelko is a U.S. Navy brat whose father is stationed in Hawaii on the USS *Arizona*. Adam and his friends are fishing in a boat in the harbor when the first bombs begin to fall from Japanese planes. Mazer's books introduce readers to the situation that many islanders found themselves in at a time when Hawaii was not yet a state and many of its Hawaiian and Japanese residents' loyalties were suddenly suspect.

Good companion reads to Mazer's novel are Graham Salisbury's **Under the Blood-Red Sun** and **Eyes of the Emperor**, both of which take place in Hawaii just before and during World War II. In the first book, fourteen-year-old Tomi Nakaji and his family have come to Hawaii from Japan, and Tomi just wants to be a normal American kid. But after the Japanese bomb Pearl Harbor, life becomes increasingly difficult, especially after his father and grandfather are sent to internment camps. In **Eyes of the Emperor**, set in 1941 (and based on true events, which gives even more of a punch to this moving novel), Eddy Okubo lies about his age and enlists in the U.S. Army, but he doesn't get sent to the battlefield; instead he and other Japanese Americans are used as bait to train dogs who will hunt and destroy Japanese combatants throughout the Pacific theaters of war.

Four Steps to Death by John Wilson is not a particularly uplifting read, but it's one of the few (perhaps only?) books for this age group to deal with the Russian front during WWII. The story of the strategically important battle for Stalingrad in 1942 is told from the point of view of a German tank commander, a Russian foot soldier, and a young boy whose city becomes a major battleground.

DRAGON TALES

D ragons, fire-breathing or not, have a long history in children's literature. Perhaps J. R. R. Tolkien's fabulously evil Smaug, outwitted by Bilbo Baggins in **The Hobbit**, comes closest to the traditional concept of "dragon," with his brilliant armor, piles of treasure, and a mesmerizing stare, but there are others to read about, too, as you can see here.

Dragon Rider by Cornelia Funke includes out-of-the-ordinary creatures (the main ones are dragons, of course) and daring deeds by unexpected heroes.

Dealing with Dragons is the first in the high-spirited Enchanted Forest Chronicles, by one of the best fantasy writers for children and young adults (indeed, for adults, too), Patricia C. Wrede. Witty, well-written, and featuring a dynamite pair of heroines—the indomitable, improper Princess Cimorene (but how on earth does one pronounce that?) and the dragon Kazul—this and its sequels make enchanting reading.

In Jason Hightman's **The Saint of Dragons**, the creatures are far less benign—they are, as one of the characters says, "the source of all that is rotten in the world." And worse, they are highly evolved and walk upright, so you can't tell who's a dragon and who's not.

Illustrator Michael Hague has chosen a collection of tales featuring these fearsome beasts in **The Book of Dragons**, which includes selections from writers as diverse as Padraic Colum, E. Nesbit, and Elizabeth Coatsworth.

When the main character of **Jeremy Thatcher, Dragon Hatcher** by Bruce Coville is entrusted with a dragon's egg, which must be hatched under the light of a full moon (sounds simple enough, right?), he learns that taking care of a baby dragon can create unexpected complications in the life of a sixth-grader.

And if young readers are interested in every aspect of dragon lore, no matter how esoteric (or fact-based), hand them the delightfully comprehensive **The Dragonology Handbook: A Practical Course in Dragons** by Dugald Steer, which purports to be a facsimile of a manuscript published in the 1890s by Dr. Ernest Drake, a noted scholar and founding member of London's Secret and Ancient Society of Dragonologists, and its companion (also really by Steer), **Dragonology: The Complete Book of Dragons**.

DEWEY LOVE NONFICTION?
DEWEY EVER!

When I was a children's librarian, back in the Dark Ages (although we did have electricity), children's nonfiction wasn't particularly something that book people paid a lot of attention to. Oh, there were plenty of books on different topics available for reports, but that's pretty much all they were being written for—to help someone with his or her homework. (Another difference was that the kids didn't get assigned that much homework, or at least not nearly as much as today's kids, and the homework assignments usually didn't begin until the upper elementary grades.) I don't remember being excited about a children's book of nonfiction, ever. But all that's changed in the last decade or so. What parents, librarians, and teachers find now is that many of the best books for kids are nonfiction. And using these books is often the best way to get nonreaders reading, because you can always find books that fall into the category of what the child is interested in. Sports? Try the 700s. Creepy crawlies or dinosaurs? Take a look at the 500s. Want to share some funny poems with your kids? Try the books described in the 800s. Visiting New York City? You'll find lots of quality stuff in the 900s.

The titles in this section range in suitability for first- through sixth- or seventh-graders, but most are appropriate for eight- to twelve-year-olds. I think that, in general, older kids can certainly use adult books, although there's not the quantity of quality nonfiction there that you'll discover in the children's departments of libraries and bookstores.

100s

Bryan Magee's **The Story of Philosophy** is just what its subtitle states: "The essential guide to the history of Western philosophy." It includes philosophical theories and great thinkers from the ancient Greeks to the late twentieth century, and is well-illustrated, authoritative, and fascinating reading for children and adults alike.

200s

Mary Pope Osborne's **One World, Many Religions** incorporates photos of children worshipping in the traditions of the major religions, including Judaism, Christianity, Islam, Hinduism, Buddhism, Confucianism, and Taoism (all religions with a written tradition) in this outstandingly informative overview that also includes a timeline and a useful glossary.

Celebrating Ramadan with text by Diane Hoyt-Goldsmith and photos by Lawrence Migdale, and **Ramadan**, written by Suhaib Hamid Ghazi with evocative illustrations by Omar Rayyan, both use the experiences of a young boy to introduce young readers to Islam and the Muslim month of prayer and fasting. One nice sidelight of Goldsmith's book is the way it shows that Islam is a worldwide religion, with some of the family's relatives coming from Egypt, and others from Bosnia.

300s

In **Fireboat: The Heroic Adventures of the *John J. Harvey***, Maira Kalman links the year 1931—when the *John J. Harvey*, one of twelve fireboats in New York City, was first launched—to September 11, 2001, when the little boat came out of retirement to fight the fires following the disaster at the Twin Towers.

Fantasy fans (or those addicted to horror novels) won't want to miss Judy Sierra's **The Gruesome Guide to World Monsters**, and **The Essential Worldwide Monster Guide** by Linda Ashman, both of which offer spine-tingling descriptions of ghoulies, ghosties, long-legged beasties, and things that go bump in the night.

There are two very cool aspects of **The Shipwrecked Sailor** by Tamara Bower: It's based on a story found on a papyrus scroll now in the Hermitage Museum in Saint Petersburg, Russia, which scholars believe dates from the nineteenth century BCE, and Bower has included hieroglyphs from the original papyrus, along with their literal meanings, so readers can actually get a sense of what this ancient writing looks like. She also includes a bibliography of titles (mainly aimed at adult readers, unfortunately) in case readers want to explore the subject further.

It's instructive to read about how an election works from beginning to end, from campaigning to recounts, in **Vote!** by Eileen Christelow. Or at least how it should ideally work.

Phineas Gage: A Gruesome but True Story About Brain Science by John Fleischmann unravels the mysteries of the brain by describing the situation of a mid-nineteeth-century man who lived for eleven years after a thirteen-pound iron rod was shot through his brain; although he could function normally, his personality changed a lot.

Virginia Hamilton wrote, and Leo and Diane Dillon illustrated, **The People Could Fly: American Black Folktales**, a collection of stories that were first told by slaves and have remained part of African American history and culture to this day.

The twenty women profiled in Kathleen Krull's **Lives of Extraordinary Women: Rulers, Rebels (and What the Neighbors Thought)** include Indira Gandhi, Queen Victoria, Marie Antoinette, Harriet Tubman, Wilma Mankiller, and Eva Perón, among others. The writing is lively and the information is useful both for school reports and as a stepping stone to further reading.

Eric A. Kimmel retells a Jewish legend about Rosh Hashannah, the Jewish New Year, in **Gershon's Monster**, illustrated by Jon J Muth.

Jacqueline Mitton is a Fellow of Britain's Royal Astronomical Society (and has an asteroid named after her and her husband), so she's well qualified to write **Zodiac: Celestial Circle of the Sun**, explaining the myths surrounding each of the twelve zodiac constellations; it's sumptuously illustrated by Christina Balit.

The journey of immigrants to America is detailed in **Shutting Out the Sky: Life in the Tenements of New York, 1880–1915**, in which Deborah Hopkinson uses archival photographs and actual diary entries to tell the story of five immigrants, representative of the twenty-three million people who came to America from all over the world during those years.

400s

WordPlay Café, written and illustrated Michael Kline, is filled with, as the subtitle has it, "Cool Codes, Priceless Punzles & Phantastic Phonetic Phun," from "amazing grapes" to "inflated language," and including, in Chapter Fore: Deep-Fried Diction for Two (Or More!). Lots of fun.

Most kids love codes, and James Rumford's **Seeker of Knowledge: The Man Who Deciphered Egyptian Hieroglyphs** tells the story of Jean-François Champollion, the Frenchman who figured out the key to the Rosetta stone (which is on display in the British Museum).

500s

Don't miss Robert Sabuda's incredible pop-up books, **Encyclopedia Prehistorica: Dinosaurs** and **Encyclopedia Prehistorica: Sharks and Other Sea Monsters**. (See the "Christmas Is Coming!" section in Part I for more examples of Sabuda's marvelous work.)

The Voyager's Stone: The Adventures of a Message-Carrying Bottle Adrift on the Ocean Sea by Robert Kraske uses a story format to explain different aspects of oceanography, including tides, the current, and the many denizens of the deep.

Susan E. Goodman's text and photographs by Dorothy Handelman strikingly demonstrate how inventions (like umbrellas or camouflage clothing) have been borrowed from nature in **Nature Did It First!**

If only every kid could have Ms. Frizzle for a science teacher—using the Magic School Bus, she helps the students in her class explore various topics in books such as **The Magic School Bus at the Waterworks**, **The Magic School Bus Inside the Earth**, **The Magic School Bus Inside the Human Body**, **The Magic School Bus on the Ocean Floor**, **The Magic School Bus Lost in the Solar System** (my personal favorite), and **The Magic School Bus in the Time of the Dinosaurs**. One of the best things about these books by Joanna Cole is that kids tend to love them, although I know at least one mother who confessed how tired she got as she read them all out loud to each one of her three sons. (Some of these are shelved in the 500s, and some in the 600s, depending on the subject. I've put them all here in the 500s for convenience.)

In April Pulley Sayre's **Secrets of Sound: Studying the Calls and Songs of Whales, Elephants, and Birds**, readers learn about the work that three acoustic biologists perform through following their research from beginning to end.

Bob Barner's **Dem Bones** combines the well-known song ("Toe bone connected to da foot bone") with factual information about our bone structure. Did you know there are twenty-two bones in your feet and a built-in arch support? I didn't, until I read this helpful and amusingly illustrated (with skeletons, of course) book.

Life on Earth: The Story of Evolution by Steve Jenkins uses a combination of instructive text and lively illustrations to provide a basic introduction to evolutionary science. One of the most interesting parts of the book is a timeline showing the history of the Earth as a single day—Earth is formed at 12:00 a.m., life appears at 4:47 a.m., the first dinosaurs and other mammals don't evolve until 10:42 p.m., and humans don't show up on the scene until 11:58:30 p.m.—four and a half billion years or almost twenty-four hours later.

G is for Googol: A Math Alphabet Book by David M. Schwartz explains twenty-six mathematical terms, from abacus to zillion, in language that certainly children (and even the most math-challenged adult) will find comprehendible.

The 500s are where you find the books about animals, so it's a very popular area for kids to browse through. Here are some choices to check out: **Growing Frogs** by Vivian French (who can make even the yucky parts interesting to someone who's not particularly a huge frog lover, as I still am not); **Grandma Elephant's In Charge** by Martin Jenkins (and illustrated by Ivan Bates), which explores life in an African elephant herd, where grandma's rule is absolute.

Owen & Mzee: The True Story of a Remarkable Friendship describes the loving relationship between a baby hippopotamus and a giant tortoise 130 years old that arose following the devastating tsunami in Southeast Asia, told by Isabella and Craig Hatkoff, along with Dr. Paula Kahumbu (who is the director of the sanctuary where the friends now reside), and photographs by Peter Greste.

600s

Eight cool cats explain the process of creating a book from the author's first ideas to the finished product in the hands of the excited reader (with many stops in between) in **How a Book Is Made** by the incomparable Aliki. (I found this description very useful in understanding what was happening to my books after I sent them off to the publisher.)

David Macauley's **The New Way Things Work: From Levers to Lasers, Windmills to Web Sites, a Visual Guide to the World of Machines** is really a book for adults, but it's useful for kids who want to know everything about, say, metal detectors, or why self-winding watches really do keep on ticking. No comprehensive list of nonfiction for readers of all ages is complete without it.

Another book filled with up-to-date topics is **Transformed: How Everyday Things Are Made** by Bill Slavin, which describes what goes into making everything from blue jeans to tea to wax candles and cola drinks. (Believe me, if your child has dreams of winning a lot of money on a quiz show, he or she can't do better than study Macauley's and Slavin's books—together, they're pretty comprehensive.)

Patrick O'Brien offers lots of interesting tidbits of information in **The Hindenburg**. The zeppelins, before one exploded in 1937 in the sky over New Jersey, had a glorious history of flight for more than thirty-five years. (It's books like this that convince me that if you want to know the basics about almost any topic, your first step should be a children's book on the subject.)

From its arresting cover—a skeleton peering through a microscope—to its informative (and relevant) text, charts, and illustrations, **Outbreak: Plagues That Changed History** by Bryn Barnard demonstrates that learning about science can be both interesting and educational. Jim Murphy focuses on one outbreak plague in particular (that I'd never heard of before, in fact) in **An American Plague: The True and Terrifying Story of the Yellow Fever Epidemic of 1793**.

One of the best sex-education books around is Robie H. Harris's **It's Perfectly Normal: Changing Bodies, Growing Up, Sex and Sexual Health**. Its matter-of-fact tone is reassuring, and the content is invaluable to answer the questions—asked and unasked— of any child.

If there's a child in your life who wonders about outer space or dreams of being an astronaut, give him or her Faith McNulty's **If You Decide to Go to the Moon**, illustrated by Steven Kellogg. This fact-filled, tender, and entirely wonderful book opens up the world of space for young readers. (I learned stuff from this book that I didn't know before, and I bet you will, too.)

700s

Any reader with adventure in his or her blood will definitely enjoy Steve Jenkins's **The Top of the World: Climbing Mount Everest**, a slim book filled with facts (including what equipment you'll need when you go) and descriptions of the ascent. The illustrations alone are worth the read.

I Hear America Singing!: Folk Songs for American Families, collected and arranged by Kathleen Krull, is an outstanding collection of sixty-two folk songs, almost two dozen of which are on an accompanying CD.

Quentin Blake uses pictures from an exhibit he developed at London's National Gallery to promote early art appreciation in **Tell Me a Picture**, and Jan Greenberg uses the art of a well-known African American painter to tell his story in **Romare Bearden: Collage of Memories**.

Bruce Koscielniak's **The Story of the Incredible Orchestra** would be a good text for an elementary school Music 101 class; it includes the history of orchestras and their various instruments, with useful (and entertaining) drawings to accompany the text. Who would have thought that there was a time—not so long ago, really, prior to 1600—when there were no orchestras? Or that composers didn't indicate which instruments they had in mind for their written compositions?

You can't skim through the pages of Yann Arthus-Bertrand's amazing **Earth from Above**—the aerial photographs, along with Robert Burleigh's sensitive and thoughtful text, offer such a fascinating view of our world that you'll want to pore over each page with your child. Whether it's an artificially constructed lake in Africa's Côte d'Ivoire (Ivory Coast), a farmer tilling his field on the island of Crete, the Grand Prismatic Spring in Yellowstone National Park, or rice fields in Bali, each photo makes us look closely and think deeply.

All of David Macauley's books about how various buildings are constructed are worth sharing with children (or even just reading yourself), but **Mosque** is particularly relevant to today's world. It would be a very nice follow-up to **Ramadan** by Suhaib Hamid Ghazi.

Wolfgang Amadeus Mozart, Charles Ives, Nadia Boulanger, Woody Guthrie, and Scott Joplin are among the twenty musicians profiled in Kathleen Krull's **Lives of the Musicians: Good Times, Bad Times (and What the Neighbors Thought)**; it's filled with all sorts of inside (and fascinating) information—kind of like reading a well-written *People* magazine article about each of them. For kids especially interested in music, give them Mordicai Gerstein's **What Charlie Heard**, a short but enticing biography of composer Charles Ives, and **When Marian Sang** by Pam Muñoz Ryan, with gorgeous illustrations by Brian Selznick, which tells the story of the life of Marian Anderson and her triumphant concert—at the behest of Eleanor Roosevelt—on the steps of the Lincoln Memorial in Washington, D.C.

All she ever wanted to do was pitch on a professional baseball team—a daunting career goal for anyone, but especially for an African American woman during the 1950s, when the major leagues were still racially segregated. But, as Michelle Y. Green demonstrates in her inspiring **A Strong Right Arm: The Story of Mamie "Peanut" Johnson**, nothing is impossible if you want it enough—Mamie Johnson was one of only three women to play pro ball in the Negro Leagues.

Heroes of Baseball, by *New York Times* columnist Robert Lipsyte, describes the lives and accomplishments of everyone from A. G. Spaulding (a star during baseball's early years) to Ty Cobb, Babe Ruth, and the headline-grabbers of tomorrow.

A diverse (African American, Asian American, Jewish, Hispanic, Native American) group of artists offers brief looks at their lives in **Just Like Me: Stories and Self-Portraits by Fourteen Artists**, edited by Harriet Rohmer. Rohmer also edited **Honoring Our**

Ancestors: Stories and Pictures by Fourteen Artists, with contributions from many of the same artists.

In 1974, when the two towers of the World Trade Center in New York City were being completed, a high-wire walker named Philippe Petit strung a line between the two buildings and walked high, *high*, HIGH above the ground between them—his feat is beautifully envisioned in Mordicai Gerstein's Newbery Award–winning **The Man Who Walked Between the Towers**.

Peter Golenbock's **Teammates** tells the story of the friendship of Jackie Robinson and Pee Wee Reese, players on the Brooklyn Dodgers baseball team. The illustrations include both vintage photos and watercolor paintings by Paul Bacon.

Stunning paintings by Michele Wood (I wish I could get copies of the originals and frame them—I never get tired of looking at them) and an informative text by Toyomi Igus are perfectly integrated in **I See the Rhythm**, a history of African American music, including the birth of the blues, ragtime, bebop, jazz, and rap.

800s

From Sea to Shining Sea: A Treasury of American Folklore and Folk Songs, edited by Amy L. Cohn and illustrated by some of the leading contemporary children's book artists (including Jerry Pinkney, Chris Van Allsburg, David Wiesner, and Trina Schart Hyman), is an indispensable addition to any child's book collection. Some of the 140 examples it includes are the words and music to "The Big Rock Candy Mountain" and "Git Along, Little Dogies," Martin Luther King Jr.'s "I Have a Dream" speech, Emma Lazarus's poem about the Statue of Liberty, "The New Colossus," and tales of Johnny Appleseed and Paul Bunyan.

Teen (and adult) fantasy readers will adore Diana Wynne Jones's travel guide through the pretty much hitherto uncharted realm of fantasy, **The Tough Guide to Fantasyland**, which describes, with witty accuracy, the landscape, attractions, and people (dwarfs, elves, wizards, vampires, demons, et al.) that you'll encounter on a trip there. This is, as the cover of the book says, "The essential guide to fantasy travel." The more fantasy a child reads, the more they'll enjoy this. (The same is true for adult readers.)

The distinctly American genre of music, the blues, is explored in both poetry and art in Walter Dean and Christopher Myers's collaborative **Blues Journey**; it has a glossary of words associated with the genre, as well as a timeline beginning in 1865 highlighting the various singers and songwriters, including Ma Rainey, Bessie Smith, and Leadbelly.

Another stunning use of poetry and art—and a book that's appropriate for kids and adults of all ages—is found in **Jazz A B Z**, with poems by jazz great Wynton Marsalis and portraits by Paul Rogers. The book celebrates in poetry everyone who's anyone in the jazz world, from Louis Armstrong, Sonny Rollins, and Art Blakey to Miles Davis and Thelonius Monk. There's also a brief biography of each musician (written by jazz historian Phil Schaap) at the end of the book.

A Wreath for Emmett Till by Marilyn Nelson is not an emotionally easy collection of poetry to read. But these poems, about the lynching death of a fourteen-year-old African American boy in Mississippi in 1955, have a strength and power that draws the reader in and doesn't let go.

900s

Because I'm a history buff, the 900s are my favorite section of the Dewey run. And there's so much good stuff here! It only supports my belief that a good place to begin in the search for information about nearly any topic is the nonfiction section of your library or local bookstore. I've arranged the books that follow in the order in which you'd probably find them on the shelves. Browse away:

I doubt a lot of people have even heard of Ibn Battuta, one of the great travelers of all time, let alone are familiar with his journeys. In James Rumford's **Traveling Man: The Journey of Ibn Battuta, 1325–1354**, you'll discover a fascinating and intrepid individual who left his native Morocco for Mecca when he was twenty-one and never looked back. Text and illustrations, which resemble Persian miniatures and include Chinese and Arabic writings, combine to make almost anyone want to learn more about this remarkable man.

Extraordinarily detailed pictures by Stephen Biesty (with text by Stewart Ross) illustrate daily life in Egypt circa 1200 BCE, in **Egypt in Spectacular Cross-Section** (and the word spectacular here is not misused). Fans of Biesty's approach will want to take a look at his books on ancient Rome, castles, and fighting ships.

The eruption of Mt. Vesuvius in August of AD 79 buried the Italian towns of Pompeii and Herculaneum in hot ash; they were essentially lost to history until the late eighteenth century, when workmen (digging an underground canal) uncovered slabs of marble and the remains of a wall painting. In **Pompeii: Lost and Found**, Mary Pope Osborne takes the fascinating story from that point on, aided by incomparable illustrations by Bonnie Christensen.

Another look at the same event can be found in James M. Deems's **Bodies from the Ash: Life and Death in Ancient Pompeii**. In **Auschwitz: The Story of a Nazi Death Camp**, Clive A. Lawton includes photos and documents, as well as original text, to give readers a sense of the Holocaust. Lawton's book is useful to read along with biographies and autobiographies that cover the same period. Bartoletti's book, below, makes a good companion read.

The Queen's Progress by Celeste Davidson Mannis goes through the alphabet to show the annual holiday that Queen Elizabeth I takes—along with members of her court, her servants, and others. The illustrations by Bagram Ibatoulline help make this a great selection for any history fan.

Susan Campbell Bartoletti brings home to readers just what it was like to live in Germany in the 1930s as Hitler rose to prominence, in **Hitler Youth: Growing Up in Hitler's Shadow**, an outstanding example of nonfiction for young adults.

10,000 Days of Thunder: A History of the Vietnam War by Philip Caputo, whose **A Rumor of War** (written for adults) was one of the best memoirs written about the war in Vietnam, uses maps, photos, and text to describe both the war's history and what it was like to be a soldier there.

Brothers in Hope: The Story of the Lost Boys of Sudan by Mary Williams (illustrated by R. Gregory Christie) is told from the point of view of eight-year-old Garang; when his village is destroyed he begins the long trek that will—at last—take him to America.

Alice Provensen's **Klondike Gold** portrays the dangers and excitement of the Canadian gold rush through the experiences of a young man who comes west from New England to search for gold.

Kids looking for an interesting aspect of the Civil War to write a report on can hardly do better than Sally M. Walker's **Secrets of a Civil War Submarine: Solving the Mysteries of the H. L. Hunley**, the story of a Confederate underwater boat that, in 1864, was the first submarine ever to destroy an enemy ship. How the sub was found and recovered is a rousing tale of history and archaeology.

Young people are mainly taught about the Civil War in terms of the great land battles such as those at Appomattox or Gettysburg. When it comes to warfare at sea, perhaps a few of us (adults or young readers) could dredge up some memory of the encounter between the ironclad ships *Monitor* or *Merrimack*, but as George Sullivan shows in **The Civil War at Sea**, there were many key naval battles that certainly helped turn the tide (yes, I intended that pun) in favor of the North.

Both Dennis Brindell Fradin's **The Founders: The 39 Stories Behind the U.S. Constitution** and **The Signers: The 56 Stories Behind the Declaration of Independence** offer short and lively biographies of the men involved in bringing the United States together as one nation. The woodblock-like illustrations by Michael McCurdy are quite appropriate to the period. These two books are good fodder for history projects, but they also make entertaining reading for history buffs.

An excellent read, as well as a choice resource for reports, is Gary McGowan's **Freedom Roads: Searching for the Underground Railroad**, which also gives readers a useful sense of how historians work.

It's difficult to find good, accessible information (except in an encyclopedia) for young readers about the period immediately following the Civil War, so Tonya Bolden's **Cause: Reconstruction America, 1863–1877**, with its illuminating narrative and excellent illustrations (many of them vintage photographs) is particularly valuable. In addition to helping with homework assignments, the book rewards anyone looking for thorough nonfiction on American history.

In **Free at Last!: Stories and Songs of Emancipation**, Doreen Rappaport explores the experiences of black Americans through letters, memoirs, poetry, and music, describing the experiences of both well-known and ordinary people from right after the Civil War to the 1954 Supreme Court decision that made "separate but equal" illegal. The oil paintings by Shane W. Evans give the book added depth and a visceral power.

The blizzard of 1888 struck the East Coast, from New York to Virginia, with a vengeance—three days of powerful winds, strong snow, and deadly cold. The story of the survivors and the victims is told in gripping prose—frequently using the words of the people who were there—by Jim Murphy, in **Blizzard!**

Lynn Curlee's **Liberty** tells the story of the how the idea for the Statue of Liberty came about, how a French sculptor was commissioned to design it, and how it was finally assembled in the New York harbor. There's also a useful compendium of facts about the statue and a timeline of important dates in its history.

It turns out that it wasn't the fault of Mrs. O'Leary's cow that Chicago nearly burned down in 1871, as related in Jim Murphy's fascinating **The Great Fire**. It's as useful and interesting for adult history fans as it is for middle and high school history assignments. (Anything by Jim Murphy is worth reading.)

The women of the West usually get short shrift in histories of the period, but Candace Savage's **Born to Be a Cowgirl: A Spirited Ride Through the Old West** should go a long way to remedying that. Using both original sources and vintage photos, Savage shows the important role that cowgirls played in the settling of Western America.

Another excellent offering in the 900s includes **American Heroes: Fifty Profiles of Great Americans Who Set Out, Spoke Up, Stood Tall, Fought Hard, or Truly Dared to Dream** by Marfé Ferguson Delano, which includes such varied folks as William Penn, Theodore Roosevelt, Alice Paul (a suffragist leader I had never heard of), Margaret Mead, Thurgood Marshall, Queen Lili'uokalani, and Jonas Salk, among others.

DOGGONE IT, SHE SAID HO(A)RSELY

Between the ages of about seven and ten, basically all I read were horse and dog books. I could probably walk into the Parkman Branch Library in Detroit today and stroll unerringly to the section of the library where they were then shelved. It wasn't until Miss Frances Whitehead bribed me by offering to let me be the first to check out a new dog or horse book if I would just read another book that she absolutely knew I would love, that I gradually found there were other areas of the library that had titles I enjoyed reading, too.

I didn't own many books when I was a kid, but the ones I did have were, of course, about dogs and horses—Anna Sewell's **Black Beauty**, Marguerite Henry's **Misty of Chincoteague** (which the author autographed for me at a book fair); **The Magnificent**

Barb by Dana Faralla (which I borrowed from a friend and conveniently never returned); Walter Farley's **The Black Stallion's Blood Bay Colt**; Marshall Saunders's very sad **Beautiful Joe**; **Us and the Duchess** by Edward Fenton; and **Bonny's Boy**, the story of a cocker spaniel puppy by F. E. Rechnitzer. You'll want to try to find some of these classics of the past as well as the newer titles to satisfy a reader who craves animal stories.

Many of the more recent dog stories are written from the point of view of the animal himself. Two good ones are Ann M. Martin's **A Dog's Life**, the story of a stray dog named Squirrel (the plot grew out of the author's volunteer activities with an animal rescue organization) and Avi's **The Good Dog**, in which McKinley, a malamute, is torn between his settled life and the lure of a wolf named Lupin. (Fans of this book may want to go back and read both of Jack London's now classic tales, **Call of the Wild** and **White Fang**.)

Another book told from the point of view of the dog characters (indeed, most of the characters—except for the villain—are dogs) is Dodie Smith's **The 101 Dalmatians**, which became, of course, a Walt Disney film. Even if you and your child have seen the movie, don't miss this little gem of a novel, which is much more complex (and satisfying) than the screenplay.

Here are some of my other favorite dog and horse stories.

Dogs

Carol Ryrie Brink's **The Highly Trained Dogs of Professor Petit**

Kate DiCamillo's **Because of Winn Dixie**

Eleanor Estes's **Ginger Pye**

Fred Gipson's **Old Yeller**

William H. Armstrong's **Sounder**

Eric Knight's **Lassie Come-Home**

Phyllis Reynolds Naylor's **Shiloh**, and its two sequels, **Shiloh Season** and **Saving Shiloh**

Wilson Rawls's **Where the Red Fern Grows**

Horses

Walter Farley's **The Black Stallion** and its sequels, especially **The Black Stallion and Satan**

Lynn Hall's **The Something-Special Horse**

Marguerite Henry's Newbery Award–winning **King of the Wind**; **Sea Star: Orphan of Chincoteague**; **Justin Morgan Had a Horse**; and the one I most loved, **Born to Trot**

Will James's **Smoky, the Cow Horse** (which won the 1927 Newbery Award)

John Steinbeck's **The Red Pony**

DOLLS AND DOLLHOUSES

As a child, when I wasn't at the library or lying on my bed reading, I was playing with my dollhouse. It makes sense, then, that some of the books I remember with the most fondness are those that took place in dollhouses, or at least had as their central characters dolls who just happened to have the ability to come alive occasionally (always when humans weren't around to witness it). Be sure to take the dollhouse lover in your family to the Museum of American History in Washington, D.C., where's there's an amazing dollhouse on permanent display. Meanwhile, here are some superb books to savor:

Edward Tulane would not want to be included in this category, since the main character in Kate DiCamillo's **The Miraculous Journey of Edward Tulane** would argue that he is not a doll at all. And he'd be right. But where else would I include this moving novel about the power of love to transform even a most proper (not to say full of self-pride) three-foot-tall rabbit? Edward lives a serene (not to say boring) and most self-important life under the care of a little girl named Abilene, until the unforeseen and unthinkable happens and he's unwillingly set on a challenging series of adventures, none of which he's prepared for and, especially at the beginning, none of which he welcomes.

Ann M. Martin and Laura Godwin's **The Doll People** introduces brave Annabelle, a member of the Doll family that lives in a house in eight-year-old Kate Palmer's bedroom. She decides to search for the whereabouts of her Auntie Sarah, who disappeared forty-five years before. There's lots of fun (among much else, there's a Baby Doll who belongs to another dollhouse family entirely but whom the entire Doll family loves because she's theirs) and drama to be found in Martin and Godwin's inventive dollhouse world, such as their descriptions of the Dolls trying to coexist with The Captain, the Palmers' dangerous cat, or avoid the fate of Doll State or—worse!—permanent Doll State, and yet have a fulfilling and non-boring life (just what we all want). When they meet the Funcrafts, a new dollhouse family, things really start to happen. The pictures by Brian Selznick help make this book special for anyone who loves playing with a dollhouse. The adventures continue in **The Meanest Doll in the World**.

I would bet almost anything that Godwin and Martin loved **Big Susan** by Elizabeth Orton Jones (originally published in 1947) as much as I did, because when I read their book, I was so reminded of Jones's story of a group of celluloid and china dolls who come alive only on one special night a year. Again the illustrations, by Jones herself, are just perfect for this gentle and beautiful book.

Although there are no dollhouses in Rachel Field's **Hitty: Her First Hundred Years** (which won the Newbery Award in 1930), this story of a doll carved out of a piece of mountain ash wood in Maine in 1829 and her grand adventures over the next century as she passes from owner to owner never loses its freshness and appeal, despite some language and situations that may not sit well with politically correct readers.

Rosemary Wells addressed these issues in **Rachel Field's Hitty: Her First Hundred Years**, a rewriting of Field's masterpiece, which adds new scenes and eliminates, for example, the cringe-causing references to "savages" and "heathens" and changes the ending altogether. While I am sympathetic to the reasons behind Wells's revision (and while I enjoyed Susan Jeffers's radiant illustrations), I think the original remains the one I'll give my granddaughters to read.

The eponymous Miss Hickory, whose body is a just-the-right-shaped twig from an apple tree and whose head is an acorn, finds her formerly pleasant life in a corncob house upended when the family she lives with moves away, in Carolyn Sherwin Bailey's **Miss Hickory**. It's only with the help of Crow and Mr. T. Willard-Brown, a plain-speaking cat, that Miss Hickory realizes she might be meant for a different sort of life. (For some reason, I found this book incredibly sad when I was a child, although I'm sure it's intended to be comforting in many ways.)

Rumer Godden wrote many books about dolls and dollhouses, including **Miss Happiness and Miss Flower**; **The Doll's House** (which has a most unpleasant doll character named Marchpane); **Impunity Jane** (about a doll who didn't want a comfortable life in a dolls' house, but rather a life of adventure and excitement—and finally got her wish); **The Fairy Doll**; and **Candy Floss**.

Kathryn Reiss adds a dash of supernatural scariness to her dollhouse books, which include **Time Windows** and **Sweet Miss Honeywell's Revenge**.

Even though the characters in Mary Norton's **The Borrowers** are not dolls, I think both that book and its sequels belong here. I am quite fond of Arrietty Clock, who, along with her father, Pod, and mother, Homily (as well as several other Borrower families), resides in a large country house, side by side with humans who are quite unaware of their existence. When Arrietty makes the unforgivable error of allowing a human boy to see her, the Borrowers' whole future becomes problematical. Norton's books are a splendid choice for imaginative children who love the idea of (usually) unseen "little people" sharing their lives.

While most of the books in this section are generally thought of as being aimed at girls, Lynne Reid Banks's **The Indian in the Cupboard** and its sequels are well loved by both boys and girls, and doll lovers of both sexes will also enjoy **Lady Daisy** by Dick King-Smith, the story of nine-year-old Ned, who becomes the focus of teasing and trouble when he decides to keep Lady Daisy Chain, an old-fashioned wax doll that speaks only to him.

DOUBLE TROUBLE

D ouble the fun, double the stress, and double the mishaps! At least that's the way it appears when you encounter a pair of twins in a good book—excitement, misunderstandings, and mischief abound. Most people are familiar with the two sets of Bobbsey twins—Nan and Bert, Flossie and Freddie—but there are lots more twins to read about. From identical to fraternal, from realistic portrayals of sibling rivalry to fantasies of twins with supernatural abilities, each of these books shows that life as a double is never ordinary. You can certainly multiply the pleasure of middle-grade reading with these books.

Never Mind: A Twin Novel by Avi and Rachel Vail introduces a set of very different fraternal twins; Edward is the class clown, while Meg goes to a school for gifted students. Told in alternating chapters by each sibling, readers get a glimpse into the life of a pair of twins who, although different, may be more alike than they think in this humorous, lively novel. (The fact that Avi himself has a twin sister certainly adds a bit of authenticity to the story.)

In **Sea Legs** by Alex Shearer, rather than spend more boring time with their grandparents, twin brothers Clive and Eric stow away on the luxury cruise liner where their father works. As Eric tells it, although the boys try to steer clear of their father, trouble follows, which makes for a humorous and sometimes suspenseful read.

Ten-year-old twins Pauline and Arlene absolutely hate each other in **January 1905**, a historical novel by Katharine Boling told in alternating first-person, present-tense chapters. Arlene, who has a crippled foot, works at home cleaning and cooking, while Pauline puts in long hours at the nearby cotton mill. Each believes the other has it easier (although both seem pretty difficult existences to me), and each dreams of living the other's life. How they come to respect each other's lot in life makes for a satisfying conclusion.

Adventure fans will be happy to meet Grace and Mary, the thirteen-year-old fraternal twins in **Cryptid Hunters** by Roland Smith who are stranded in the Congo while on a trip with their uncle. Dinosaurs, possibly mythical animals, and a ruthless killer add to the suspense, as the twins realize that although they have their own special talents, their strength lies in working together.

The main characters in P. B. Kerr's Children of the Lamp series are fraternal twins descended from a long line of djinni—John and Philippa Gaunt's adventures begin in **The Akhenaten Adventure** and continue in **The Blue Djinn of Babylon**.

Other twin books to look for are **The Twin in the Tavern** by Barbara Brooks Wallace; **Double Act** by Jacqueline Wilson; **Angela and Diabola** by Lynne Reid Banks; Stephanie S. Tolan's **Ordinary Miracles**; **Ruby Holler** by Sharon Creech; **The Well-Wishers** by Edward Eager; and Beverly Cleary's **Mitch and Amy**.

FRIENDS MAKE THE WORLD GO ROUND

Making friends is sometimes hard. Keeping them is often even harder, but always worth working at. A good friend can make the hardest times in someone's life a little easier. Many of these novels explore unexpected friendships that cross cultures, ages, race, and certainly gender, but never in a heavy-handed or didactic way. Here are some of my favorite books about friendship in all its (sometimes unusual) permutations, all written with honesty and (occasionally) humor.

April and Melanie's friendship is cemented by their common love of all things Egyptian, but when a game they're playing takes an unexpected (and possibly sinister) turn, they wonder if they've gone too far, in **The Egypt Game** by Zilpha Keatley Snyder. **Jennifer, Hecate, MacBeth, William McKinley, and Me, Elizabeth** by E. L. Konigsburg (which is a Newbery Honor book) is a tale in which the friendship of two fifth-grade girls overcomes both loneliness and racial differences, as Jennifer and Elizabeth bond together through their interest in witchcraft and particularly in coming up with an ointment that will enable them to fly.

With her beloved grandmother Miss Eula away for a visit to a new grandbaby, nine-year-old Ruby Lavender has no one to share adventures and good times with in her hometown of Halleluia, Mississippi, until Melba Jane proves to be less of an enemy and more of a friend, in Deborah Wiles's delightful **Love, Ruby Lavender**. (Incidentally, the audio book, narrated by Judith Ivey, is top notch as well.)

Other outstanding "friendship" reads include **Crossing Jordan** by Adrian Fogelin; **How Do You Spell Geek?** by Julie Anne Peters; **P.S. Longer Letter Later** and **Snail Mail No More** by Paula Danziger and Ann M. Martin (can two thirteen-year-olds stay friends though they live in different cities?); **The Storyteller's Beads** by Jane Kurtz (set in Ethiopia in the 1980s); **The Friends** by Kazumi Yumoto (translated from the Japanese by Cathy Hirano); Nikki Grimes's **Meet Danitra Brown** (a series of poems about the friendship between two young girls); Farley Mowat's **Lost in the Barrens**; **The Tulip Touch** by Anne Fine; Frances O'Roark Dowell's **The Secret Language of Girls**; Jean Thesman's **In the House of the Queen's Beasts**; and Michael Morpurgo's **Kensuke's Kingdom**.

G AND T'S: GIFTED AND TALENTED

So what it's like to be really, really smart? The view from the outside in is fun to read, as can be seen in the books described below:

All through school, Nora, now in the fifth grade, has managed to fool everyone into thinking that she's just a normal kid, but that's all about to end when she decides to help her friend Stephen feel better about himself after he does poorly on some standardized tests, in **The Report Card** by Andrew Clements.

Possibly the smartest person of prehistoric times, Ug is always inventing things to make life in the Stone Age easier for everyone, in Raymond Briggs's delightful **Ug: Boy Genius of the Stone Age**.

Other G and T's to meet are found in Wendelin Van Draanen's **Secret Identity**, the first in her Shredderman series about ultra-brainy Nolan ("Nerd") Byrd, whose brains lead him to ultimately outdo the fifth-grade class bully; **Someday Angeline** by Louis Sachar; Eoin Colfer's **Half Moon Investigations**; Sheila Greenwald's **Alvin Webster's Surefire Plan for Success (And How It Failed)**; and Jacqueline Woodson's **Maizon at Blue Hill**.

GIRL POWER!

Sometimes the best part of reading a particular book is that you can find yourself in its pages, or that you can find a braver, more exciting, more beautiful, smarter, kinder, or just more interesting you. The books below are filled with all sorts of girls, solving all sorts of problems, living all kinds of lives.

Everyone has problems, but as is made clear in Gail Carson Levine's **Ella Enchanted** (a very loose retelling of *Cinderella*), when a fairy gives you the dubious gift at birth of always having to be obedient, it does make life difficult, especially when you have some pretty mean stepsisters and fall in love with the prince of the kingdom. Anyone who loved the world where *Ella Enchanted* is set will also want to read **Fairest**, a story about a girl who doesn't believe she can be loved for herself.

If your name was Pippilotta Delicatessa Windowshade Mackrelmint Ephraim's Daughter Longstocking, wouldn't you want to change it to Pippi? And if your name were Pippi, wouldn't you want to live with only a monkey in your own house, called Villa Villekulla? And be busy having all sorts of adventures? It's hard not to want be the irrepressible heroine of **Pippi Longstocking** by Astrid Lindgren.

Can you imagine Larry McMurtry writing a book for nine- to twelve-year-olds? If so, you'll have a good idea what the charms of **The Misadventures of Maude March** by Audrey Couloumbis are: plucky girls, nonstop adventures, and a killer who may or may not have a heart of gold.

Harriet loves to eavesdrop (and keep notes) on other people's lives, but she runs into trouble when her notebook falls into the hands of some people who aren't thrilled with her life as a spy, in Louise Fitzhugh's **Harriet the Spy**.

A thirteen-year-old Inuit girl runs away from her Alaskan home to escape an arranged marriage and ends up living with a pack of wolves in **Julie of the Wolves** by Jean Craighead George.

What would you do if you were ten years old and woke up one fine day to find a silver crown on your pillow, your parents mysteriously gone (well, that part might be okay with a lot of kids!), and an unmistakable threat from something called the Hieronymous Machine that wants your crown? Ellen faces all that and more in Robert C. O'Brien's **The Silver Crown**, now available in a beautiful new edition.

Heidi, the main character in **So B. It** by Sarah Weeks, sets out to unravel the mysteries surrounding her life with her mentally retarded mother.

Baby Island by Carol Ryrie Brink is the story of two sisters shipwrecked on a small island along with four babies. How they survive (and even prosper) after meeting the local version of Daniel Defoe's Friday makes this book a grand read for boys and girls alike. (It was one of my favorites when I was a child.)

Other books with really cool girl characters include **The True Confessions of Charlotte Doyle** by Avi; **Zeely** by Virginia Hamilton; Rumer Godden's **An Episode of Sparrows**; **The Star of Kazan** and **Which Witch** by Eva Ibbotson; Shannon Hale's **The Princess Academy**; **The Hero and the Crown** by Robin McKinley and its sequel (which can actually be read on its own), **The Blue Sword**; and Diane Duane's iconic pre–Harry Potter fantasy, **So You Want to Be a Wizard**, the first of the Young Wizards series, all starring Nita Callahan, who gets her wizardry start as a result of a visit to a library; others in the series include **Deep Wizardry**, **High Wizardry**, and **Wizard's Holiday**.

GONE BUT NOT FORGOTTEN

Keep an eye out for these winners, all published more than four decades ago. They may be hard to find, but they're wonderful choices for your middle-grade readers. It's highly unlikely that they'll ever be reissued, unfortunately. I would love to hear from anyone who's read them, too—I sometimes fear I'm the only one (besides my sister and daughters) who remembers them.

Anne Barrett's **Caterpillar Hall** (a lovely story about a magical umbrella that allows its young owner, Penelope, to see into people's pasts)

Ruth Christoffer Carlsen's **Mr. Pudgins** (I don't understand why the books about Mary Poppins remain in print, while this cheerful tale of an eccentric babysitter has been unavailable for years)

Richard Church's **Five Boys in a Cave** (I don't actually know of any other fiction book about spelunking written for grades four through eight, and this is a thrilling adventure, indeed)

John Keir Cross's **The Other Side of Green Hills** (probably one of the most inventive and scary fantasies a child can read)

Norman Dale's **The Casket and the Sword** (a thrilling adventure tale marked by an unlikely villain and a long lost treasure)

Jennie Dorothea Lindquist's **The Golden Name Day** (one of those quiet books that a certain type of girl—who loves the Betsy-Tacy books, for example—will very much enjoy)

Dean Marshall's **The Invisible Island, Dig for a Treasure**, and **Wish on the Moon** are probably close to impossible to find (they were published more than fifty years ago but are still—I just reread them—reasonably contemporary in tone and thoroughly enjoyable family stories)

Robb White's **Long Way Down** and **Lion's Paw**

GOOD SPORTS

I like to use sports stories to entice reluctant middle school readers into putting aside their antipathy for (or indifference to) books. The novels that follow usually have a moral (good sportsmanship, primarily, and the different forms it can take), but the moral is never presented in a preachy or hectoring way. So find the sport that your nonreader likes best, and try these. (And don't forget the sports books found in the 700s in the "Dewey Love Nonfiction" category.)

The baseball novels of John R. Tunis and Duane Decker were popular when I was a kid, and I still remember how much I enjoyed them. So even though a lot has changed (most notably for the Tunis books, the Dodgers are no longer in Brooklyn, alas), the themes remain current and the details of the game are the same as they were way back when the grass was green and the sky over the stadium was blue. My favorite Tunis novels are **The Kid from**

Tomkinsville (now available in a brand-new edition), **World Series**, and **Keystone Kids**.

There's a book for every position on the Blue Sox, Duane Decker's fictional team; each one follows roughly the same outline—the main character is contending for a job with either a star veteran player, someone who's seemingly more talented than he is, or his own demons of self-doubt. Of course, at the end of each book Jug Slavin, the manager, has sorted it all out: the good are rewarded and those with lack of dedication are punished (or at least sent down to the minors, forced to retire, or traded to another, less insightful team). You might have to dig these up at used bookstores or search over the Internet, but they're worth it. I can heartily recommend them all to sports fans, but my favorites are **Good Field, No Hit**; **Fast Man on a Pivot**; and **Long Ball to Left Field**.

Another, more current baseball book is sportswriter Mike Lupica's first book for kids, **Heat**. The main character, Michael Arroyo, lives in the shadow of Yankee Stadium and is the star of his Little League team; all he wants is the chance to realize his father's dream and play professional baseball—but Michael also has a secret, and if the wrong people find out, all of his dreams will be derailed.

John R. Tunis also wrote two novels about high school basketball that I remember with great fondness—**Yea! Wildcats!** and **Go Team, Go!**, and Bruce Brooks, author of many excellent books for kids and teens, wrote the introduction to the 1989 edition of **Yea! Wildcats!**

My favorite sports novel of Brooks's has always been **The Moves Make the Man**, because it's not only good on basketball, but also excellent in its handling of racism and more ordinary issues that teens face. Wherever there's a potential for heaviness, it's leavened by Brooks's sense of humor. Here's an example: thirteen-year-old African American Jerome Foxworthy, one of the two main characters, describes the game of baseball this way: "Bunch of dudes in kneepants standing up straight and watching each other do very little."

Other high school basketball novels include Carl Deuker's **Night Hoops** and **On the Devil's Court** (has Joe Faust traded his soul to be a champion basketball player?); Walter Dean Myers's **Slam!**; **Airball: My Life in Briefs** by L. D. Harkrader; and **Last Shot: A Final Four Mystery** by veteran sports writer John Feinstein, who brings his inside knowledge of the game to a novel that will please both basketball fans and mystery readers. Sports fans (especially tennis lovers) will want to read about the new adventures of Susan Carol Anderson and Stevie Thomas in **Vanishing Act: Mystery at the U.S. Open**.

With the immense popularity of NASCAR, I think it would be great if some publisher reissued the sports car racing novels of William Campbell Gault, which were originally published in the late 1950s. Besides telling a good story, Gault is a master at first lines—as you can see in the opening of **Rough Road to Glory**: "Blood is thicker than methanol and that could be the story of Walt and Eddie and why I had all the trouble with Walt." What sports fan could stop there? Gault's other books about gasoline alley include **Thunder Road** and **Speedway Challenge**, which opens:

> The Triple-A boys don't stop at Oak Grove any more.
> When my dad was alive, Oak Grove was considered
> one of the best maintained dirt tracks in America. But
> my dad died fifteen years ago.
> At Oak Grove, on the north turn.

Doesn't it make you want to read on and learn who's narrating and what's going to happen to him?

Gault also wrote a couple of fine football stories—**Mr. Quarterback** ("Peter Pulaski, that was his name, and a part of the trouble.") and **Mr. Fullback**, which, considering they were both written fifty or so years ago, are amazingly modern.

Short pieces about sports are another marvelous way of enticing reluctant readers. They're also good for reading aloud in a relatively short amount of time. Take a look at these collections: **Girls Got Game: Sports Stories and Poems**, edited by Sue Macy (with contributions by authors as well known as Jacqueline Woodson and Virginia Euwer Wolff, as well as writers not so familiar, such as Christa Campion and Lucy Jane Bledsoe); and **Rimshots: Basketball Pix, Rolls, and Rhythms** by Charles R. Smith Jr., a striking combination of photographs, prose, and poetry.

And don't forget these: Kathy Mackel's **A Season of Comebacks**; **The Million Dollar Shot** by Dan Gutman (what's it like for an eleven-year-old boy to be on the free-throw line with one chance to make a million dollars?) and **The Million Dollar Kick** (same plot, but this time the game is soccer and the main character is a thirteen-year-old girl); both **Finding Buck McHenry** and **The Trading Game** by Alfred Slote are solid stories about baseball trading cards, rather than the game itself; the many books by Matt Christopher, which second- through fifth-grade readers tend to love; and Jerry Spinelli's humorous **There's a Girl in My Hammerlock**.

GOOSEBUMPS

I n the 1990s, R. L. Stine became famous for writing an immensely popular series of scary books for middle-grade readers. The first Goosebumps book was **Welcome to Dead House**, and kids have gobbled them up at an amazing rate ever since. But what happens when readers come to the end of the series? Why, recommend these:

When Lewis comes to live with his Uncle Jonathan in **The House With a Clock in Its Walls** by John Bellairs, he discovers that his uncle is a warlock, his next-door neighbor is a witch, and Lewis himself has a part to play in saving the world from the forces of evil. The same characters are also found in **The Figure in the Shadows** and **The Letter, the Witch, and the Ring**.

There's witchcraft and wizardry, trouble and terror, fear and fun, in Debi Gliori's **Pure Dead Brilliant**, **Pure Dead Wicked**, **Pure Dead Magic**, and **Pure Dead Trouble**, all featuring the Strega-Borgia family along with various servants and pets, including Nanny McLachlan, Latch the butler, Multitudina, the Illerat, and Tarantella, a spider with attitude.

When Darren Shan goes to a rather clandestine freak show, all sorts of gruesome and unusual adventures follow for him and his best friend, Steve. They're described in a growing series of surprisingly plausible but highly unlikely (I devoutly hope), often *very scary* novels, beginning the **Cirque Du Freak: A Living Nightmare** . . . and continuing with (ah, here's a clue to what the action entails) **The Vampire's Assistant**. Evidently not one to rest on the horror laurels he's already received, Shan's begun another series, Demonata, in which yet another teenage boy finds himself confronted with unspeakable evil, in **Lord Loss**. (See the "Up All Night" section for more suggestions of scary reads for older teens.)

Other spellbinding novels for middle-grade readers to gnaw on include **My Friend the Vampire**, **The Little Vampire Moves In**, and **The Vampire in Love** by Angela Sommer-Bodenburg; Edward Bloor's **Story Time**; Eva Ibbotson's rather lighthearted tales of ghostly doings in **Dial-a-Ghost** and **The Great Ghost Rescue**; **Raven's Gate** and **Evil Star**, books I and II of The Gatekeepers by Anthony Horowitz (evil in a remote village in Yorkshire, England); Philip Pullman's **Count Karlstein**; Neil Gaiman's **Coraline** and **The Wolves in the Walls** (neither to be read when you're alone in the house); **The Empty Mirror** by James Lincoln Collier; and three novels about a girl who realizes her job is to help the dead become at peace with themselves or else revenge themselves on their living enemies, **The Ghost of Fossil Glen**, **The Ghost and Mrs. Hobbs**, and **The Ghost of Cutler Creek** by Cynthia DeFelice.

These goosebumpy books usually work well with reluctant readers, but sometimes what's even better is to offer these collections of stories, which are perfect for those not inclined to take on a whole book. Among the tested and true are R. L. Stine's **Beware!: R. L. Stine Picks His Favorite Scary Stories** (which includes stories from authors like William Sleator, Roald Dahl, and Jane Yolen); **A Creepy Company: Ten Tales of Terror** by Joan Aiken; Alvin Schwartz's **Scary Stories to Tell in the Dark** and its sequels; **A Terrifying Taste of Short and Shivery: Thirty Creepy Tales** and **Even More Short and Shivery: Thirty Spine-Tingling Stories**, all retold by Robert D. San Souci; and **The Headless Horseman and Other Ghoulish Tales**, eerie stories from around the world collected and retold by Maggie Pearson.

GREEK MYTHS

The Greek myths have it all: they're classic tales of bravery, love, violence, heroes, trickery, warfare, and dastardly villains (both mortal and immortal, humans and gods). You can introduce students to the subject through some of the entertaining books below. Take a look, too, at the books in "It Might as Well Be Greek" in Part III for more suggestions for slightly older readers.

For fiction, try these:

As if they've come into the twenty-first century straight out of a mythology book, the Greek gods, including Zeus, Dionysus, and others, enter twelve-year-old Percy Jackson's life with a vengeance, and now he's been accused of stealing Zeus's primary lightning bolt. To save his reputation (not to mention his life) Percy has to discover who really took it, before all hell breaks loose on Mount Olympus, in Rick Riordan's **The Lightning Thief** and its worthy sequel, **The Sea of Monsters**, the first two books in the Percy Jackson and the Olympians series.

Jane Yolen and Robert J. Harris combined to write The Young Heroes series, retelling the great myths with true élan. The series includes **Odysseus and the Serpent Maze, Hippolyta and the Curse of the Amazons, Atalanta and the Arcadian Beast,** and **Jason and the Gorgon's Blood.**

Kate McMullan offers up the lighter side—lots of puns and other word play—in her Myth-o-Mania series, including **Have a Hot Time, Hades!**, **Phone Home, Persephone!**, **Go for the Gold, Atalanta!**, and more. These are great to read aloud, and may inspire listeners to go ahead and read more on their own.

Rosemary Sutcliff makes good use of her prodigious talent for bringing the past to life in **Black Ships Before Troy: The Story of the Iliad** and **The Wanderings of Odysseus: The Story of the Odyssey**.

In a twist of our sympathies, Tobias Druitt pairs his hero, Corydon (born with a goat's foot and therefore considered a freak), and the Greek monsters—including Medusa, the Sphinx, two Gorgon girls, and the Minotaur—against the less noble heroes and gods who want to imprison them, in **Corydon and the Island of Monsters**.

GUARANTEED TO GRAB YOU— MEMORABLE FIRST LINES

I love first lines of books. I can't imagine a better feeling than opening up a book to the first page and coming across a line or two that is so compelling you just can't stop reading. Here are some of my favorites.

Millicent Min, Girl Genius by Lisa Yee begins, "I have been accused of being anal retentive, an over-achiever, and a compulsive perfectionist, like those are bad things."

Deborah Wiles starts **Each Little Bird That Sings** with this come-hither line: "I come from a family with a lot of dead people."

"Every night, around nine o'clock in Cold Shoulder Road, the screaming began," is how Joan Aiken begins **Cold Shoulder**

Road—and don't you want to find out what the screaming is all about?

Philip Pullman starts **The Scarecrow and His Servant** this way: "One day old Mr. Pandolfo, who hadn't been feeling at all well, decided to make a scarecrow."

Roderick Townley's **The Great Good Thing** begins with this intriguing sentence: "Sylvie had an amazing life, but she didn't get to live it very often."

"Ma, a mouse has to do what a mouse has to do," is the intriguing first line of **Ragweed** by Avi.

Who could resist reading further than this sentence that opens **Three Terrible Trins** by Dick King-Smith: "At six o'clock on the morning of her birthday, Mrs. Gray's husband was killed and eaten. It was her first birthday, and he was her third husband."

"If your teacher has to die, August isn't a bad time of the year for it," is how Richard Peck's **The Teacher's Funeral** begins.

The opening line of M. T. Anderson's **Feed** is, "We went to the moon to have fun, but the moon turned out to completely suck."

"Daddy killed Mama today, just like he told her he would," begins Betty Monthei in her terribly sad first novel, **Looking for Normal**.

And "There was a boy called Eustace Clarence Scrubb, and he almost deserved it," is the way C. S. Lewis introduces **The Voyage of the *Dawn Treader*.**

HICKORY, DICKORY, DOCK

O f course there's probably a well-worth-learning back-story of why the mouse ran up the clock, but until we find out what it is, readers can have a wonderful time meeting the mice in these books. One word of warning: rats! They're nearly always the enemy.

Redwall Abbey is the setting for a series of books by Brian Jacques, who, despite his last name, is British. These exciting, frightening, sometimes a bit violent, and well-written epics, which will remind adult readers of the books of J. R. R. Tolkien, are about the eternal battle between good and evil (mice and rats, respectively). The series begins with **Redwall** and continues with **Mossflower**, **Mattimeo**, and more.

And fans of Jacques's books will immediately want to turn to The Deptford Mice Trilogy by Robin Jarvis, including **The Dark Portal**, **The Crystal Prison**, and **The Final Reckoning**, all about an ongoing war between the rats (once again the bad guys) and the mice (our heroes) that will determine the future of London, England.

Heather Vogel Frederick's Spy Mice series, including **The Black Paw** and **For Your Paws Only**, features Gloria Goldenleaf, private eye, who, along with her human pal, fifth-grader Oz Levinson, does her best to combat the evil (and intelligent) rats who intend to rid the world of mice under the leadership of the loathsome tough guy (rat), Roquefort Dupont. (Clearly the author owes a debt of grati-tude to Margery Sharp, author of **The Rescuers** and its sequels, probably some of the earliest fantasies for children featuring mice; who could forget Miss Bianca, Bernard, and the Mouse Prisoners' Aid Society?)

Kate DiCamillo's **The Tale of Despereaux: Being the Story of a Mouse, a Princess, Some Soup, and a Spool of Thread** concerns Despereaux Tilling, a most unusual mouse: not only does he love to read, but he also falls in love with a very human princess. This Newbery Award–winner makes for a great read-aloud, too.

Brother and sister Jennifer L. and Matthew Holm's **Babymouse: Queen of the World!**, **Babymouse: Our Hero**, and **Babymouse: Beach Babe** are graphic novels featuring an energetic and adorable nine-year-old who just happens to be a mouse—like Ramona Quimby, in fact, if you can imagine her with furry ears and a little tail.

Other mice to meet include the characters in Peter Dickinson's **Time and the Clockmice, Etcetera,** the story of three mice families (the Hickorys, the Dickorys, and the Docks, of course) who live happily in the Branton Town Hall Clock until the day it breaks down; Terry Pratchett's **The Amazing Maurice and His Educated Rodents** (rats, rather than mice, but I couldn't resist putting it in here because kids needs to be introduced to Terry Pratchett's fertile imagination in every possible category!); **The Mousewife** by Rumer Godden; **The Mouse and His Child** by Russell Hoban (a lovely story to read aloud at Christmas time); **Abel's Island** by the dependable William Steig; Robert C. O'Brien's **Mrs. Frisby and the Rats of NIMH** (here the mice and rats are allies); **The Mouse and the Motorcycle**, **Ralph S. Mouse**, and **Runaway Ralph** by Beverly Cleary; Michael Hoeye's stories about the debonair mouse and watchmaker, Hermux Tantamoq, including **Time Stops for No Mouse, The Sands of Time**, and **No Time Like Show Time**; and **Stuart Little** by E. B. White.

"I" BOOKS

W hen I was in the fourth grade, Miss LaFramboise, the art teacher, came once a week to give our homeroom teacher, Mrs. Syllagi, an hour break. To pass the time, she started reading Eleanor Estes's Newbery Award–winning **Ginger Pye** out loud to the class. Early in this delightful family story about a lost dog, the reading habits of nine-year-old Rachel and ten-year-old Jerry are described this way:

> They both always opened a book eagerly and suspiciously looking first to see whether or not it was an "I" book. If it were they would put it aside, not reading it until there was absolutely nothing else. . . . But, being an "I" book, it had to be awfully good for them to like it. Only a few, **Robinson Crusoe**, **Treasure Island**, and **Swiss Family Robinson**, for example, survived the hard "I" book test. These were among their best beloved in spite of the obvious handicap.

None of us, including Miss LaFramboise, knew what an "I" book was. We had to ask Mrs. Syllagi, and she explained—how could we have missed it?—that it was a book told in the first person. Of course, no one could quarrel with Rachel and Jerry Pye's three "best beloved" books, but I'd like to think that they'd also really enjoy the books described below:

Norma Fox Mazer has made a career out of (and won numerous awards for) writing thought-provoking books about very real kids. In **What I Believe**, Vicki describes her feelings about the changes her family faces when her father loses his job, and she makes an impulsive choice with a potentially tragic outcome.

In **Dovey Coe** by Frances O'Roark Dowell, which takes place in the mountains of North Carolina in 1928, the eponymous twelve-year-old relates the events that follow an accusation that she murdered her sister's suitor.

When her parents drop her off to stay with a woman she's never met before, Bethany realizes that something is wrong—but it takes a lot of sleuthing before she learns the shocking truth about herself and an older sister she never knew she had, in Margaret Peterson Haddix's **Double Identity**.

Primrose Squarp doesn't believe her parents died at sea in a terrible storm, even though everyone else in her hometown of Coal Harbour, British Columbia, does. Although she grows to love her Uncle Jack, with whom she goes to live, she'd rather spend her time with Miss Bowzer, the owner and cook of a little restaurant called The Girl on the Swing, where all the food that's ordered—from steak to waffles—is served on a waffle. Replete with recipes and a happy ending, Polly Horvath serves up a heartwarming tale in **Everything on a Waffle**. Pass the maple syrup, please.

Sue Stauffacher's **Harry Sue** is the story of an eleven-year-old girl trying to cope with an abusively neglectful grandmother, parents in prison, and a best friend who's a paraplegic. So you think you have problems?

Everything changes for Ida B when her mother is diagnosed with cancer: her family has to sell off part of their orchard (Ida B used to love visiting with various trees) and, worst of all, she's no longer going to be taught at home but must attend public school. Katherine Hannigan's **Ida B . . . and Her Plans to Maximize Fun, Avoid Disaster, and (Possibly) Save the World** shows what can happen when a little girl's upside-down world makes her absolutely furious and she can't imagine being happy again.

Did you ever wonder where Shahrazad got those 1001 stories with which she charmed her husband, the Sultan, into letting her live day after day, and night after night, when he'd killed off numerous wives before? Susan Fletcher's **Shadow Spinner** introduces Marjan, a young crippled servant in the Sultan's harem, who tells her own story of supplying Shahrazad with the stories to tell.

Ruth White's **Belle Prater's Boy** is the story of how two cousins—Gypsy, whose father committed suicide years before, and Woodrow, the cross-eyed son of Belle Prater, who up and left her family in Virginia without any explanation—become each other's best friends.

IN THE FOOTSTEPS OF NANCY DREW AND THE HARDY BOYS

There is a wonderful time in every child's reading life when he or she discovers the pleasure of the mystery story. Clues to discover, ideas to chase down, and a crime to solve; nothing is more rewarding than digging into a good mystery story and trying to figure it out before the detective does. While Nancy Drew and the Hardy Boys provide an almost endless list of titles to explore and Encyclopedia Brown is always ready to pose his mind-bending riddles, the mysteries in this category are filled with fun, fancy, and, just as in adult mysteries, settings all over the map, ranging from England to Switzerland to Manhattan to ancient Rome.

Anthony Horowitz's novels about fourteen-year-old Alex Rider (a James Bond type in training who is frequently asked by England's security agency MI-6 to take on a top-secret job) are page-turners filled with descriptions of neat gadgets to help Alex subdue enemies and escape from dangerous situations. The series opens with **Stormbreaker** and continues with **Point Blank, Skeleton Key, Eagle Strike**, and **Scorpia**.

My favorite mystery starring the intrepid girl sleuth Sammy Keyes is the first, **Sammy Keyes and the Hotel Thief**, which won an Edgar Award for best children's mystery novel, but each of the volumes in this popular series by Wendelin Van Draanen's has its own charm.

William Shakespeare, the whereabouts of a missing diamond worth more than a million dollars, a very cute eighth-grader named Danny Cordova, and the travails of being the new kid in the sixth grade occupy Hero Netherfield in Elise Broach's **Shakespeare's Secret**, which in addition to having a fast-moving plot also manages to work in a lot of Elizabethan history and raises the issue of whether or not Shakespeare was the author of the plays attributed to him.

Double Life and **Shadow Beast** are the first two books in the Invisible Detective series by Justin Richards, which features, along with Brandon Lake, the aforementioned invisible sleuth and a group of young criminologists bent on eradicating evil and wrongdoing wherever it's found. But since no one can see him, does Brandon really exist?

From its title with a double meaning to the fast-moving, often very funny plot, **Minerva Clark Gets a Clue** by Karen Karbo offers entertainment for fifth- to eighth-graders. When a bolt of lightning during a rainstorm interferes with a computer art project by her older brother—in which she's playing the central role—Minerva wakes up to find that all of her self-hatred (too tall, too clumsy, too ugly, too weird) and self-consciousness (what she really likes to do is make up rebuses and play with Jupiter, her pet ferret) have disappeared. And when a bookstore clerk is murdered and her beautiful cousin is taken to jail in handcuffs, Minerva sets out to discover whodunit.

You might want to start at the very beginning of the A to Z Mysteries by Ron Roy—Dink, Josh, and Ruth Rose's adventures commence with **The Absent Author**. These are good for second-through fourth-graders, as are the Jigsaw Jones mysteries by James Preller (start with number one, **The Case of Hermie the Missing Monster**).

Other quality mysteries to try (and many are books in a series) include **Mr. Chickee's Funny Money**, Christopher Paul Curtis's clever story set in his hometown of Flint, Michigan; **Chasing Vermeer** by Blue Balliett; **The Westing Game**, **The Tattooed Potato and Other Clues**, and **The Mysterious Disappearance of Leon (I Mean Noel)** by Ellen Raskin; **The Headless Cupid** by Zilpha Keatley Snyder; the series by James Howe about Sebastian Barth, including **Stage Fright**, **What Eric Knew**, and **Eat Your Poison, Dear**; and Henry Winterfeld's **Detectives in Togas**, a good mystery as well as an enjoyable way to learn Roman history.

THE KIDS NEXT DOOR

I know that many readers wish they lived next door to the kids featured in these books (I just wanted to live next door to a library), but unfortunately the only place we can meet them is in the pages of their stories.

Judy Blume's Margaret Simon, in **Are You There God? It's Me, Margaret**

Betty Brock's Annabel Tippins, in **No Flying in the House**

Beverly Cleary's Henry Huggins, in **Henry Huggins, Henry and Ribsy, Henry and the Paper Route**, and others; Beezus and Ramona Quimby, in **Beezus and Ramona**; Ellen Tebbits, in **Ellen Tebbits**

Paula Danziger's Matthew Martin, in **Everyone Else's Parents Said Yes** and Sarah Kate (otherwise known as Skate) Tate, in **United Tates of America**

Lois Lowry's Anastasia, in **Anastasia Krupnik** and sequels

Arthur Ransome's Nancy and Peggy Blackett (who have a small sailboat called the *Amazon*) and John, Susan, Titty, and Roger Walker (their boat is called the *Swallow*), whose adventures are recounted in **Swallows and Amazons, Swallowdale, We Didn't Mean to Go to Sea**, and others

KIDS TO THE RESCUE

I nstead of calling in the Ghostbusters, as the movie would have it, it's sometimes better to call in the kids to save the world. These are good books to offer a reluctant reader, or the one who thinks books can't be as exciting as a video game.

An excellent choice for kids ages eight to twelve is Terry Pratchett's **Only You Can Save Mankind**, the first novel in a trilogy featuring Johnny Maxwell. Originally written more than a decade ago (during the first Gulf War, in fact, which is an integral part of the plot), Johnny, a computer-war-game-playing twelve-year-old, discovers that game space and real space/time are—shockingly—related, when the aliens in the computer game "Only You Can Save Mankind" send Johnny a note that they have chosen to surrender to his forces. This is a great introduction to many years of reading Terry Pratchett's clever, good-humored, and inventive novels.

In **The Merlin Conspiracy**, fantasy writer extraordinaire Diana Wynne Jones introduces Roddy and Nick, who come from two different worlds, Earth and Blest (they're similar, but with subtle differences), battle three evil people who try to turn the magic that runs through all the hundreds of worlds into the dangerous sort.

Whales on Stilts by M. T. Anderson is the story of Larry, a mad scientist (half whale, half man) who intends to take over the world with the help of his cetacean cohorts. The only three people who can possibly stop him are twelve-year-old Lily Gefelty (a perfectly ordinary kid whose father happens to work for Larry) and her two best friends, the decidedly unordinary Katie Mulligan—the heroine of her own series of horror novels for kids (all based on Katie's own experiences)—and the equally extraordinary Boy Technonaut and retro super-geek, Jasper Dash. (Who could resist a book that begins, "On Career Day Lily visited her dad's work with him and discovered he worked for a mad scientist who wanted to rule the earth through destruction and desolation."?) The three reappear in another thrilling tale, **The Clue of the Linoleum Lederhosen**.

The paradoxes inherent in working with time are difficult to get your mind around: if you go back in time and accidentally kill your great-great-grandfather, would that mean that you'd never exist? Questions like this take on new meaning when someone starts playing not very funny tricks with time on seventh-grader Dorso Clayman, who, along with his best friend Frank, has to discover the brains behind the capers before the world ends up in serious trouble, in Gary Paulsen's **The Time Hackers**.

Other excellent books that fall into this category include the Billy Clikk series by Mark Crilley, including **Creach Battler** and **Rogmasher Rampage**; and Colin Bateman's **Running with the Reservoir Pups** and **Bring Me the Head of Oliver Plunkett**, two adventures of Eddie and the Gang with No Name.

KING ARTHUR

The legend (and reality) of King Arthur has captured the imagination of readers of all ages looking for historical tales of heroism, magic, danger, treachery, and the sundering of the Round Table over the love of a woman. Of course, these elements appear in greater or lesser quantities, depending what age group the Arthurian novels are aimed at. The books recommended here concentrate on the heroism, magic, and danger aspects:

One of the first Arthurian novels for middle-grade readers is T. H. White's **The Sword in the Stone**, a wonderful story about how Arthur—known here as Wart—innocently pulls the sword Excalibur from a stone in a churchyard and becomes the High King, after a thorough training by Merlin in the responsibilities of kingship. Although the books that follow—**The Queen of Air and Darkness, The Ill-Made Knight**, and **The Candle in the Wind**—grow increasingly dark and are definitely for older readers, the first one was clearly written with this age group in mind.

Howard Pyle wrote (and illustrated in a sort of Pre-Raphaelite style) several books about Arthur and his companions. **The Story of King Arthur and His Knights, The Story of Sir Launcelot and His Companions, The Story of the Champions of the Round Table**, and **The Story of the Grail and the Passing of Arthur** are old-fashioned retellings of the great tales of chivalry and knighthood, stories of the rescue of damsels in distress, and fighting the good fight in tournaments, all of which capture the pure romance of the time.

T. A. Barron's Lost Years of Merlin series concentrates on the life and adventures of the great Arthurian wizard in the years before Merlin meets Arthur and comes, as it were, into the public consciousness. It all begins with a boy washed up on the coast of Wales with no memory of where he came from or who he is, in **The Lost Years of Merlin**. The adventures continue in **The Seven Songs of Merlin**, **The Fires of Merlin**, **The Mirror of Merlin**, and **The Wings of Merlin**.

In **The Seeing Stone, At the Crossing-Places**, and **King of the Middle March**, Kevin Crossley-Holland uses the legend of King Arthur as background for a story about a twelfth-century boy (also named Arthur) who has received a mysterious gift from his friend Merlin—a seeing stone that allows him to observe what's happening in King Arthur's time while his own life has some uncanny echoes of the past.

Jane Yolen wrote two winning novels about Arthur, including **Sword of the Rightful King**, in which Merlinnus (who is known as Merlin in most accounts) devises a plan to prove to the doubting citizens that Arthur is the true King of England, and **The Dragon's Boy**, in which young Arthur learns wisdom and grace from a druid priest who's conjured up a dragon.

Rosemary Sutcliff uses the legends as described by Sir Thomas Malory, the fifteenth-century writer to whom all subsequent Arthurian books are indebted, to tell the Arthurian saga in **The Light Beyond the Forest: The Quest for the Holy Grail**, **The Sword and the Circle: King Arthur and the Knights of the Round Table**, and **The Road to Camlann: The Death of King Arthur**. (Sutcliff also wrote about Arthur for older readers;

see "Historical Fiction" in Part III for more suggestions by this terrific British novelist.)

Younger readers in this age group can get a taste for the days of King Arthur and his Knights of the Round Table in Clyde Robert Bulla's **The Sword in the Tree**, as young Shan fights for his family's survival against the wickedness of his uncle Lionel, as well as in Jane Yolen's trilogy **Passager, Hobby**, and **Merlin**.

Other portrayals well worth taking a look at include the classic Roger Lancelyn Green's **King Arthur and His Knights of the Round Table; Sir Gawain and the Loathly Lady** by Selina Hastings (a solid introduction to one of King Arthur's best knights); **Parzival: The Quest of the Grail Knight**, retold by Katherine Paterson; Nancy Springer's **I Am Mordred: A Tale from Camelot** (a sympathetic look at the young man who grew up hating King Arthur, his father, and was fated to kill him—Oedipus, anyone?); and Mark Twain's **A Connecticut Yankee in King Arthur's Court**.

For use in school assignments, or just because kids often want to know what *really* happened, Kevin Crossley-Holland's **The World of King Arthur and His Court** is chock-full of information and is, as well, a pleasure to read. He separates fact from fiction, offers brief biographies of all the important Arthurian players, and includes a useful map of Arthur's Britain. The illustrations by Peter Malone resemble the illuminated manuscripts of the Middle Ages.

And just for fun, try **Wizardology: The Book of the Secrets of Merlin** by Dugald Steer, one in the luxe packaged series that also includes **Egyptology: Search for the Tomb of Osiris, Being the Journal of Miss Emily Sands; Pirateology: The Pirate Hunter's Companion;** and **Dragonology: The Complete Book of Dragons**.

LET'S TALK ABOUT IT:
GOOD BOOKS FOR DISCUSSION

I f you're involved in a parent/child book group, or you're leading a discussion group for kids, try the titles described here. While everyone may not love them, they're guaranteed to elicit strong reactions and lots of good conversation.

In a world where families are only allowed to have two children, Luke, the third child in his family, must always stay hidden so the government won't learn of his existence. But when he meets a girl about his own age who also has two siblings and wants Luke to take part in a challenge to the Population Law, he must decide whether to risk the status quo for the unknown, in Margaret Peterson Haddix's **Among the Hidden**, the first in The Shadow Children series, which also includes **Among the Brave**, **Among the Enemy**, and others.

Kids in the third grade and up will be interested in talking about **Pink and Say** by Patricia Polacco. Set during the Civil War, this is (be forewarned!) the tragic story of two teenage Union soldiers (one white, the other a former slave) who are sent to the infamous Andersonville Prison. But it's also a story of how human connections can transcend death, as the adult Say tells his children (who tell their children and so on down through the generations) about how Pink once shook hands with Abraham Lincoln, and how Say touched the hand that touched the President's hand. . . .

In Madeleine L'Engle's **A Wrinkle in Time**, Margaret Murry—with the help of her brilliant younger brother, Charles Wallace, and the assistance of three strange women (Mrs. Whatsit, Mrs. Who, and Mrs. Which)—figures out how to rescue her father from the clutches of evil (in the form of a giant brain).

Three siblings, the children of the military ruler of Zimbabwe in 2194, set off on what they think will be just be a little adventure and find much more than they bargained for, in Nancy Farmer's **The Ear, the Eye and the Arm**.

Other exceptional discussion books for middle-grade readers include Lloyd Alexander's **The Gawgon and the Boy**; **The Slave Dancer** by Paula Fox; David Almond's **Kit's Wilderness**; **Skeleton Man** by Joseph Bruchac; **Sahara Special** by Esmé Raji Codell; Christopher Paul Curtis's **The Watsons Go to Birmingham—1963**; **Rifles for Watie** by Harold Keith; Kyoko Mori's **Shizuko's Daughter**; Gregory Maguire's **Seven Spiders Spinning**; **The Great Gilly Hopkins** by Katherine Paterson; and Robert C. O'Brien's **Z for Zachariah**.

LOL: LAUGH OUT LOUD

Kids of all ages love funny books; in my experience the broader and more ridiculous the humor is, the more they enjoy the tale. Children in this age group can probably take a bit of subtlety, but too much may turn them off. Offer them books with odd but loveable characters, impossible situations, and strange settings, and you'll see what I mean. Perhaps it's needless to add that the books here all make for prime reading out loud, but they do. Think about picking one or two to share on your next car trip.

Boys and girls in Mrs. Piggle-Wiggle's neighborhood love to visit her because of her upside-down house, the fresh-baked cookies (always available), and her pet cat, Lightfoot, and dog, Wag. But their parents love her as well, and the reasons for that can be seen in Betty MacDonald's **Mrs. Piggle-Wiggle** and its sequels, which tell of her ingenious (and very funny) cures for common childhood (mis)behaviors such as refusing to bathe, eating too slowly, never wanting to go to bed, and more. Move over, Dr. Spock.

Helen Cresswell's books about the eccentric Bagthorpe family include **Ordinary Jack**, **Absolute Zero**, and **Bagthorpes Unlimited**, among others. Reluctant readers, especially boys, tend to devour them. Do read them in order, though.

You always know you're in for a guffaw or two with the books of Daniel Pinkwater, and **The Hoboken Chicken Emergency** is no exception—what else can you expect when one of the characters is a 166-pound chicken named Henrietta, who happens to love oatmeal cookies? Try Pinkwater's Werewolf Club series, as well, beginning with **The Magic Pretzel**.

Meeting Homer, the hero of **Homer Price** and **Centerburg Tales: More Adventures of Homer Price** by Robert McCloskey, is one of the not-to-be-missed experiences of childhood. Whether it's the tale of a lost diamond bracelet in a donut shop, the one about a bet involving a BIG ball of yarn, or the story of a skunk that proves useful in apprehending some criminals, Homer's escapades have delighted readers since they were originally published way back in 1943.

Because Philip Pullman's best-known books are those in the His Dark Materials trilogy (**The Golden Compass**, **The Subtle Knife**, **The Amber Spyglass**), which—though wonderful—are not exactly intended to elicit laughter from readers, it's sometimes easy to forget that he's written some certifiable laugh-out-loud books. Don't miss three of his best, **The Scarecrow and His Servant**, **Spring-Heeled Jack**, and **I Was a Rat!**

One fine day Tiffany Aching is both minding her own business on her parents' sheep farm and babysitting her little brother, Wentworth, when a group of blue, fierce, and decidedly very small men show up, all shouting what seem to be warnings to her. It turns out there's a killer witch in the nearby stream who has more than a passing interest in Wentworth, brat or no. What to do? Turn him over to the hag? Or try to vanquish her? The laughs and surprises keep coming in page after page of Terry Pratchett's **The Wee Free Men** and its sequels, which serve as a great introduction to this prolific and terrific author.

Poor Mr. Popper: he's always wished that before he settled into his present pleasant (but boring) life, he'd done something exciting, even heroic, like accompanying Admiral Drake in his journey to the South Pole. Reading about polar expeditions just doesn't cut it. But when a fan letter to Admiral Drake results in the gift of a penguin—well, life's about to change at 432 Proudfoot Avenue, in Richard and Florence Atwater's **Mr. Popper's Penguins**.

Other humorous books include **Skinnybones** by Barbara Park; **The Sixth Grade Nickname Game** by Gordon Korman; **Chancy and the Grand Rascal**, a (very) tall tale by Sid Fleischman; Louis Sachar's **Sideways Stories from Wayside School** and **Wayside School is Falling Down**; and Paul Rosenthal's **Yo, Aesop! Get a Load of These Fables**.

MELTING POTS AND SALAD BOWLS

Novels about immigrants coming to America in pursuit of the American dream are a favorite choice of many adult readers. The same is true for middle-grade readers. Lucky for them there are many superb novels that deal with what it's like to come to a new home where you look different and/or talk differently than your schoolmates and neighbors. In a subtle and nondidactic way, the books described here will help readers imagine just what that's like. All of them are excellent choices for parent/child book discussion groups; teachers will find that they make fine introductions to lessons on our multicultural society, as well.

In Bette Bao Lord's autobiographical novel, **In the Year of the Boar and Jackie Robinson**, the author describes the experiences of Shirley Temple Wong, who moves to Brooklyn with her family in 1947 and finds making friends easier after she becomes a fan of the great infielder Jackie Robinson, star of the Dodgers, the local professional baseball team.

When Jenny's fourth-grade class is given an assignment to pretend they're mice and write letters to second-graders, Jenny is assigned to a girl named Sameera, who never answers her letters. Jenny learns that Sameera has recently come to America from Saudi Arabia, and she has to figure out how to communicate with her pen pal, in Ann Whitehead Nagda's **Dear Whiskers**.

Donna Jo Napoli's **The King of Mulberry Street** is told from the point of view of Beniamino, who comes to America, alone, from Naples, Italy, in the last years of the nineteenth century and makes his way to adulthood on the dangerous streets of New York City.

Other books about immigrants and refugees that will broaden a middle-grade reader's perspective include **Home Is East** by Many Ly, the story of a Cambodian immigrant family; **The Memory Coat** by Elvira Woodruff, about two Jewish cousins who come to America in the first decade of the twentieth century from their home in a small Russian village; the similarly plotted (although for slightly younger readers) **When Jessie Came Across the Sea** by Amy Hest; **How I Became an American** by Karen Gündisch, translated from German by James Skofield; Carolyn Marsden's **The Gold-Threaded Dress**; and Lensey Namioka's **Yang the Youngest and His Terrible Ear**. (How can Yang reconcile his immigrant family's expectations and at the same time become a regular American boy? There's more about the family in **Yang the Third and Her Impossible Family** and **Yang the Second and Her Secret Admirers**.)

MYTHS, LEGENDS, FOLK AND FAIRY TALES

One of the best ways to give children a sense of the similarities and differences among the people and cultures of our diverse world is to introduce them to the various myths and legends that have come down to us from ages past and countries and societies far away.

Neil Philip arranged **The Illustrated Book of Myths: Tales and Legends of the World** under topics such as creation accounts, gods and animals, and gods and men, and includes familiar stories from the Greeks and Romans as well as less well-known tales from Polynesia, South America, and Africa. The appealing illustrations, by

Nilesh Mistry, make this book a keeper. (The pair also collaborated on **The Illustrated Book of Fairy Tales**.)

There are thirty-three tales (again, including some quite well known to a western audience—such as the story of Theseus—and less familiar—the Japanese tales about Izanagi and Izanami, for example) in **A World Treasury of Myths, Legends, and Folktales: Stories from Six Continents** as told by Renata Bini. The style of Mikhail Fiodorov's pictures changes to reflect the origins of the tale each illustrates, which adds to the pleasure of the reading experience.

Although there are no illustrations in **Best-Loved Folktales of the World**, as selected (and with an introduction) by children's author Joanna Cole, this is an excellent one-volume collection of more than two hundred stories from Laos to Ireland, and from Scandinavia to Africa.

Other collections of folk tales include Howard Norman's **Between Heaven and Earth: Bird Tales from Around the World**, a group of five stories told by students in the author's class on folklore, with engaging illustrations by Leo and Diane Dillon; Ingri and Edgar Parrin d'Aulaire's classic **D'Aulaires' Book of Greek Myths**, which is often the first book of myths a child encounters (and a good first choice it is), along with their **D'Aulaires' Book of Norse Myths**; and **Can You Guess My Name? Traditional Tales Around the World**, selected and retold by Judy Sierra and illustrated by Stefano Vitale, which takes familiar stories like *The Three Little Pigs* and *Hansel and Gretel* and shows their counterparts in stories from other countries.

For the myths and legends of specific areas of the world, take a look at these classics: Roger Lancelyn Greene's **Tales of Ancient**

Egypt; Kevin Crossley-Holland's **The Norse Myths; American Indian Myths and Legends** by Richard Erdoes; **Swedish Folktales and Legends** by Lone Thygesen Blecher and George Blecher; and Henri Pourrat's **French Folktales**.

Way back in the late nineteenth century, Andrew Lang, a novelist, psychic researcher, and friend of Robert Louis Stevenson, started collecting fairy tales from around the world that were popular then and remain so today. The series is composed of **The Blue Fairy Book, The Brown Fairy Book, The Crimson Fairy Book, The Green Fairy Book, The Grey Fairy Book, The Lilac Fairy Book, The Olive Fairy Book, The Orange Fairy Book, The Pink Fairy Book, The Red Fairy Book, The Violet Fairy Book,** and **The Yellow Fairy Book**. Taken together, this is surely one of the most comprehensive collections we have available, although it's good to keep in mind that these are heavily bowdlerized and sanitized versions of the original tales by the Brothers Grimm, Charles Perrault, Hans Christian Andersen, and others, which tended to be much grimmer and more violent.

When I was a children's librarian, I relied heavily on The Pantheon Fairy Tale and Folklore Library when I was looking for stories to introduce young readers to fairy tales from different countries, time periods, and regions of the world. Some that I found most useful include Aleksandr Afanas'ev's **Russian Fairy Tales; The Victorian Fairy Tale Book** by Michael Patrick Hearn; **The Complete Grimm's Fairy Tales; Chinese Fairy Tales and Fantasies** by Moss Roberts; **Legends and Tales of the American West** by Richard Erdoes; and Angela Carter's **The Old Wives' Fairy Tale Book**.

Michael Hague edited (and illustrated) **The Book of Fairies**, in which contributors run the gamut from poet Christina Rossetti ("The Goblin Market") to Hans Christian Andersen. Hague also illustrated **The Book of Pirates**, in which stories by Rafael Sabatini and J. M. Barrie (among others) make an appearance.

One of my favorite collections of folk tales is **Sweet Land of Story: Thirty-Six American Tales to Tell** by Pleasant DeSpain, himself a superb storyteller.

NOT A DRY EYE IN THE HOUSE

One of the reasons these books are so popular with middle-grade readers is that it's usually at this age when the reality of death and loss hits home. Although the cliché is that kids think they'll live forever, in fact they're now capable of understanding death in a way they weren't when they were reading picture books like Judith Viorst's **The Tenth Good Thing About Barney** or Tomie dePaola's **Nana Upstairs and Nana Downstairs** (see the "Death and Dying" section in Part I). The books described here, with main characters around their own age, help readers sort out their own feelings, as well as offer just plain good (although sad) reading.

The death of a friend is handled with great sensitivity in Katherine Paterson's **Bridge to Terabithia**, which has not lost any of its power to move readers since its original publication in 1977.

After her mother is killed outside the family's home (the gunmen were really aiming at her father, an outspoken journalist in Lagos), Sade and her brother Femi are sent to England out of concern for their safety, not knowing whether they will ever see their father again. What follows is worthy of Dickens; it's heart-tugging and in places almost too painful to read. Beverly Naidoo has captured the experience of modern-day displaced refugees in **The Other Side of Truth**, which won England's 2000 Carnegie Medal and other major awards. And most unusual for a children's book, there's no happy ending here.

It takes a car trip with her grandparents to allow Sal to finally come to terms with the death of her mother, in **Walk Two Moons** by Sharon Creech.

Sadako and the Thousand Paper Cranes by Eleanor Coerr is a story based on the life and death of a real person, Sadako Sasaki, a young girl dying of radiation poisoning after the bombing of Hiroshima. After a friend tells her that many Japanese believe if a sick person folds one thousand paper cranes, the gods will grant her one wish, Sadako decides that's what she'll do. Although this is ostensibly a picture book (with illustrations by Ronald Himler), its subject is really more appropriate to fourth-graders and above.

When May, who's been Summer's foster mother for the past six years, dies, both Summer and May's husband, Ob, are inconsolable. It takes Cletus, one of Summer's seventh-grade classmates, a visit to a woman who supposedly can contact the dead, and a mysterious owl to finally give Summer (and Ob) the comfort they need to go on, in Cynthia Rylant's **Missing May**.

Eleanor Estes has written other books that are happier than **The Hundred Dresses**, but none has the whopping emotional impact of this tale of fourth-grade cruelty about when Maddie and a group of her friends unmercifully taunt Wanda Petronski for wearing the same ugly, faded blue dress to school every day. It's a book that brings home a lot of lessons, but does so very subtly.

Other books to cry over include **Each Little Bird That Sings** by Deborah Wiles; **Defiance** by Valerie Hobbs; **Sort of Forever** by Sally Warner (which explores the longtime friendship between two twelve-year-olds and what happens when one is diagnosed with an incurable cancer); Audrey Couloumbis's **Getting Near to Baby** (the death of her baby sister rocks Willa Jo's world); **Olive's Ocean** by Kevin Henkes (about the death of a classmate); Alfred Slote's **Hang Tough, Paul Mather** (a real tearjerker about an eleven-year-old Little Leaguer with leukemia); Gary D. Schmidt's **Lizzie Bright and the Buckminster Boy** (based on a true event that took place in Maine in 1912); **Because of Winn-Dixie** by Kate DiCamillo; and Cynthia Kadohata's **Kira-Kira** (in which a young girl tries to understand the death of her beloved older sister).

O PIONEERS!

The pioneer period in American history makes for enthralling reading on many levels; stories about this time are usually relatively fast-moving tales filled with excitement and danger. And many authors have chosen as their main characters young girls who are thrust into events that they find challenging. Many children's first introduction to pioneer stories are the Little House books by Laura Ingalls Wilder, and *Book Crush* wouldn't be complete without including **Little House in the Big Woods** and its sequels, **Little House on the Prairie, Farmer Boy, On the Banks of Plum Creek, By the Shores of Silver Lake, The**

Long Winter, **Little Town on the Prairie**, and **These Happy Golden Years**. These autobiographical stories of pioneer life grow along with the boy or girl reading them: second- and third-graders can probably read the first two on their own, and as they mature they can follow along as Laura grows up, moving from the woods of Wisconsin to, finally, De Smet, South Dakota. (And the illustrations by Garth Williams are perfection themselves.) These books are also wonderful for read-alouds on long car trips. I know families who have visited all of the places Laura writes about, and I once saw a bumper sticker that made me smile: "I am a Laura Ingalls Wilder freak," it declared. (I recently spent a lovely day in De Smet, South Dakota, where the last four books take place.)

For another view of the same general historical period, try Louise Erdrich's rich and involving story **The Birchbark House**, told through the eyes of a seven-year-old Ojibwa girl named Omakayas, or Little Frog, who lives on an island on Lake Superior with her adopted family. All the everyday details of a particular slice of Native American life in 1847 are described in prose that will captivate young readers.

Other enjoyable pioneer stories for this age group include Paul Fleischman's **The Borning Room**; Nancy Smiler Levinson's **Prairie Friends**, in which she describes both the camaraderie and loneliness of life on the prairie; **The Cabin Faced West** by Jean Fritz (set back when western Pennsylvania was the frontier); Carol Ryrie Brink's **Caddie Woodlawn** and **Magical Melons**; **I Have Heard of a Land** by Joyce Carol Thomas (about an African American pioneer in Oklahoma Territory in the late nineteenth century); Elizabeth George Speare's **The Sign of the Beaver**; Lois Lenski's oldie but goodie, **Prairie School**; **Weasel** by Cynthia

DeFelice; Jennifer Armstrong's **Black-Eyed Susan** (the same setting as the Wilder books); and Jennifer L. Holm's **Our Only May Amelia** (Washington State at the end of the nineteenth century).

ONE WORD IS WORTH A THOUSAND PICTURES (OR SOMETHING LIKE THAT)

Sometimes you don't need more than one word as a title to invite readers into a book—and these books are the sort where you absolutely want to accept the invitation.

When he was eleven years old, Sterling North adopted a baby raccoon—and he describes his adventures with his beloved pet (as well as his Saint Bernard, Wowser) in **Rascal**, a memoir much beloved by animal lovers young and old.

Nobody writes about really awful adults better than Roald Dahl (which may explain why he tends to be more popular with kids than with their parents and teachers), and few fictional parents are as loathsome as Mr. and Mrs. Wormword in **Matilda**, not to mention the inexorable Miss Trunchbull, Matilda's headmistress at school. Only Miss Honey (Matilda's teacher) and Mrs. Phelps (the librarian who introduces Matilda to the world of literature) make her life worth living. (And don't forget Spiker and Sponge, James's truly horrible, really evil aunts in **James and the Giant Peach**. Of course, James dispatches them, in spades, by having them crushed to death by a rolling piece of guess what fruit.)

Carl Hiaasen's **Hoot** and **Flush** are both entertaining stories combining Hiaasen's passion for the importance of protecting the environment (played out in his books for adults as well) with fast-moving plots and realistic young male protagonists.

Hatchet by Gary Paulsen is not only one of the most exciting novels for kids and young adults ever written, it's also one of the best books to give to reluctant readers. It's the story of a boy's survival in the wilderness against seemingly insurmountable odds.

Other one-word wonders include **Hush**, Jacqueline Woodson's moving story of a family forced to go into the witness protection program; **Milkweed**, Jerry Spinelli's wrenching novel of a Jewish orphan trying to get by in Nazi-occupied Warsaw; David Almond's fantasy novel **Skellig**, about a young boy who finds a mysterious creature—part angel, part bird—in the garage of his new house; and Andrew Clements's **Frindle**, which answers the question of how words get added to our everyday vocabulary. It's an excellent choice for third and fourth graders.

ORPHANS ABOUNDING

I've often wondered why there are so many orphans as main characters in children's books—is it because it's a common fear that kids can relate to? Or, contrariwise, is it because children sometimes feel that having parents is more of a burden than a blessing? Or maybe, reading about these kids who somehow manage to come out on the other side of a tragedy—always successfully (at least in books), through pluck or brains or simply good luck—can help children be aware of and appreciate their own inner resources.

Perhaps everyone's favorite orphan is Anne Shirley, heroine of Lucy Maud Montgomery's series beginning with **Anne of Green Gables**, when Anne goes to live with Matthew and Marilla Cuthbert on their farm on Prince Edward Island, Canada (although they had asked for a boy, to help with the chores), and ends, many books (and years) later, with **Rilla of Ingleside**, the story of Anne's youngest daughter. (My favorite, though, has always been the oh-so-romantic **Anne of the Island**, when she goes off to college, rejects her longtime suitor, and meets the man who she's sure is the love of her life.)

Then there are the other now classic orphans: Mary Lennox (**The Secret Garden**) and Sara Crewe (**A Little Princess**), both by Frances Hodgson Burnett; J. K. Rowling's Harry Potter (**Harry Potter and the Sorcerer's Stone** and sequels); **Heidi** by Johanna Spyri; David Balfour (**Kidnapped** by Robert Louis Stevenson); and the Baudelaire kids—Violet, Klaus, and Sunny—in Lemony Snicket's Series of Unfortunate Events, which begins with **The Bad Beginning** and continues (with great glee) over many, many books.

But here's a wildly diverse selection of other books—some fantasy, most realistic—in which orphans play a leading role; they're probably less familiar, but, as kids will discover when they're reading them, they're no less fun to get to know:

> Franny Billingsley's **The Folk Keeper**
> Gary Blackwood's **The Shakespeare Stealer** and **Shakespeare's Scribe**
> Eve Bunting's **Train to Somewhere**
> Georgia Byng's **Molly Moon's Incredible Book of Hypnotism** (give this to Lemony Snicket fans)
> Christopher Paul Curtis's **Bud, Not Buddy**
> Karen Cushman's **Rodzina**
> Helen Fern Daringer's **Adopted Jane**
> Elizabeth Enright's **Thimble Summer**
> Dorothy Canfield Fisher's **Understood Betsy**

Sid Fleischman's **The Midnight Horse**
Rumer Godden's **The Story of Holly and Ivy**
Elizabeth Goudge's **The Little White Horse**
Erik Christian Haugaard's **The Samurai's Tale**
Eva Ibbotson's **Journey to the River Sea**
Gail Carson Levine's **Dave at Night**
D. Anne Love's **The Puppeteer's Apprentice**
Betty McDonald's **Nancy and Plum**
Tor Seidler's **Brainboy and the Deathmaster**
Jerry Spinelli's **Maniac Magee**
Noel Streatfeild's **Ballet Shoes**
Jean Thesman's **The Ornament Tree**
Cynthia Voigt's **Homecoming**
Barbara Brooks Wallace's **Sparrows in the Scullery** and
   Peppermints in the Parlor (give the latter book to fans
   of **The Little Princess**)

OTHER TIMES, OTHER PLACES

One of the best reasons to read the books in this category
is that they offer glimpses of other worlds, different ways
of living, and take children into the lives of people they
would never otherwise have the chance to get to know.

Twelfth-century Korea is the setting for Linda Sue Park's Newbery
Award–winning **A Single Shard**, the story of Tree-Ear, who longs
to help one of the village's potters make the famed celadon pitcher.
Park also set **When My Name Was Keoko** in Korea, but this
time it's just before and during the Second World War, when the
Japanese Emperor decreed that every Korean had to take a Japanese

name. Told from the alternating points of view of a brother and sister, Park explores what it means to be forced to give up your culture and identity—and what bravery means in the shadow of war.

In Arthur Dorros's **Under the Sun**, thirteen-year-old Ehmet leaves his war-ravaged city in Bosnia to try to find a place he's only heard rumors of—a children's village where young people of all ethnicities from the former Yugoslavia come together to live in peace.

London in 1677 comes alive in **At the Sign of the Star** by Katherine Sturtevant, the story of Meg Moore, who likes nothing better than working with her widowed father in his bookstore (and meeting the leading literary figures of the day). Meg's life turns upside down, however, when her father marries a woman determined to turn Meg into a "lady." Meg's story is continued in **A True and Faithful Narrative**.

Karen Hesse's **Stowaway** shows that in the hands of a gifted writer, even the most obscure of facts can be made interesting. Here she begins with a real person, eleven-year-old Nicholas Young, who stowed away on Captain Cook's HMS *Endeavour* in 1768, and accompanied his crew as they searched for a continent at the bottom of the world. Drawing on Cook's own diary of the trip, as well as the writings of the famed naturalist Joseph Banks, Hesse has written this spellbinding adventure as though it were Nick's own journal.

Other too-good-to-miss titles in this category—books guaranteed to take kids away from their ordinary, everyday lives—are **Catherine, Called Birdy** by Karen Cushman (set during the Middle Ages, with a very modern and determined thirteen-year-old heroine); and Mildred D. Taylor's **Roll of Thunder, Hear My**

Cry and its sequel, **Let the Circle Be Unbroken** (about a black family living in heavily segregated and prejudice-filled Mississippi during the Depression years).

THE PLEASURES OF POETRY

I think that children would be natural poetry lovers if we only gave them the chance by introducing them to the books that I've included here. The rhymes and rhythms, the imagery, even the subject matter will engage a child's imagination, stimulate his creativity, and broaden his or her language skills. And best of all, poetry is written to be read aloud, so you'll have a wonderful experience sharing them, too.

Paul B. Janeczko (text) and Chris Raschka (illustrations) combined to produce two colorful, useful, and, most important, entertaining books of poetry. The first, **A Kick in the Head: An Everyday Guide to Poetic Forms**, is a guide, with examples, of different forms of poetry, including couplets, quatrains, pantoums, and sonnets. The second is **A Poke in the I: A Collection of Concrete Poems**. Concrete poems (we learned in **A Kick in Head**) look like their subject matter, and Janeczko offers some of the best here. Don't miss these poems: "Giraffe" by Maureen W. Armour, "Tennis Anyone?" by Monica Kulling, and John Hegley's "I Need Contact Lenses," all brightly illustrated by Raschka. I thought, as I read through this book, that composing and illustrating a concrete poem would be a great school assignment for all grades.

Poetry Speaks to Children is an anthology of poetry for kids, including selections from William Shakespeare to James Stevenson, Rita Dove to Christina Rossetti, Carl Sandburg to

Roald Dahl, Langston Hughes to J. R. R. Tolkien, and Eugene Field to Sylvia Plath, edited by Elise Paschen and illustrated in several different styles by Judy Love, Wendy Rasmussen, and Paula Zinngrabe Wendland. It's accompanied by a CD of more than half the poems, many read by the authors themselves, others recorded especially for this project.

Sing a Song of Popcorn: Every Child's Book of Poems, selected by Beatrice Schenk de Regniers, is illustrated by nine Caldecott Medal winners, including Marcia Brown, Leo and Diane Dillon, Maurice Sendak, Arnold Lobel, and Margot Zemach.

A Family of Poems: My Favorite Poetry for Children is a wide-ranging anthology assembled by Caroline Kennedy, including poems by everyone from A. A. Milne to Robert Frost, and Edward Lear to William Wordsworth.

One of the most beautiful combinations of art and poetry I've ever seen is **Heart to Heart: New Poems Inspired by Twentieth-Century American Art**, edited by Jan Greenberg. The art includes works by Frank Stella, Grant Wood, Andy Warhol, and Georgia O'Keeffe; the poets included are Nancy Willard, Naomi Shihab Nye, and Marvin Bell, among others.

For those young readers who love Shel Silverstein's **Where the Sidewalk Ends** and **A Light in the Attic**, Jack Prelutsky's **The New Kid on the Block**, and other books of light verse, it's time to try Douglas Florian. His clever and amusing poems can be found in **Bow Wow Meow Meow: It's Rhyming Cats and Dogs**; **Mammalabilia** (poems about Bactrian camels, mules, and aardvarks: "Aardvarks aare odd, / Aardvarks aare stark, / Aardvarks look better / By faar in the dark"); **Laugh-eteria**; **Summersaults**; **Bing Bang Boing**; **In the Swim**; **On the Wing**; **Beast Feast**; **Lizards,**

Frogs, and Polliwogs; and **Insectlopedia**. And Florian himself—multitalented as one person can be—did the paintings that illustrate these books (as, of course, did Shel Silverstein in his books). Try Florian's books on your second- and third-graders, as well.

For Laughing Out Loud: Poems to Tickle Your Funnybone is a collection of poems by writers like Ogden Nash, Karla Kuskin, Judith Viorst, and John Ciardi, all selected by Jack Prelutsky, with illustrations by Marjorie Priceman.

Canadian poet laureate Dennis Lee's classic contribution to the silly-poetry genre, **Alligator Pie**, is still a crowd-pleaser, though it was originally published more than thirty-five years ago.

The accessible free verse written by Valerie Worth in **Peacock and Other Poems** will both entertain and help young readers discover the poetry within them. (Of course, few of us will be lucky enough to have our books illustrated by Natalie Babbitt.) This is a valuable choice for teachers who want to do creative writing with their classes, as well as for parents interested in sharing poetry with their children.

Poems in both Spanish and English express a little boy's memories of his home in El Salvador and how his uprooted family moved far away to San Francisco's Mission District, in Jorge Argueta's **A Movie in My Pillow**.

Another bilingual collection of poetry is **Angels Ride Bikes and Other Fall Poems**, written by Francisco X. Alarcón with colorful illustrations by Maya Christina Gonzalez that are reminiscent of the great Mexican muralists. You can find more of their collaborative work in **Laughing Tomatoes and Other Spring Poems**, **From the Bellybutton of the Moon and Other Summer Poems**, and **Iguanas in the Snow and Other Winter Poems**.

Other books of poetry to be checked out and shared are Nancy Willard's award-winning **A Visit to William Blake's Inn**; **The Llama Who Had No Pajama** by Mary Ann Hoberman ("Balloons to blow / Balloons to burst / The blowing's best / The bursting's worst!"); Bobbi Katz's **Once Around the Sun** (a month-by-month's worth of poetry), illustrated by LeUyen Phamany; Robert Louis Stevenson's **A Child's Garden of Verses** (if you can find the edition illustrated by Brian Wildsmith your child is in for a true treat); Jack Prelutsky's **Read-Aloud Rhymes for the Very Young** (illustrated by Marc Brown, author of the "Arthur" books); **If Not for the Cat** (a collection of haiku); and Prelutsky's very funny poems about dinosaurs, **Tyrannosaurus Was a Beast**. Prelutsky also edited two excellent collectionns: **The Random House Book of Poetry for Children** and **The 20th Century Children's Poetry Treasury**.

REAL PEOPLE YOU OUGHT TO KNOW

The goal of the biographer, it seems to me, is both to bring his or her subject to life and to illuminate the time period in which the biographee lived. Through offering readers an entrée into the mind and experiences of another person, biographers give readers the opportunity to step outside their own lives. A good biography can lead readers down many different pathways and open a lifetime of reading opportunities. Here are some first-rate ones for the middle-grade reader:

Laurie Lawlor's **Helen Keller: Rebellious Spirit** conveys not only the Keller that many children may be familiar with, but also gives a good sense of a fun-loving and lively child, who lost little of her vivaciousness as she grew up. A companion for Lawlor's is the fine biography by Joan Dash, **The World at Her Fingertips**. Together they provide a well-rounded and informative portrait of Keller.

Dash also wrote **The Longitude Prize**, which tells the story of John Harrison, a British clockmaker who spent his life trying to find a way for sailors to figure out their longitude at sea.

She presents the life and work of a much better-known man in **A Dangerous Engine: Benjamin Franklin from Scientist to Diplomat**. It's hard to write a dull biography of a man as interesting as Benjamin Franklin, and Dash's is no exception, nor is Rosalyn Schanzer's **How Ben Franklin Stole the Lightning**, which includes accounts of many of Franklin's creative experiments and inventions.

Walter Dean Myers captures the mercurial nature of an amazing boxer in **The Greatest: Muhammad Ali**, covering his childhood, his career as a boxer, his decision not to fight in Vietnam, and his later career. (Teen readers won't want to overlook **King of the World**, a biography of Ali by David Remnick.)

In **Sigmund Freud: Pioneer of the Mind**, Catherine Reef offers a comprehensive picture of the father of psychoanalysis, whom she describes as "an archaeologist of the mind"; she doesn't shy away from discussing the controversial nature of some of his beliefs.

Fans of the Robinson Crusoe story will want to check out Robert Kraske's **Marooned**, a biography of the "real" Crusoe, Alexander Selkirk.

In 1833, Prudence Crandall, a young, white, single schoolteacher living in Canterbury, Connecticut, decided to open a school for African American teens. Suzanne Jurmain highlights the difficulties

Crandall and her students faced, especially in dealing with the townspeople's anger, in **The Forbidden Schoolhouse**.

Until 2001, African American Matthew Henson's contributions to the success of Robert Peary's 1909 trek to the North Pole weren't given full due, but **Onward: A Photobiography of African-American Polar Explorer Matthew Henson** by Dolores Johnson should remedy that. The inspirational text and outstanding photographs are just what you would expect from a National Geographic Society publication.

Russell Freedman is one of the best biographers around, whether you're talking about books for adults or kids. I look forward to reading and recommending each of his books as it appears (not often enough, in my opinion!). Here are five of my favorites: **The Voice That Challenged a Nation: Marian Anderson and the Struggle for Equal Rights**; **Confucius: The Golden Rule**, which not only offers us a biography of the fifth-century Chinese philosopher, but also serves as a fine introduction to Eastern thought; his Newbery Award–winning **Lincoln: A Photobiography**, which is an excellent introduction to the life and career of the president known as the Great Emancipator; **The Wright Brothers: How They Invented the Airplane**, the story of the two eccentric men who changed history through their inventions; and **The Life and Death of Crazy Horse**, a good way to meet the chief of the Lakota Indians and understand the world he lived in.

The story of a man who worked tirelessly to improve the lot of America's migrant workers is movingly recounted in Kathleen Krull's **Harvesting Hope: The Story of Cesar Chavez**.

Josephine Poole and Angela Barrett have combined to write and illustrate two biographies for young readers: **Joan of Arc** and **Anne**

Frank are both superb introductions to these indomitable girls who came to sad ends. (Although I suppose some smart kid could argue that Joan of Arc came to a glorious end.)

Charles Darwin was first and foremost one of the nineteenth century's most respected naturalists; in a text mostly taken from Darwin's own writings and accompanied by commentary and detailed illustrations, Peter Sís helps young readers (and the adults in their lives) understand Darwin and his ideas, in **The Tree of Life**.

Maritcha: A Remarkable Nineteenth-Century American Girl by Tonya Bolden combines Maritcha's own words, vintage photographs, reproductions of newspaper articles, and more to animate the life of a young woman who was the first African American to graduate from Providence High School, in Rhode Island.

Other recommendable biographies for this age group include **Dickens: His Work and His World** by Michael Rosen; **Saladin: Noble Prince of Islam** by Diane Stanley, the story of a great man who was known for his generosity of spirit toward his friends and enemies alike; **Good Brother, Bad Brother: The Story of Edwin Booth and John Wilkes Booth** by James Cross Giblin (one was a great classical actor and the other, the man who assassinated Abraham Lincoln); and **Bill Pickett, Rodeo-Ridin' Cowboy** by Andrea Davis Pinkney (the story of the great African American bulldogger).

RELATIVITY

Sometimes I think that—at least in books, but probably also in real life—strangers can be, uh, strange, but family can be decidedly quirky.

A visit from their father's very odd sister, Aunt Sally, gives the three Anderson siblings—ten-year-old Melissa, eight-year-old Amanda, and six-year-old Frank—a chance to learn some surprising family history in Polly Horvath's **The Trolls**, which is one of those books that teaches an important truth without hitting the child over the head with it. Horvath is also the author of the wild and wonderful **The Canning Season**. Ratchet Clark is sent by her uncaring mother to stay with her ninety-one-year-old twin great-aunts, Penpen and Tilly, in their big old house in the woods of Maine. There, Ratchet, along with Harper, another teenager summarily dumped on the twins' doorstep grows up hearing tales both gory and amusing of Penpen's and Tilly's lives. And just what is that deformity on Ratchet's shoulder that so disgusts her mother?

When twelve-year-old Hattie's mentally ill uncle Adam comes home to small town Millerton to live with his mother and father, she learns that some people help you grow up in unexpected, not always happy ways, in Ann M. Martin's moving **A Corner of the Universe**.

Eleven-year-old Angel has to be the adult in the family—her father's in jail for murder and robbery, and her alcoholic mother has proven herself unfit to take care of Angel and her younger brother, Bernie, in **The Same Stuff as Stars** by Katherine Paterson.

Albert Rosegarden (who, according to the principal of his school, is on his way to becoming a career criminal) really, really wants an adventure that will take him away from his badly misnamed Mountain View, Idaho, home—and he gets his wish when his eccentric (and ex-con) grandfather Wendell involves him in an elaborate plot to scam a scammer in **The Bamboozlers** by Michael de Guzman.

SCIENCE FICTION:
FUTURE POSSIBILITIES

S cience fiction—as opposed to fantasy—is set within the realm of possibility. However improbable they seem, the events in these books might happen. They're set in a world we know—technologically advanced, perhaps, but quite familiar nonetheless. There are, in general, no dragons, quests, or magical rings to be found here. The plots often revolve around the theme of humanity vs. technology, or extrapolations of current issues becoming major problems (e.g., population growth or global warming). These stories are exciting and fast moving, so they're good for reluctant readers. The majority of them (especially those written more than a decade ago) feature male heroes, but that's changed a bit in recent years.

Although I've chosen to put this section in Part II, most of these books will also be enjoyed by young teens. Older teens will want to move into the whole adult science fiction genre, where they'll find outstanding writers like Isaac Asimov, Kim Stanley Robinson, Dan Simmons, Lois McMaster Bujold, and Greg Bear.

It's still the case, after all these many years, that when someone asks me to suggest books for boys twelve to fourteen, the first ones that come to mind are the great space adventure tales by Robert A. Heinlein. Really, you don't want readers to miss **Red Planet**, **Time for the Stars**, **Between Planets**, **The Star Beast**, **Space Cadet**, **Have Spacesuit, Will Travel**, or **Podkayne of Mars** (the main character is a girl, which is unusual for books in this category).

Here are some other goodies:

John Christopher's **The White Mountains, The City of Gold and Lead**, and **The Pool of Fire** (known collectively as The Tripods Trilogy) are about a group of boys who try to escape being "capped," a form of mind control practiced by the otherworldly Masters who have taken control of humanity. Christopher is also the author of **The Guardians**, set in a society where being discontented is forbidden.

More choices include Eleanor Cameron's **The Wonderful Flight to the Mushroom Planet** and Ellen MacGregor's **Miss Pickerell Goes to Mars**, which have delighted the eight- to ten-year-old set since the 1950s, when they were first published; **The Random House Book of Science Fiction Stories**, edited by Mike Ashley; Mel Gilden's **Pumpkins of Time**; **Space Race** and **Earthborn** by Sylvia Waugh; T. A. Barron's **Heartlight**; H. M. Hoover's **The Winds of Mars** and **Another Heaven, Another Earth**; Kathy Mackel's **Can of Worms** (is thirteen-year-old Mike an alien, or just an alienated kid?); Louis Slobodkin's **The Space Ship Under the Apple Tree**; Bill Brittain's **Shape-Changer**; and **Aliens in the Family** by Margaret Mahy. Don't forget Jules Verne's classic, **A Journey to the Center of the Earth**, as well.

SLAVERY AND THE CIVIL WAR

There's often a school assignment for fourth- to eighth-graders on one aspect or another of the black experience, beginning with the Middle Passage (when the slaves were brought to the United States from Africa) and continuing through the Civil Rights movement of the 1960s. The assignment often involves reading one of the classic (and still best) stories about the Civil War for kids this age, Irene Hunt's **Across Five Aprils**, but make sure your readers don't miss these lesser-known titles:

Shelley Pearsall's **Trouble Don't Last** begins this way: "Truth is, trouble follows me like a shadow. To begin with, I was born a slave when other folks is born white." What follows is the story of an eleven-year-old boy's escape from slavery via the Underground Railroad in 1859.

The first battle of the Civil War is brought to vivid Technicolor life through the alternating viewpoints of sixteen characters from different backgrounds in Paul Fleischman's not-soon-forgotten novel **Bull Run**.

Julius Lester has written sensitively about the black experience over his long career, using both fiction and nonfiction to help kids this age get a sense of what slavery was really like. His powerfully moving first book, **To Be a Slave**, uses the chronologically arranged reminiscences of slaves and then ex-slaves to tell their experiences from their early years in Africa, to their lives under the yoke of slavery, on through the Civil War and Reconstruction years, concluding with their experiences in the early twentieth century.

Lester's novel **Day of Tears** begins with a documented event, an 1859 slave auction in Georgia (the largest in history). Then, using both real people and imagined characters, employing dialogue and monologues only, he shows the repercussions of the sale on a large cast of characters.

In **Under the Quilt of Night**, author Deborah Hopkinson collaborated with illustrator James E. Ransome to produce a moving story of a young girl's escape from slavery via the Underground Railroad. Even adults will be interested in the information here about the use of quilts to signal a house that's willing to hide fleeing slaves. And if your children enjoy that story, give them Hopkinson and Ransome's **Sweet Clara and the Freedom Quilt**, another poignant tale of quilting and slavery.

THE WITCH TRIALS— SALEM AND BEYOND

One of the most frightening and tragic times in American history was the last decade of the seventeenth century, when the Puritan residents of Salem, Massachusetts, were caught up in a frenzy of hunting down suspected witches among the women of the town. The novels described here all make for entertaining and educational reading; each offers a slightly different look at the events that culminated in the Witch Trials of 1692. (These trials are the inspiration for Arthur Miller's great play *The Crucible*, which older teen readers may want to check out as well.)

Ann Petry's **Tituba of Salem Village**, Elizabeth George Speare's Newbery Award–winning novel **The Witch of Blackbird Pond**, and Kathryn Lasky's **Beyond the Burning Time** all present a chilling picture of the witch hunts. In the first two, the main characters are themselves accused of being witches, while in Lasky's novel Mary Chase's mother is accused of witchcraft.

The Minister's Daughter by Julie Hearn broadens the canvas a bit by including the experiences of three girls growing up in a small village in Puritan England in the 1640s, where a belief in the power of witches to do harm is played out in an accusation that Nell, granddaughter of the village's midwife, is a witch, and continues across the ocean, into the Salem of the witch trials, where one of the girls, now an adult, offers testimony on recent events.

Ann Rinaldi's historical novels are always worth reading, and **A Break with Charity** is no exception—weaving the tragic events in Salem with a young teen's desire to be accepted by her peers, and the horror that results.

Ten-year-old Abigail Faulkner, who's always been in trouble for her unladylike behavior, relates what it's like to be accused of working with witches and forced to stand trial in Kathleen Benner Duble's gut-wrenching **The Sacrifice**. In the process she must decide whether or not she should accuse her mother of witchcraft in order to save herself and her sister from certain death at the hands of the witch-hunters.

If, after reading these books, your child wants to find out what *really* happened, give him or her Marc Aronson's **Witch-Hunt: Mysteries of the Salem Witch Trials**.

TEEN READERS
AGES 13–18

PART III

AFTER SAM SPADE AND
KINSEY MILLHONE

There are plenty of mysteries shelved in the adult section of the library that are perfectly wonderful for older teens: Ross Macdonald's books featuring Lew Archer (especially **The Instant Enemy** and **The Galton Case**); Sue Grafton's alphabet series (**A Is for Alibi**, etc.); Susan Wittig Albert's cozy English mysteries based on the life of beloved children's author Beatrix Potter (the first is **The Tale of Hill Top Farm**); of course, Arthur Conan Doyle's tales of Sherlock Holmes; Agatha Christie's Hercule Poirot and Miss Marple books (the Marple books tend to be slower paced); and Dashiell Hammett's whodunits featuring Sam Spade. (You can find many more good mysteries for teens in the "I Love a Mystery" section in *Book Lust* and "Ms. Mystery" in *More Book Lust*.) Given so many choices, a teenage reader might wonder why there's any reason to browse the young adult shelves to find a gripping mystery. Well, here's why—you don't want to miss these:

In **Finding Lubchenko** by Michael Simmons, wealthy teenage slacker Evan Macalister has to change his ways—sort of—when his father is arrested for murder and Evan realizes that he can prove his dad innocent, but only by confessing that he's been stealing computer equipment from his father's business and then selling it on the Internet. The only solution? Find the guilty party himself.

Philip Pullman is best known for his fantasy trilogy, His Dark Materials, made up of **The Golden Compass**, **The Subtle Knife**, and **The Amber Spyglass**, but if you're looking for mysteries featuring strong, brave (not to say foolhardy) young women, you can't go wrong with his series set in Victorian England. Everyone's favorite (and I agree) is the first, **The Ruby in the Smoke**, in which Sally Lockhart investigates—at great personal peril—the mysterious death of her father. The sequels, equally atmospheric and high on entertainment value, are **The Shadow in the North** and **The Tiger in the Well**.

Other marvelous mysteries for teens include Marsha Qualey's **Close to a Killer** (a group of female ex-cons all work at a beauty shop called Killer Cuts, run by Barrie's mother—they've all killed once, but are any of them responsible for two recent murders?); and **Down the Rabbit Hole** by Peter Abrahams, a veteran adult thriller writer, which takes place in Echo Falls, "home of a thousand secrets." The second secret Echo Falls is hiding is revealed in **Behind the Curtain**, another taut, page-turning story. I can't wait for the third in the series. . . .

ALWAYS SHORT AND SOMETIMES (BUT USUALLY NOT) SWEET

T he stories in these collections have one thing in common: they're short. Beyond that, however, they range wildly from humorous to serious, from realistic to fantastical. And, of course, they're all good reading.

> **Am I Blue?: Coming Out from the Silence**, edited by Marion Dane Bauer (includes contributions by M. E. Kerr, Bruce Coville, and Jane Yolen, all on the topic of homosexuality)
> **Baseball in April and Other Stories** by Gary Soto
> **Being Dead: Stories** by Vivian Vande Velde (there's a ghost in each one)

Black Juice by Margo Lanagan (evocative and unsettling short stories—many almost science fiction-y—that linger in the mind long after the last words are read)

Girl Goddess #9 by Francesca Lia Block (marvelous tales about love in all its many guises)

An Island Like You: Stories of the Barrio by Judith Ortiz Cofer (teen life in a mostly Puerto Rican neighborhood in Patterson, New Jersey is explored with gusto, grit, and great writing)

Necking with Louise by Rick Book (a collection of bitter-sweet tales about growing up in the middle of the 1960s in a small town in Saskatchewan, Canada)

Past Perfect, Present Tense: New and Collected Stories by Richard Peck

13: Thirteen Stories That Capture the Agony and Ecstasy of Being Thirteen, edited by James Howe (includes stories by some of the most talented contemporary writers in the young adult pantheon, including Bruce Coville, Alex Sanchez, and Carolyn Mackler)

Visions: Nineteen Short Stories by Outstanding Writers for Young Adults, edited by Donald R. Gallo

A Walk in My World: International Short Stories About Youth, edited by Anne Mazer (includes such outstanding writers as Germany's Heinrich Böll, India's Anita Desai, Egypt's Nobel Prize winner Naguib Mahfouz, and Chile's Antonio Skarmeta, among many others)

Who Am I Without Him? Short Stories About Girls and the Boys in Their Lives by Sharon G. Flake (often tragic and always thought-provoking stories encompass universal themes, told from the point of view and in the vernacular of African American teens)

Highly regarded teen librarian Michael Cart asked some of the best writers around to contribute original stories for three out-standing anthologies for older teens. And did they ever rise to the occasion! Writers in one or more of the collections include Joyce Carol Thomas, Michael Lowenthal, Sonya Sones, Lois Lowry, Joan Bauer, Jon Scieszka, Chris Lynch, and Emma Donoghue, among others. (Teens will likely find their favorite authors represented in one or more of these collections.) You can't really go wrong with any of them, so give all of them a try. They include **Necessary Noise: Stories About Our Families As They Really Are**; **Tomorrowland: 10 Stories About the Future**; and **Love & Sex: 10 Stories of Truth**.

CHICKLET LIT: FOR GIRLS ONLY

There are some books that seem to be written expressly for teenage girls—it's hard to imagine any boys warm-ing to them (unless they're sucked in by the covers). But girls—well, it's pretty safe to say that they'll love them. Many of these novels are clearly influenced by the Helen Fielding's **Bridget Jones's Diary** phenomenon, which produced countless numbers of humorous novels about single, hip, frequently overweight, self-absorbed and -aware women in their thirties, and spawned a new genre of women's fiction called "Chick Lit." The phenomennon ricocheted into the teen fiction market as well, bringing us humor-ous novels with teen heroines looking for boyfriends, worrying about their weight and their acne, trying to deal with difficult

parents and difficult schoolwork, and suffering from teenage angst.
Here are some can't-misses:

You can usually tell a chicklet lit book by its title—take a look at
Louise Rennison's **Angus, Thongs and Full-Frontal Snogging:
Confessions of Georgia Nicolson; On the Bright Side I'm
Now the Girlfriend of a Sex God; Knocked Out By My
Nunga-Nungas: Further, Further Confessions of Georgia
Nicolson**, and the others in the series, which are the über-books
of this genre; fans of Rennison (and they are legion) will also
delight in **Girl, 15, Charming but Insane** and **Girl, Nearly
16, Absolute Torture** by Sue Limb, as well as Katie Maxwell's
The Year My Life Went Down the Loo and **They Wear *What*
Under Their Kilts?**

After Ginny's wannabe artist Aunt Peg dies of cancer, Ginny gets a
mysterious letter from her—the first of thirteen letters that Ginny is
told to open one at a time, after she fulfills the instructions contained
in each letter. These letters take Ginny from New York to London
to Scotland to Greece, a trip of a lifetime that allows Ginny not only
to learn more about her aunt and her life, but also to understand
herself better, in **13 Little Blue Envelopes** by Maureen Johnson.

A pair of secondhand jeans that seem to magically change their
size and shape with each new wearer helps Bridget, Lena, Tibby,
and Carmen, four fifteen-year-old closer-than-close friends, stay
in touch over a summer separated from one another, in Ann
Brashares's **The Sisterhood of the Traveling Pants**. It's followed
by **The Second Summer of the Sisterhood**, **Girls in Pants**,
and **Forever in Blue**.

In **The Earth, My Butt, and Other Big Round Things** by
Carolyn Mackler, fifteen-year-old Virginia struggles with self-esteem,

loneliness, her weight, and surviving an essentially dysfunctional family. While adults may find the characters crudely cast (Virginia's hypocritical, emotionally distant mother is a psychiatrist specializing in troubled adolescents), teens have no trouble relating to Virginia's life battles and cheer her on as she learns to stand up for herself in a sometimes unfair world.

Ashley's totally uninterested in her senior prom—she's concentrating on finishing her senior year and moving in with her loser boyfriend TJ—but when it appears that the prom will be cancelled (because a teacher at school embezzled the money that was to pay for it) and her best friend Natalia is heartbroken by the prospect of no senior prom, Ashley swings into action, in Laurie Halse Anderson's **Prom**. (This is a much lighter book, both in tone and subject matter, than Anderson's well-regarded **Speak**, but the characters here are also three-dimensional and the situations are realistic.)

Can Sari and Jess's long friendship survive ninth grade at a new school, especially when Sari's fallen head over heels in love with a senior boy? Mariah Fredericks explores the consequences in **The True Meaning of Cleavage**. (Note: The title and the cover art are the raciest parts of this good-hearted novel.)

Joan Bauer's **Rules of the Road**, which introduces Jenna, a high school sophomore who works after school selling shoes and always worries about her father's alcoholism, always leaves teens wanting to know more about Jenna's life; so give them **Best Foot Forward**, which focuses on Jenna's junior year.

CRY ME A RIVER

For sad and ultimately satisfying (if not entirely cheering) novels, try these:

In Alison McGhee's novel **All Rivers Flow to the Sea**, Rose tries to figure out how to live with the aftereffects of the car accident that put her sister Lily into an irreversible coma.

In 1955, Lyric, her older sister Summer, and Poppy, her father, leave the hills of Virginia for Flint, Michigan, where Poppy hopes to get work in the automobile industry. Summer can't seem to adjust to the changes, and her behavior, which Lyric thought once was only quirky, deteriorates into serious mental illness, in Ruth White's sad and evocative **Memories of Summer**.

You might want to have a handkerchief handy when you begin Jacqueline Woodson's **If You Come Softly**, a novel that realistically explores first love, racial prejudice, lost opportunities, and tragic outcomes as they're played out in the relationship between Jeremiah and Elisha, two students at a tony private school. There's a sequel, **Behind You**, too.

Private Peaceful by Michael Morpurgo is the story of Thomas Peaceful, who lies about his age to follow his older brother, Charlie, into the British Army during World War I. His experiences on the battlefields in France illuminate a little-known practice the Army followed: men (and a great many were just boys, like Tommo and his brother) who fell asleep on sentry duty were executed as traitors.

Other books that are practically guaranteed to bring at least a tear or two include Alice Hoffman's lyrical **Green Angel**; Bruce Brooks's collection of three stories about teens dealing with different aspects of grief and loss, **All That Remains**; **True Confessions of a Heartless Girl** by Martha Brooks; **Freewill**, a thought-provoking novel (one of many) by Chris Lynch about a teenage boy who believes that he may be responsible for the suicides of his classmates; **Rockbuster** by Gloria Skurzynski (a really interesting novel about a boy coming of age during the early years of the labor movement); and Gary Paulsen's **Nightjohn**, the story of a slave who risked his life to teach other slaves to read—a true testimony to the possibility of grace in a period of the nation's shame.

DRAGOONED BY DRAGONS

It's interesting that despite the plethora of dragon tales available for younger readers, there's still no dearth of them for teens, too. If jewel-hoarding, fire-breathing horrors sound good to your older readers, give them these:

Dragonsbane by Barbara Hambly is a dark fantasy that pits average heroes against both the wily dragon Morkeleb and a wicked (but beautiful) sorceress. In a similar vein, **The Hunting of the Last Dragon** by Sherryl Jordan features a peace-loving English boy named Jude, who must rid the countryside of the ill-tempered fire-breather that incinerated his village.

Perhaps even more frightening than a possible violent death is the prospect of *becoming* a dragon, which is the fate that awaits Gavril, the new Lord Drakhaon of Azhkendir in **Lord of Snow and Shadows**, the first in the Tears of Artamon series by Sarah Ash.

The queen of dragon lore, Anne McCaffrey, created the world called Pern, in which humans and dragons work together to protect civilization from a natural phenomenon called Thread. In the first of the series, **Dragonflight**, Lessa escapes slavery to take part in a ceremony of "impressing" and bonds with the dragon hatchling, Ramoth. Her next task is to save the endangered clan of dragon riders, and, of course, the world. There are twenty-one Pern books in the series (as I write this); the latest is **Dragonsblood** by Todd McCaffrey, Anne's son. Within the larger series is a mini-series composed of **Dragonsong**, **Dragonsinger**, and **Dragondrums**. They're known as the HarperHall-Pern trilogy.

No list of recommended dragon fantasy stories would be complete without mentioning Christopher Paolini's **Eragon** and its sequel, **Eldest**. In the first adventure, Eragon, a poor farm boy, finds a dragon egg, loses his family, and embarks on a quest to become a dragon rider. In **Eldest**, Eragon must seek a deeper knowledge of magic. Great stuff!

For some shivery fun, try **Heir Apparent** by Vivian Vande Velde, which places Giannine in a virtual reality game called Heir Apparent where she must beat impossible odds (and a dragon) to win the crown. But a glitch in the game makes winning more than a game—it becomes a matter of life and death.

In the first of the Pit Dragon series, fifteen-year-old Jakkin realizes that his only route to escape from thralldom in Master Sarkhan's dragon barns is to steal a baby dragon and train him to be a champion, in **Dragon's Blood**, another of Jane Yolen's top-notch novels. It's followed by **Heart's Blood** and **A Sending of Dragons**.

FANTASTIC FANTASIES

I t's a crowded marketplace for teen fantasies, and hard to figure out from a cover, a jacket blurb, or a title what's good, bad, or indifferent. Here are some suggestions to get you started with the best.

In **Water Mirror**, the first in the Dark Reflections trilogy by Kai Meyer, readers are introduced to a medieval Venice where magic is part of the real world—police riding stone lions patrol the streets, mermaids inhabit the many canals, and Merle, one of the two main characters, has a magic mirror. How Merle and Serafin, her friend who was once a skilled thief, help to find the Flowing Queen and defeat the Egyptian invaders (with their mummy warriors) makes for a thrilling read.

Murkmere by Patricia Elliott (isn't the title evocative?) takes place in a country ruled by a puritanical government (some adult readers may recognize the setting as more or less England under Oliver Cromwell). The main character is teenage orphan Agnes, who has been brought to Murkmere as companion to the lord's daughter, Leah, whom people suspect as being one of the feared *avia*—half bird, half human, and outlawed by the government. But is she?

Other outstanding fantasies for teens include Peter Dickinson's **The Ropemaker**; **The Naming** by Alison Croggon, the first volume in the Pellinor series; **Firegold** by Dia Calhoun; Robin

McKinley's first (of many, I'm so happy to report) novel, **Beauty**, a retelling of *Beauty and the Beast*; Donna Jo Napoli uses the same fairy tale as the basis for her novel, **Beast**; Lian Hearn's Tales of the Otori, all set in a recognizable feudal Japan, but clearly fantasy, beginning with **Across the Nightingale Floor** and continuing with **Grass for His Pillow** and **Brilliance of the Moon**; **Sabriel** (and sequels) by Garth Nix (how do you destroy Death, the greatest of enemies?); Ursula K. Le Guin's **Gifts**; **Treasure at the Heart of the Tanglewood** by Meredith Ann Pierce; Catherine Fisher's **The Oracle Betrayed**; **The Truth-Teller's Tale** and **The Safe-Keeper's Secret** by Sharon Shinn; Vivian Vande Velde's slightly humorous and slightly gruesome **Never Trust a Dead Man**; Clive Barker's **Abarat**; and **The Princess Bride: S. Morgenstern's Classic Tale of True Love and High Adventure** by William Goldman (one of the few books ever that became an almost equally good film).

GETTING TO KNOW ME: MEMOIRS

What I especially like about these memoirs, many of which are about the authors' teenage years, is that they encourage healthy self-reflection. Several of the books recount painful periods in the lives of the writers, so that teens (and adult readers, looking back at adolescence) may finish reading them feeling like "thank goodness that's not *my* life." But hey, it's not always an easy world out there. I found all of these books to be honest, compelling, and well worth sharing with teen readers. Many of them are not shelved in the teen section of libraries or bookstores, but rather with the adult nonfiction. Some deal with sensitive subjects, such a rape or abuse, so if you're at all concerned, do read the books before you hand them over to a teen.

Rick Bragg's **All Over But the Shoutin'**

Augusten Burroughs's **Running with Scissors**

Chelsea Cain's **Dharma Girl: A Road Trip Across the American Generations**

Hillary Carlip's **Queen of the Oddballs: And Other True Stories from a Life Unaccording to Plan**

Esmé Raji Codell's **Educating Esmé: Diary of a Teacher's First Year**

Edward Conlon's **Blue Blood**

Pat Conroy's **My Losing Season**

Lynne Cox's **Swimming to Antarctica: Tales of a Long-Distance Swimmer**

Chris Crutcher's **King of the Mild Frontier: An Ill-Advised Autobiography**

Andie Dominick's **Needles** (not drugs—diabetes)

Dave Eggers's **A Heartbreaking Work of Staggering Genius**

Zlata Filipović's **Zlata's Diary: A Child's Life in Wartime Sarajevo** (these are the diary entries the author kept from age eleven to thirteen)

Jack Gantos's **Hole in My Life** (about the year he spent in prison for drug smuggling—it's hard to believe that kid grew up to write **Rotten Ralph**, the Joey Pigza books, and other children's favorites)

Lori Gottlieb's **Stick Figure: A Diary of My Former Self**

Lucy Grealy's **Autobiography of a Face**

Linda Greenlaw's **The Hungry Ocean: A Swordboat Captain's Journey**

Julie Gregory's **Sickened: The Memoir of a Munchausen by Proxy Childhood**

Elva Trevino Hart's **Barefoot Heart: Stories of a Migrant Child**

Marya Hornbacher's **Wasted: A Memoir of Anorexia and Bulimia**

Francisco Jiménez's **The Circuit: Stories from the Life of a Migrant Child** and its sequel, **Breaking Through**

Mary Karr's **The Liars' Club**

Susanna Kaysen's **Girl, Interrupted**

Jesse Lee Kercheval's **Space**

Anita Lobel's **No Pretty Pictures: A Child of War** (growing up during the Holocaust)

Hans J. Massaquoi's **Destined to Witness: Growing Up Black in Nazi Germany**

Mark Mathabane's **Kaffir Boy**

J. R. Moehringer's **The Tender Bar: A Memoir**

Walter Dean Myers's **Bad Boy: A Memoir**

Dawn Prince-Hughes's **Songs of the Gorilla Nation: My Journey Through Autism**

Brent Runyon's **The Burn Journals**

Mark Salzman's **Lost in Place: Growing Up Absurd in Suburbia** and **True Notebooks: A Writer's Year at Juvenile Hall**

Marjane Satrapi's **Persepolis** and **Persepolis II**

Julia Scheeres's **Jesus Land: A Memoir**

Alice Sebold's **Lucky: A Memoir** (an account of the author's rape when she was a freshman in college)

Lauralee Summer's **Learning Joy from Dogs Without Collars**

Rebecca Walker's **Black, White, and Jewish: Autobiography of a Shifting Self**

Jeanette Walls's **The Glass Castle: A Memoir**

Ma Yan's **Diary of Ma Yan: The Struggles and Hopes of a Chinese Schoolgirl**

GHOSTS I HAVE LOVED

A dolescent love is tough enough without adding the supernatural to the volatile mixture of hormones, identity crises, and the shame of not having a date on Saturday night. Nonetheless, these books do add the magical to the mundane, to great effect. So for those interested in supernatural (but not really horror-filled) novels, try these:

Eve Bunting's **The Presence**

Louise Hawes's **Rosey in the Present Tense**

Sollace Hotze's **Acquainted with the Night** (set in Maine, just after the Vietnam War ends)

Elizabeth Marie Pope's **The Sherwood Ring** (a girl, a suitor, several ghosts, a wicked uncle, and some unfinished Revolutionary War doings)

Gary Soto's **The Afterlife**

Elswyth Thane's **Tryst** (a totally romantic novel with no graphic sex at all—in fact, there's barely any sex to speak of)

Laura Whitcomb's **A Certain Slant of Light** (teenage ghosts whose desire for one another leads them into a complex situation involving two real teens)

GIRLS KICK BUTT

Somehow, in recent years especially, girls seem more likely to kick butt in fantasy fiction, rather than in the more realistic sort, which, it seems to me, makes for a pretty sad state of affairs. Still, these novels are awfully entertaining reading, and the main characters provide strong role models for young women in the real world, as well.

If you want an example of the sort of heroine who figures in this category, look no further than the words of Thirrin Freer Strong in the Arm Lindenshield, heir to the throne of the Icemark, in **The Cry of the Icemark** by Stuart Hill. As she faces death at the hands of a werewolf, Thirrin says, "Make it quick, wolfman, and make sure all the wounds are in front. I don't want anyone saying I died running away." Wow! Who wouldn't want to read about a young woman like that? Who wouldn't want to *be* a young woman like that?

In Shannon Hale's fantasy **The Goose Girl**, Princess Anidori, faced with a series of betrayals, is forced to disguise her identity until she can make her real self known and reclaim her crown. It's followed by **Enna Burning** and **River Secrets**.

Life during the reign of King Arthur is the setting for Patricia Malone's **The Legend of Lady Ilena** and **Lady Ilena: Way of the Warrior**, both fast-moving, action-filled adventure novels with a well-drawn setting and a brave and passionate heroine.

Louis A. Meyer introduces a brave (although she believes she's a coward) and ready-for-anything adventurer in **Bloody Jack: Being an Account of the Curious Adventures of Mary "Jacky" Faber, Ship's Boy**. Thirteen-year-old Mary, orphaned and living hand to mouth on the streets of eighteenth-century London, disguises herself as a boy and joins the Royal Navy, encountering high seas, friends and enemies among the crew, a true love, and pirates. Her adventures continue in **Curse of the Blue Tattoo: Being an Account of the Misadventures of Jacky Faber, Midshipman and Fine Lady** (the powers that be actually try to turn her into a proper lady) and **Under the Jolly Roger: Being an Account of the Further Nautical Adventures of Jacky Faber**. You won't find better historical adventures than these, except for Celia Rees's **Pirates!: The True and Remarkable Adventures of Minerva Sharpe and Nancy Kington, Female Pirates**. After reading these, girls will want to take to the seas immediately.

Following her mother's unexpected death in India in 1895, sixteen-year-old Gemma Doyle is sent to a stuffy boarding school in England, where her education on the mores of high society is complicated when she discovers that she is the link between the world she lives in and other, magical (and possibly dangerous) realms, in Libba Bray's **A Great and Terrible Beauty**. Gemma's adventures are continued in **Rebel Angels**.

The coming of a great woman warrior is prophesied among the followers of the Great Alta, and it slowly becomes clear to

Jenna that she is the Anna, the one who was foreseen to both save and destroy, in Jane Yolen's superior fantasy **Sister Light, Sister Dark** (followed by **White Jenna** and concluding with **The One-Armed Queen**).

Other great fiction featuring unstoppable young women includes Sylvia Engdahl's **Enchantress from the Stars**; Betsy James's The Seeker Chronicles (which includes **Long Night Dance**, **Dark Heart**, and **Listening at the Gate**); Charlotte Brontë's **Jane Eyre**; **Jenna Starborn**, Sharon Shinn's retelling of *Jane Eyre* (as science fiction); Emily Brontë's **Wuthering Heights**; and Jane Austen's **Emma**.

GLBTQ

GLBTQ, as many people know, is shorthand for Gay, Lesbian, Bisexual, Transsexual, and Questioning; this section is filled with excellent fiction for teens on these topics. With a few notable exceptions (such as Rosa Guy's **Ruby**; **The Man Without a Face** by Isabelle Holland; and Sandra Scoppettone's **Trying Hard to Hear You**, all published in the 1970s; Nancy Garden's **Annie on My Mind**, which [warning: pun to follow] came out in 1982; and Francesca Lia Block's **Weetzie Bat**, published in 1989 and still going strong), there weren't many YA novels with gay and lesbian characters written before the last years of the twentieth century. A gay or lesbian teen who wanted to "find" him- or herself in a book was pretty much out of luck. Even today, the number of books with gay and lesbian protagonists is relatively small. Books with bisexual or transgender characters are even fewer, although older teens will probably enjoy Carol

Anshaw's **Lucky in the Corner**, Chris Bohjalian's **Trans-Sister Radio**, and Jeffrey Eugenides's **Middlesex**.

Here are some of the very best teen novels featuring gay, lesbian, transsexual, or bisexual characters:

Stephen Chbosky's **The Perks of Being a Wallflower**

Garret Freymann-Weyr's **My Heartbeat**

Jack Gantos's **Desire Lines**

Brent Hartinger's **Geography Club**

A. M. Homes's **Jack**

James Howe's **The Misfits** and its sequel **Totally Joe** (this one written in the form of twenty-six diary entries, one for each letter of the alphabet)

Maureen Johnson's **The Bermudez Triangle**

M. E. Kerr's **Deliver Us from Evie**, **"Hello," I Lied**, and **Night Kites**, published in 1995 and the first young adult novel I'm aware of that deals with AIDS

David Levithan's **Boy Meets Boy**

Lisa Papademetriou and Chris Tebbetts's **M or F?**, an entertaining combination of Edmund Rostand's *Cyrano de Bergerac* and William Shakespeare's *Twelfth Night*

Julie Anne Peters's **Keeping You a Secret**, **Far from Xanadu**, and **Luna**; her groundbreaking novel (and National Book Award finalist) about a transgender teen

Sara Ryan's **Empress of the World** (two girls at a summer program for gifted teens fall in love)

Alex Sanchez's series about three gay high school students, including **Rainbow Boys**, **Rainbow High**, and **Rainbow Road**

Shyam Selvadurai's **Swimming in the Monsoon Sea** (set in a lush Sri Lanka, this is the story of a young man's growing awareness of his sexual identity)

Andreas Steinhöfel's **The Center of the World** (good for those who enjoyed Selvadurai's novel)

Jacqueline Woodson's **The House You Pass on the Way**

Three quality nonfiction books on this topic are **Out of the Ordinary: Essays on Growing Up with Gay, Lesbian, and Transgender Parents**, edited by Noelle Howey and Ellen Samuels; **The Shared Heart: Portraits and Stories Celebrating Lesbian, Gay, and Bisexual Young People**, a collection of photographs by Adam Mastoon; and **Hearing Us Out: Voices from the Gay and Lesbian Community**, a series of interviews by Roger Sutton.

GROWING UP IS (SOMETIMES) HARD TO DO

The novels that follow are the teen equivalent of the middle-reader "family story." They're set in both contemporary times and the not too distant past, and feature teens who find that becoming an adult can be a tricky business, indeed.

When sixteen-year-old Mattie Gokey—growing up in the Adirondacks in the early years of the twentieth century—discovers a packet of letters left behind by a dead young woman that reveal a murder has taken place, her desire to go to college and become a writer grows more intense than ever, in Jennifer Donnelly's **A Northern Light**. (Interestingly, the murder that occurs in this novel is the same one that inspired Theodore Dreiser to write *An American Tragedy*.)

In **Car Trouble**, computer geek Duff takes off for a new job across the country from his home in Virginia. Jeanne DuPrau combines a road-trip novel with Duff's voyage of self-discovery.

Sarah Dessen knows teenage girls inside and out—this was eminently clear from her very first novel, **That Summer**, in which two upcoming weddings are bedeviling fifteen-year-old, too tall Haven: her father's marriage to Lorna Queen, weather girl at the local television station, and her sister Ashley's upcoming wedding to a young man who can't hold a candle to her first boyfriend, Sumner Lee—who comes back to town shortly before the wedding. For another of Dessen's outstanding novels about teen life in suburban America, try **Just Listen**, which is a bit darker than *That Summer*.

R. A. Nelson's **Teach Me** explores what happens when high school senior Nine (short for Carolina) has an affair with her youngish English teacher, Mr. Mann. The plot of this novel reminded me strongly of Elizabeth Strout's **Amy and Isabelle** (a novel you'll find in the adult fiction section—but it's appropriate for older teens as well), which also looks at the forbidden relationship between a high school student and one of her teachers.

Other good choices in this category include Kim Ablon Whitney's **The Perfect Distance** (aimed at horse-crazy girls); **Big Mouth and Ugly Girl**, the first young adult novel by Joyce Carol Oates (the voice of Ursula, self-styled Ugly Girl, is mesmerizingly real); and Annette Curtis Klause's **Freaks: Alive, on the Inside!**, about Abel Dandy, the "normal" son of performers in a freak show (the armless woman and the legless man, in fact), who learns—after many adventures—that it's not what you look like but who you are on the inside that really matters.

HEARTBREAK HOTEL

Although we tend to think that "heartbreak" simply implies love gone wrong, the possibilities for a broken heart are almost endless, as can be seen from the following titles, which range from the pain and sadness of losing a parent, to the problems of returning home after fighting in a war, to becoming physically incapacitated. Read on. . . .

When Anna realizes that she was conceived in order to be a donor match for her older sister, Kate, who has a rare type of leukemia, she makes a decision that will have repercussions far beyond her original decision to stop being her family's guinea pig, in **My Sister's Keeper** by Jodi Picoult.

Callisto, the heroine of **Borrowed Light** by Anna Fienberg, keeps hoping that she can find a way to shine on her own, even as she finds herself in the shadow of her famous grandmother and charming brother, and ignored by her distant mother and work-absorbed father.

In John Green's impossible to put down **Looking for Alaska**, Miles chooses to attend his dad's alma mater, Culver Creek Prep, an Alabama boarding school, where he's drawn into the web of his roommate, Chip, and Chip's best friend, the enigmatic temptress Alaska.

Set in a sunny, small fishing village in Guam, **Keeper of the Night** by Kimberly Willis Holt is the story of Isabel, who tries to make order out of the chaos caused by her mother's suicide by compiling lists and helping to care for the rest of the family.

Raised by her uptight but loving single mother and grandmother in a working-class neighborhood, Josie attends a private school on scholarship, meets her father for the first time in seventeen years, and lusts after two completely different boys. Melina Marchetta explores the choices that Josie faces in **Looking for Alibrandi**.

Anna's dreams of a black belt and future championships in karate are shattered when she breaks her neck in a car accident. Although some of her friends and family treat her as if she is too frail and broken to recover, she realizes that she must be stronger than ever to overcome the physical and psychological pain, in Wendy Orr's **Peeling the Onion**.

Though Imani is the child of a rape, Tasha loves her daughter with all her heart and is determined to make a better life for her in a world that seems to offer only obstacles to success, in Connie Porter's moving **Imani All Mine**.

What do you do when your closest friend—your blood brother—starts hanging out with the wrong people, who are certain to increase the likelihood of his death at an early age in your inner-city neighborhood? Jesse tells the story of the life and death of Rise, in Walter Dean Myers's **Autobiography of My Dead Brother**, with illustrations by Christopher Myers.

HISTORICAL FICTION

Why read historical fiction? The easiest answer is, of course, why not? Besides the innate pleasure these well-written, well-researched, and interesting novels provide, they may also start readers on the path to a lifelong interest in history. Plus, if these books click with readers, they also point the way to other pleasing reads—both fiction and nonfiction. They're all useful for teachers seeking to turn students on to particular historical time periods, as well.

The Turkish genocide of its Armenian citizens from 1915 to 1918 is the subject of Adam Bagdasarian's **Forgotten Fire**, which is based on his great-uncle's experiences. Teens live with Vahan as he tries to adjust to the cataclysmic changes going on around him, including the deaths of friends and family, the loss of all he knows, and finding love in unexpected places. (A follow-up for this novel is Peter Balakian's memoir, **Black Dog of Fate**.)

Laurie Halse Anderson's **Fever 1793** is the story of Matilda Cook, a young woman trying to survive the yellow fever epidemic on her own in what was then the nation's capital, Philadelphia.

Marie Dancing by Carolyn Meyer illuminates the life of a little-known historical figure, Marie van Goethem, the young woman who was the model for Degas's sculpture *Petite Danseuse de Quatorze Ans*; it offers, as well, an accurate picture of the life of a ballet dancer in the late nineteenth century. Meyer also did a series of historical novels about well-known women in Tudor England, including **Mary, Bloody Mary**; **Doomed Queen Anne**; and **Beware, Princess Elizabeth**; collectively known as the Young Royals series.

The twelfth-century crusades by King Richard I of England to retake the Holy Land from the Muslim infidels led by Saladin are vividly portrayed in K. M. Grant's **Blood Red Horse** (the first in the De Granville trilogy), as seen through the experiences of two English brothers, their adopted sister, a young Muslim warrior, and a horse named Hosanna. Grant doesn't take sides in the conflict, and best of all, doesn't glorify the events on the battlefield.

The late twelfth and early thirteenth century in Europe is also the setting for an engrossing quartet of novels by Catherine Jinks, all featuring Pagan, an orphan who joins the Knights Templar to escape from the slums of Jerusalem. Readers follow Pagan as he becomes an adult and is finally appointed the Archdeacon of Carcassone, in **Pagan's Crusade**, **Pagan in Exile**, **Pagan's Vows**, and **Pagan's Scribe**.

I've known a few teenagers who counted the historical novels of Rosemary Sutcliff among the best books they'd ever read, but to be quite honest, it's an abysmally small number. Probably the majority of teen readers are likely to be put off by the smallish type and the dense narrative of Sutcliff's prose. Readers who do make it even a little way into these outstanding books will find, however, that Sutcliff animates a historical era like no other author I've ever read, making us care deeply about her characters and their (often fraught) situations. Her best books for teens feature main characters who are themselves in their teens or early twenties, and all take place in Roman Britain. These include **The Eagle of the Ninth** (set in AD 133), **The Silver Branch** (set about a century and a half later), **The Lantern Bearers** (set in the fifth century, when the Roman troops were all pulled out of Britain by their emperor), and **Dawn Wind**, with the main character being the great-great-grandson of the hero of **The Lantern Bearers**. Once readers finish these, it's a natural progression to go on to Sutcliff's great Arthurian novel (although Arthur appears as a character in **The Lantern Bearers**), **Sword at Sunset**.

In Richard Peck's **The River Between Us**, set in 1915 and the Civil War period, the author makes adroit use of flashbacks to discuss race, war, and family secrets, while telling a grand story at the same time.

Jamila Gavin has a talent for creating exciting plots and vivid settings, as can be seen in both **Coram Boy**, set in eighteenth-century England (you can go to Russell Square in London even today and see the setting for this book) and **The Blood Stone**, which takes place in Venice and Hindustan in the seventeenth century.

The importance of not only knowing yourself, but also your place in the world is the subject of Aidan Chambers's **Postcards from No Man's Land**, which combines two tales. One, set in contemporary times, is about seventeen-year-old Jacob Todd, who comes to Amsterdam from his home in England to honor his grandfather who died in World War II. The other is the story of his grandfather, as told to Jacob by a now elderly nurse who knew him during the war. This challenging and sometimes disturbing novel is most appropriate for older teens.

More recent history—the period immediately following the attack on the World Trade Center on September 11, 2001—is conjured up in Suzanne Fisher Staples's **Under the Persimmon Tree**. The lives of two people—one a girl disguised as a boy and the other an American convert to Islam—intersect at a refugee camp in Pakistan, where kindness and friendship manage to flourish in unlikely places. As she did in this book, Staples brings the Middle East alive for teen readers in her other books, **Shabanu** and **Shiva's Fire**.

IMMIGRANTS AND REFUGEES

Being a hyphenated American is especially hard during adolescence, when there's such a need to find a sense of oneself and discover where one fits into the world. These books (all of which can lead to fruitful discussions) take place in many different decades of the twentieth century. They offer a nice balance between normal teen issues and the special problems that being an immigrant or being adopted from another country can impose, such as how to balance traditional family ways with a new life in a new culture, or the embarrassment that accompanies the knowledge that older relatives don't seem to fit into their adopted country.

The Triangle Shirtwaist Factory fire in 1911 is the background for Mary Jane Auch's **Ashes of Roses**, the story of Rose, who refuses to leave her new home in America and return to Ireland with her family, only to find that working long and grueling hours in a factory is not the future she envisioned.

A Step from Heaven by An Na is a powerfully told novel that describes the differences between dreams and reality, as Ju and her family discover that America isn't the heaven on earth that everyone in their native Korea imagined it was.

Fictional stories of teenage immigrants from Kazakh to Romania, from Palestine to Sweden, from Haiti to Cambodia, written by Lensey Namioka, Pam Muñoz Ryan, David Lubar, and others, explore what it's really like to leave your homeland for an America that might not meet your dreams and hopes, in **First Crossing: Stories about Teen Immigrants**, edited by Donald R. Gallo.

In Sherry Garland's **Shadow of the Dragon**, Danny comes of age between two worlds: his American life at school, where he's just like everyone else—hoping for a date with a cute girl, studying for his driver's license, and working for good grades—and his life at home, where his family stubbornly holds on to their traditional Vietnamese customs and beliefs.

Fresh Girl by Jaira Placide is the story of Mardi, who returns to Brooklyn from her grandmother's home in Haiti when the political situation there becomes too dangerous. She finds it difficult to bond with her American classmates while at the same time trying to cope with her painful memories of the past.

You might also want to try **Esperanza Rising** by Pam Muñoz Ryan; **Born Confused** by Tanuja Desai Hidier; Rita Williams-Garcia's **Every Time a Rainbow Dies**; **Journey of the Sparrows** by Fran Leeper Buss; **Fresh Off the Boat** by Melissa de la Cruz; Linda Crews's **Children of the River**; and these excellent novels that are usually found in the adult section of the library and book-store: **China Boy** by Gus Lee; Sandra Cisneros's **The House on Mango Street**; Wayson Choy's **The Jade Peony**; and Lan Cao's **Monkey Bridge**.

IT MIGHT AS WELL BE GREEK

Teens are usually introduced to Greek mythology in the eighth or ninth grades, frequently through being assigned Edith Hamilton's classic **Mythology**. But that should just be the beginning of what can easily become a lifelong love affair with all things Greek.

I think a lot of authors feel that ancient Greece is the ideal location to set a historical novel because you have so many options open to you—you can deal realistically with the rivalry between the Greek city-states, or bring in the fantastic stories of gods and heroes, or take a new look at the classic Greek tales of Homer's *The Iliad* and *The Odyssey*. Or you can select whatever combination you want from options a, b, and c! In any event, the books described here are surefire choices.

In Adèle Geras's two fabulous novels, readers are plunged into the world of ancient Greece, and two of its most famous incidents are retold in lush and evocative language. **Troy** is the story—told from the points of view of a variety of narrators—of the Trojan War, with its great and terrible battles, the death of Hector, the anger of Achilles, and the interference in mortal lives by the bored and jealous gods on Mount Olympus. The wanderings of Odysseus and the stay-at-home life of Penelope (who waits patiently for him while he's off having the adventure of his life) are described through the eyes of Klymene, who's always regarded Penelope as her mother, in **Ithaka**.

Donna Jo Napoli has written several outstanding adaptations of Greek myths. These include **Sirena**, also set around the Trojan War, about a young woman who becomes a siren (like the ones who tempted Odysseus) despite her determination to be different from her sisters, and **The Great God Pan**, in which Napoli weaves together the various versions of the Greek myth and adds in a love story with Iphigenia, daughter of the Greek king Agamemnon.

H. M. Hoover's **The Dawn Palace** is a retelling of the story of Jason and Medea, beginning with their first meeting—it's love at first sight, at least for Medea, when Jason arrives in Medea's father's kingdom on his quest for the golden fleece—and ending with the tragic conclusion of their love story.

There's no fantasy in **The Road to Sardis** by Stephanie Plowman; it's straight historical fiction—and heartbreaking at that—about the events of the Peloponnesian War, the conflict between Athens and Sparta, which broke out in 431 BC and lasted twenty-seven long years.

Others to try include **Quiver** by Stephanie Spinner, a retelling of the myth of the huntress Atalanta (this is a nice follow-up to Jane Yolen and Robert J. Harris's **Atalanta and the Arcadian Beast**, which is for younger readers); Clemence McLaren's **Inside the Wall of Troy** and **Waiting for Odysseus**, both told from the point of view of the women (both mortal and immortal) involved in *The Iliad* and *The Odyssey*; Patrice Kindl's **Lost in the Labyrinth** (Theseus and the Minotaur); and **Goddess of Yesterday** by Caroline B. Cooney (the siege of Troy as seen through the eyes of a young princess—it's especially good if you're not that big a fan of Helen, who caused the war in the first place). **The Firebrand** by Marian Zimmer Bradley and **The King Must Die** and **The Bull from the Sea** by Mary Renault are especially sound recommendations for older teens.

IT'S A GUY THING

B oth avid and reluctant male readers will want to check out these titles. Their styles range from the humorous to the serious, and their subjects from the mundane to the unusual.

Jack Grammar can't get a date for the senior prom until his best friends Natalie and Percy put a personal ad in their school's online paper—and now there are too many girls to choose from, in Alex Bradley's amusing **24 Girls in 7 Days**.

When his evil uncles put Sandy's parents and pet chicken into a coma by means of a poisoned birthday cake, it takes all of Sandy's brains, along with help from a very cute nurse named Sunnie and the family's butler, Bentley, to put a halt to his uncles' nefarious doings in **Love Among the Walnuts** by Jean Ferris.

While he's very reluctantly (we're talking about your basic student slacker here) doing research for a science paper on smallpox, Mitty finds an envelope of century-old scabs in an old medical book, and fears that he's inadvertently infected himself and all other Manhattanites with the disease. Caroline B. Cooney ratchets up the suspense, while at the same time throwing in enough humor to keep things just scary, in **Code Orange**.

Set during the 1950s, Julian Houston's **New Boy** explores the racial issues of the decade through the story of Rob Garrett, who's the only African American student at his exclusive boarding school. Houston not only illuminates the black/white controversies, but also the division in the black community over how to approach the issue of integration.

Readers will get caught up in sixteen-year-old Steve Nugent's journal as he describes the often difficult, even violent events that led to his present circumstances: an indefinite stay at Burnstone Grove, a treatment facility for teens who are either dangerous to themselves or to others, in Adam Rapp's **Under the Wolf, Under the Dog**.

There's lighter reading to be had in Ron Koertge's **Confess-O-Rama**, in which fifteen-year-old Tony Candelaria, starting at a new high school, falls for Jordan, whose taste in clothes tends towards the exotic, and confesses his feelings to a supposedly anonymous self-help hotline . . . only guess who's on the other end of the phone.

Underachieving kids will gravitate toward Steve, the intelligent stoner at the heart of **Rats Saw God** by Rob Thomas, as he tries to explain to everyone, including himself, what it's like to be the son of a famous astronaut.

Only a writer as clever as Norma Howe could invent a character like sixteen-year-old David Schumacher, comic-book artist, crusader against handguns, investigator into the secrets of "weepless" meringue, lovesick swain of Omaha Nebraska Brown, and superhero challenger of the idea of fate—it all comes together in the smashing **The Adventures of Blue Avenger**.

In **Bucking the Sarge**, Christopher Paul Curtis spins the story of Luther, whose hard-hearted mother, "the Sarge," forces him to participate in her moneymaking scams. Luther tows the line at home and at school, plotting revenge and forming his own philosophy of life that's both hilarious and heartbreaking.

KUNG FU, THE SAMURAI CODE, AND NINJA STEALTH

K ung fu, samurai, ninjas, and plenty of action can be found in martial arts fiction, a genre that's growing in popularity (along with its close companions, manga and martial arts films). These novels all make good use of action, adventure, and the philosophy and mystery of martial arts. As you'll see, secrets are uncovered. Families break apart. There's inevitable betrayal by friends, and an adherence to the wisdom of the ancients.

Adeline Yen Mah based **Chinese Cinderella and the Secret Dragon Society** on both the kung fu stories she read as a child and the movie *Thirty Seconds Over Tokyo*, describing the life of twelve-year-old Ye Xian, or CC (Chinese Cinderella), during the Japanese occupation of Shanghai. When she's forced to leave her father's house after an argument, Ye Xian joins the Dragon Society of Wandering Knights Martial Arts Academy, and becomes involved in the Chinese Resistance.

Tiger, **Monkey**, and **Snake** by Jeff Stone are the first three novels in the Five Ancestors series, tales loosely based on the history of the Shaolin monks who lived in seventeenth-century China. Five orphans are brought up together as brothers: each is given the name of an animal and trained in the strengths of that particular beast. Every book is told from the point of view of a different brother; in **Tiger**, they're trying to foil the plans of Ying, their traitorous foster brother. Readers looking for nonstop action won't want to miss these.

There's also a lot of kung fu action in Da Chen's **Wandering Warrior**, and **Sign of the Qin** by L. G. Bass, the first in the Outlaws of Moonshadow Marsh trilogy.

A look at life through the eyes of a ninja is found in **Blue Fingers** by Cheryl Aylward Whitesel, the story of a boy captured by ninjas who realizes what role he is to play in life. (There's a useful glossary of Japanese terms in the back of the book.)

Anyone who enjoys fast-moving and well-plotted novels will enjoy the Samurai Girl series of books by Carrie Asai. In **The Book of the Sword**, nineteen-year-old Heaven (miraculously saved as a baby from the wreckage of a plane crash) realizes—at her wedding ceremony—that she doesn't love her fiancé. That realization sets off a series of events, involving an attack by ninjas, a murder, a betrayal, and a search for truth. Fans won't want to miss the other titles in the series, including **The Book of the Shadow, The Book of the Pearl, The Book of the Wind, The Book of the Flame**, and **The Book of the Heart**.

For those who enjoy samurai stories, the mysteries by Dorothy and Thomas Hoobler, set in eighteenth-century Japan, are just about perfect. The first in the series is **The Ghost in the Tokaido Inn**, in which fourteen-year-old Seikei, the son of a tea merchant, is asked by Judge Ooka, the samurai magistrate, to assist him in finding a stolen ruby. The same characters star in **The Demon in the Teahouse**; **In Darkness, Death**; and **The Sword That Cut the Burning Grass**.

MAY I HAVE THIS DANCE? OLD-FASHIONED LOVE HIP ENOUGH FOR THE JADED-AT-TWELVE CROWD

Little girls do not stay little for very long; before you know it they are reading teen novels overly full of overly sexy adolescents, and all the sweetness and innocence of first love is lost in a sea of wished-for popularity, trendy clothes, and cute little cell phones. But it's not inevitable that young girls of today have to travel the agonizing road of adolescence in the sole company of the current crop of It girls. There are books that capture the thrill of that newly heightened energy in ways that are more affirming than ironic. Perhaps it's not surprising that many were written decades ago, and while they may be dated in terms of dress and phone service, they have not aged a bit when it comes to learning about love, popular girls, and making your perilous way into the grown-up world.

Sadly out of print but worth tracking down, **The Pink Dress** by Anne Alexander is a classic fifties novel of first love, cliques, and social status. Sue Stevens goes to the Peppermint Prom in a new pink dress, and Dave Young, the coolest boy in school, asks her to dance. Not too much later he gives her his ID bracelet and first kiss. In a story a bit like a more serious *Grease* (or a less serious *Romeo and Juliet*), Sue and Dave have to negotiate the school's social divide.

Cages of Glass, Flowers of Time by Charlotte Culin (also out of print but easier to find) is set in the seventies and is a much darker work than any other described here, although relatively tame compared to a lot of contemporary young adult fiction. Claire lives with her violent alcoholic mother and struggles to make it through each day. She's an outcast at school, endangered at home, and has no outlet for her ambition to paint. Then she meets three special people: an art teacher, a musician, and a boy.

Kids discover Beverly Cleary in elementary school through the antics of the loveable Ramona Quimby, or the everyday adventures of Henry Huggins. As they grow up, girls should not leave Ms. Cleary behind until they've read her love stories, **Jean and Johnny**, **The Luckiest Girl**, **Sister of the Bride**, and my favorite, **Fifteen**. It's about Jane Purdy, who's never been asked for a date by anyone other than the unromantic and boring George. Then she unexpectedly meets Stan and her life is changed forever.

The Moonspinners is a perfect introduction to Mary Stewart. Stewart's novels—whether for adults or teens—are intriguing, romantic, often set in exotic locales, and peopled by intrepid women worth getting to know. Vacationing in Crete, Nicola Ferris discovers the wounded Mark Langley and, against his every objection, insists on helping him investigate a mystery.

Flambards by K. M. Peyton is the first book in a trilogy (followed by **The Edge of the Cloud** and **Flambards in Summer**). Set in England before World War I, it's chock-full of period detail (and includes enough stuff about horses to appeal to readers more into riding than boys). The orphaned Christina is sent to live at Flambards, the home of her uncle and his two sons, Mark and William—one of whom will introduce Christina to the heady experience of first love.

MOVING UP

There are some terrific adult novels that make perfect reading for older young adults, and often, when you ask tenth- and eleventh-graders what they're reading, the answers are not what we would call "young adult" books, but novels that are found on the best-seller lists. Those best sellers are probably fine, but if you're looking for other suggestions, try these:

Stephen King's **The Girl Who Loved Tom Gordon** is just one of this author's books that older teens love. It's less of a "horror" novel than **The Shining**, say, or **Carrie** or **The Stand**, but is just as enthralling. But don't miss my favorite, **Hearts in Atlantis** (the title story was made into a badly miscast movie, but is a marvelous read).

Mark Haddon's **The Curious Incident of the Dog in the Night-Time** is the story of a fifteen-year-old high-functioning autistic who decides to try to discover who killed the dog next door.

Both Chris Bohjalian's **Midwives** and **Amy and Isabelle** by Elizabeth Strout describe the sometimes unraveling relationship between a mother and daughter.

Older boys will be moved by Tim O'Brien's story of Vietnam, **The Things They Carried**, while older girls will be transfixed by Alice Sebold's disturbing and distressing **The Lovely Bones**.

Other novels usually found in the adult sections of libraries and bookstores that teens often love include Jack Schaefer's **Shane**; **The Secret Life of Bees** by Sue Monk Kidd; **A Tree Grows in Brooklyn** by Betty Smith; and Dodie Smith's **I Capture the Castle**.

NOT YOUR PARENTS' COMIC BOOKS

Graphic novels are probably among the most popular genres in the library—if you know where to look for them. One of the problems with finding graphic novels in the library is that many librarians still persist in shelving them in the 700s, with the nonfiction art books, rather than pulling them out in a separate section as bookstores do, to great success. And the vast majority of graphic novels and manga are fiction, in any case.

There's no generally accepted definition of graphic novels, but most people describe them as stories written in a comic-book format, with more serious, frequently complex, sometimes violent storylines (at least for this age group, as well as for adults) than a regular comic book. In the literature about graphic novels, they're often referred to as "comix" to distinguish them from comics like *Superman*, *The Green Hornet*, or even *Archie and Veronica*.

Manga is the Japanese word for comic books, and it's used in English to denote a graphic novel originally published in Japan. Manga seems to have originated in 1814 with an artist named Hokusai, who first produced a book filled with sketches in black and white—he called it "manga," meaning "involuntary drawing."

Most of these popular comix and manga are simply the first volumes in a series, so check out the rest, as well.

In Hiromu Arakawa's **Fullmetal Alchemist**, Edward and Alphose fail miserably in trying to use the powerful forces of alchemy to bring back their mother, and the price for that failure is high: Ed loses an arm and a leg, Al must take form in a suit of armor since he is now bodiless. Their only hope at restoring their original forms is to find the Philosopher's Stone, but they'll have to defeat their enemies to succeed.

Yotsuba&! by Kiyohiko Azuma features an odd little girl who is always getting herself into trouble, refusing to learn manners from her neighbors, the pretty Fuka, and her sisters.

The Kindaichi Case Files: The Opera House Murders Volume 1 by Kanenari Yozaburo is about Kindaichi, to all outward appearances a slacker but with a genius IQ. Because he's related to a famous Japanese detective, he's the obvious person to deduce who's responsible for killing his classmates à la *The Phantom of the Opera*. (Follow this whodunit up with Agatha Christie's **And Then There Were None**.)

An orphan who has endured cruel treatment by his village and classmates, Naruto doesn't know that the hatred comes from their knowledge of his true identity as the cursed nine-tailed fox demon. Hoping to harness his unpredictable power, Naruto is determined to be the best ninja of his school. Can he give up his pranks long enough to endure and master his training? The answer's in **Naruto** by Masashi Kishimoto.

Usagi Yojimbo is a ronin, a samurai without a master, in feudal Japan. As Stan Sakai describes in **Usagi Yojimbo: Ronin**, this fearless and troubled ronin, who happens to be a rabbit, is determined to redeem his shame at having been unable to protect his master. Although this series features talking animals, it's anything but silly.

In **Bone: Out from Boneville** by Jeff Smith, three cousins are ousted from Boneville because of the nasty doings of the aptly named Phoney Bone. Lost on his own in a strange valley with hungry rats, an oddly protective dragon, the beautiful Thorn, and a cow-racing grandma, Fone Bone tries to reunite with his cousins.

Tohru Honda learns a secret about the Sohma family—each of them turns into an animal of the Chinese zodiac when hugged by the opposite sex, in Natsuki Takaya's **Fruits Basket**.

There's a new kid in school and Manta seems to be the only one who knows that Yoh Asakura is a shaman who is trying to gain the powers of the spirit world in his training to become more powerful in Hiroyuki Takei's **Shaman King: A Shaman in Tokyo**.

Only constant drawing and a major crush on Raina, a girl from church camp, keep Craig sane during an often-lonely childhood filled with strict parents in **Blankets**, an intense autobiographical graphic novel by Craig Thompson.

Runaways: Pride and Joy by Brian K. Vaughan is about a group of six teens with special powers, who discover that their seemingly boring parents are supervillains calling themselves The Pride (and basically controlling the world with their evil ways). Is this the secret knowledge (or fear) of every teenager, or what?

Vaughan's also the author of **Y the Last Man: Unmanned**, in which an unknown disease has killed all the men in the world except for the geeky Yorick, who is puzzled as to why he survived and what he should do about his continued existence.

For those who have rewatched every *Buffy the Vampire Slayer* episode and are desperate for more, suggest **Fray** by Joss Whedon, which takes place in a grim future of poverty and flying cars. Melaka Fray learns of her true identity from a strange goat-like creature who trains her to battle vampires; at the same time the ghost of her dead brother haunts her and her disapproving cop sister is always shadowing her criminal movements.

Planetes by Makoto Yukimura is one of the few manga series that stops before it reaches double digits. Strictly science fiction, the plot follows the adventures of the garbage collectors of 2074. The cleanup crew of three—constantly orbiting Earth—include Yuri, who lost his wife to the damage caused by space trash; Fee, who's just looking for a good life and a place to smoke; and Hachimaki, who's saving his money to become a real astronaut.

And don't miss Judd Winick's **Pedro and Me**, the story of a friendship (played out on MTV's *The Real World*) between cartoonist Judd and his HIV-positive roommate, AIDS activist Pedro Zamora.

ONE-WORD WONDERS

Who needs more than a one-word title to describe these winning teen reads?

Although Paul Fisher is no slouch at soccer, his brother Erik is a champion football player—a placekicker on the road to a college scholarship. But is he also a violent sociopath who was responsible for the "accident" that made Paul legally blind? Brotherly love has its limits in Edward Bloor's **Tangerine**. Check out Bloor's **Crusader** too.

In Melissa Lion's **Upstream**, Marty's last year at her Alaska high school is marked by the accidental shooting death of her boyfriend the summer before.

Did you ever wonder what happens after you die? In her first novel for young adults, **Elsewhere**, Gabrielle Zevin has come up with an intriguing possibility. Nearly sixteen-year-old Lizzie is killed in a bicycle accident, and discovers that after you die, you start living your life backwards, until you're ready to return to earth and be born again. One of the side benefits of this engaging and well-written novel is meeting Lucy, an always hungry, frequently crotchety pug. (**Where I Want to Be** by Adele Griffin is a nice companion read for Zevin's novel—it's a novel narrated by two sisters, one of them dead.)

How do you deal with the fact that you were driving the car that killed your brother's girlfriend, Cameron? Anna has to live with those exact consequences in **Wrecked** by E. R. Frank. Frank's other novels, including the painfully honest and true **America** (the story of a little boy lost for more than a decade within the foster care system, and the therapist who helps him learn to live with his past and move comfortably into the future) and **Friction** (about a possibly misunderstood teacher/student relationship), are both award-winning, realistic, often heart-wrenching novels about life during late adolescence.

Donna Jo Napoli's **Zel** retells with a lovely resonance the tale of Rapunzel from three points of view: the adolescent Zel, her overly possessive mother, and Konrad, the prince who falls in love with Zel. Other clever retellings of classic fairy tales by Napoli include **Spinners** (*Rumpelstiltskin*); **Bound** (based on Chinese *Cinderella* tales); **North** (*The Pied Piper of Hamlin*); **The Magic Circle** (*Hansel and Gretel*); **Crazy Jack** (*Jack and the Beanstalk*); and **Beast** (*Beauty and the Beast*).

In **East**, Edith Pattou vividly retells the old fairy tale *East of the Sun, West of the Moon* from the point of view of four characters: a young woman named Rose, her father, her brother, and an evil troll queen who has bewitched a prince by turning him into a bear.

Other "one-word wonders" well worth reading include the humorous **Squashed** by Joan Bauer (a teenager tries to lose twenty pounds as well as grow the largest pumpkin in Iowa); **Celine** by Brock Cole; Peter Dickinson's awfully spooky **Eva**; **Smack** by Melvin Burgess (a riveting look at teenage heroin addiction); Will Hobbs's **Downriver**; Jerry Spinelli's **Crash** and **Stargirl** (which can make even grown-ups cry); **Fade** by Robert Cormier (well written and painful as all his books are); Laura and Tom McNeal's **Crushed**, **Crooked**, and **Zipped**, three tales of the ups and downs of life during high school; Gregory Maguire's **Wicked** (the real story of the Wicked Witch of the West from L. Frank Baum's *The Wizard of Oz*); Pete Hautman's provocative, painful, and sometimes controversial novels, including **Invisible** (which is almost unbearably sad) and **Godless**, winner of the National Book Award; and **Bird** by Angela Johnson.

OUR LOVE IS HERE TO STAY—OR NOT

Teenage romances will never go out of style, and here are some goodies to try:

Sarah Dessen writes what are best described as "old-fashioned teenage books in an updated world." I love them because they remind me of the books I read as a young adult, but at the same time they are totally contemporary, without a hint of the mustiness or dated-ness of the past. As Dessen so charmingly shows in **The Truth About Forever**, when your boyfriend breaks up with you via e-mail, you're stuck in a dull summer job that he arranged for you, and you're still grieving over the death of your father, meeting the crew of Wish, a catering company (including the incredibly handsome Wes), can go far in cheering up a teenage girl. Take a look at **Someone Like You** and **Keeping the Moon**, as well.

Dessen also wrote **Dreamland**, a sensitive and honest book about a girl falling in love with a boy who abuses her. Another excellent book on the same topic is **Fault Line** by Janet Tashjian.

Of course Jessica Darling fell for Marcus Flutie, who's all wrong for her, but she vows to not get burned again in her senior year. But like a moth to a flame . . . or so Megan McCafferty tells it in **Second Helpings**.

When sixteen-year-old Ruby McQueen falls for bad boy Travis Becker, it takes the efforts of a senior citizen's book club, her mother's understanding, and the story of a love that transcended years of separation to help her deal with her feelings, in Deb Caletti's

Honey, Baby, Sweetheart. (Her **Wild Roses** and **The Queen of Everything** are also wonderful.)

Gordon Korman's **Son of the Mob** is a witty updating of Shakespeare's *Romeo and Juliet*, in which the main characters— seventeen-year-old Vince Luca and his girlfriend, Kendra—are not destined to live happily ever after, all because Vince's dad is a mob boss and Kendra's father is the FBI agent assigned to find the goods on Mr. Luca and put him behind bars.

Other novels exploring high school romances include David Levithan's **The Realm of Possibility**; **Boy Girl Boy** by Ron Koertge; and Ellen Wittlinger's **Heart on My Sleeve**, which uses all the tools of modern communication, including e-mails, instant messaging, and—surprise!—actual letters, to explore Chloe and Justin's relationship.

PAGE-TURNING PLEASURES

Sometimes what teen readers want is just what a lot of adult readers are looking for in their pleasure reading—a fast-moving, exciting page-turner, where you just can't wait to find out what happens next, page by page and chapter by chapter. Here are some doozies:

Philip Reeve's **Mortal Engines**, the first in The Hungry City Chronicles, is set far in the future, when cities consume other cities—what Reeve cleverly calls "municipal Darwinism"—and the mayor of London has discovered the weapon that effectively wiped out much of humanity eons before in the "sixty-minute war." It's up to a group of teens, led by an apprentice historian named Tom, to stop him. The action, excitement, and mayhem continue in **Predator's Gold** and **Infernal Devices**.

Matt, the main character in **The House of the Scorpion** (set in an alternate future that frequently looks a lot like today—or at least like the day after tomorrow), is a clone of a powerful drug lord. As Matt starts to realize just what that means for his future, Nancy Farmer offers readers the chance to consider issues of good and evil and what it means to be human.

Danger, excitement, and romance combine to keep the action moving along at a fast clip in Philip Pullman's **The Tin Princess**, which takes place in 1882 in an imaginary kingdom nestled between Germany and Austria.

Eleanor Updale brings the Victorian period to life in her trilogy that begins with **Montmorency: Thief, Liar, Gentleman?**, about a cunning thief who uses a double identity (and the London sewers) to steal from upper-class British families all over the city. The cliff-hanging chapter endings will keep readers turning the pages quickly and immediately going on to the sequels, **Montmorency on the Rocks: Doctor, Aristocrat, Murderer?** and **Montmorency and the Assassins: Master, Criminal, Spy?**

Victoria McKernan's **Shackleton's Stowaway** is a maritime adventure based on the disastrous expedition that trapped Ernest Shackleton and his crew of the *Endurance* in the ice for months. It's told from the (imagined) point of view of a (real) stowaway, eighteen-year-old Pierce Blackborrow.

Other page-turners include **The Road of the Dead** by Kevin Brooks (a dead sister, sinister inhabitants of a small English town, and a brother determined to find who killed his sister, and why); Jackie French Koller's **The Falcon** (which partially takes place in a psychiatric ward); **Mr. Was** by Pete Hautman (time travel); Lois Duncan's **Down a Dark Hall**; and Graham McNamee's heart-pounding **Acceleration**, in which seventeen-year-old Duncan hunts down a serial killer.

PLAY THE GAME

Sometimes the best way to get reluctant teens to read is to give them fast-moving books about whatever their particular interests might be. If it's painting ceramics, you might not be able to find much out there, but if it's sports, you're in luck. Try these:

Sticky, a white foster kid who spends his days playing street basketball, realizes that his talent on the court just might offer him an escape from a dead-end life in **Ball Don't Lie** by Matt de la Peña.

Three not-to-be missed books about boxing include Robert Lipsyte's classic **The Contender**, which takes place in more or less (it was originally published in 1967) contemporary Harlem; **Fighting Ruben Wolfe** by Markus Zusak; and **The Boxer** by Kathleen Karr, about a fifteen-year-old ex-con who tries to make it as a fighter in the last years of the nineteenth century.

Hockey was all that mattered to Nick Taglio, and he was great on the ice. When he doesn't bounce back from his most recent concussion—leading to his doctor forbidding him to play again, maybe permanently—he's forced to contemplate life after hockey, and it doesn't look good, in Pat Hughes's **Open Ice**.

Many of Chris Lynch's best novels can be seen as either sports novels with a coming-of-age subtext, or as coming-of-age novels set against the world of high school sports. Three of my favorites are **Slot Machine**, about an overweight, sports-phobic teen who's sent to a Christian Brothers sports camp to get him ready for high school; **Iceman** (hockey); and **Shadow Boxer**.

Ultimate Sports, a collection of stories edited by Donald R. Gallo, is a solid introduction to some of the leading YA writers around, including Robert Lipsyte, Thomas Dygard, and Chris Crutcher. (A popular novel of Crutcher's is **Whale Talk**, about a talented teen who's always hated organized sports but decides to start a swim team made up of his school's misfits.)

Other sports fiction to try includes **The Perfect Shot** by Elaine Marie Alphin; Carl Deuker's **Painting the Black**; Gloria D. Miklowitz's prescient novel—published in 1989—about the lure and dangers of steroid use, **Anything to Win**; **Hoops** by Walter Dean Myers; **Wrestling Sturbridge** by Rich Wallace; Joyce Sweeney's **Players**; **Bull Catcher** by Alden R. Carter; Marie G. Lee's **Necessary Roughness** (football); Rich Wallace's **Playing Without the Ball**; Randy Powell's **Dean Duffy**; and **Danger Zone** by David Klass.

POEMS AS NOVELS AND
NOVELS AS POEMS

I t might be hard to get many teens to read poetry, but sometimes if the poems have all the hallmarks of their favorite novels— good characters, realistic settings, and energetic plots—voila!, the problem's close to being solved. Try recommending these novels-in-verse:

The hero of Ron Koertge's **Shakespeare Bats Cleanup** is a high school baseball player stuck at home in bed with a bad case of mononucleosis, who discovers that looking at his life through the lens of poetry is a great way to pass the seemingly interminable time until he can play again, if that ever happens.

While this isn't exactly a novel, the poems in Naomi Shihab Nye's **19 Varieties of Gazelle: Poems of the Middle East** are united by their attention to the lives of Arabs and Arab Americans. The collection begins with a poem she wrote after the terrorist destruction of the World Trade Center towers on September 11, 2001. There's also a moving and heartfelt introduction.

Besides its knockout title, **One of Those Hideous Books Where the Mother Dies**, Sonya Sones's novel of the ups and downs of a teenage girl—trying to accept her mother's death, moving across the country to live with her movie-star father (whom she's never even met), losing her first boyfriend to her best friend, and more—is one of those books where the narrator simply comes alive for the reader.

Ellen Hopkins has written two moving novels in verse: **Crank** is the almost terrifying tale of a teenage girl's infatuation with a dangerous drug, and **Burned** is the story of a teenager's search for acceptance and self-understanding after being banished by her abusive father to live with an aunt she doesn't know.

Josie, Aviva, and Nicolette all fall for the same irresistible boy and find that their lives will never quite be the same again, in Tanya Lee Stone's **A Bad Boy Can Be Good for a Girl**.

Ann Turner tackles difficult subjects (in free verse, yet) in **Learning to Swim: A Memoir** (which is really a novel).

Poignant glimpses of seven young people grappling with pregnancy, foster families, abusive parents, arrest, and sexuality form the short collection called **Keesha's House** by Helen Frost. As you read you can almost hear the rhythm of the beat driving the words along the page.

Even reluctant readers and poetry-averse teens will be drawn into Virginia Euwer Wolff's **Make Lemonade** and **True Believer**, the first two of a proposed trilogy. They're written in free verse in the voice of LaVaughn, a teen who wants more than anything a life outside the projects where she lives.

QUEENS OF FANTASY

Without fail, every teenage girl I talked to told me that I had to include Mercedes Lackey's books in *Book Crush* (not that there was any doubt I would: I'm a big fan, too). They couldn't stop raving about Lackey's ability to create a realistic fantasy world, spellbinding plots, and dynamic characters. (In fact Lackey's world, Valdemar, is so well drawn that other fantasy writers have chosen to set their books there as well.) You can read Lackey's novels in an order based on the Valdemarian timeline, or in chronological (publishing) order. Or you can start with my favorite trilogy, composed of **Magic's Pawn**, **Magic's Promise**, and **Magic's Price**, and go on from there. When you finish all the novels, take a look at **The Valdemar Companion: A Guide to Mercedes Lackey's World of Valdemar** by John Helfers et al.

Tamora Pierce almost single-handedly changed the world of teen fantasy from a place devoid of girls (except for princesses) to a world of women warriors. Her books are feminist in outlook, frank in their descriptions of sex and violence, and utterly enthralling. She writes grand stories of adventure, danger, intrigue, and heroic feats. I haven't ever met a female teenage fantasy fan who hasn't adored Pierce's books.

While Pierce has several series, probably her best known is The Song of the Lioness, a quartet of novels featuring Alanna, the archetypal girl warrior. Set in the land of Tortall, a wonderfully conjured mix of myth, magic, and an invented medieval-ish land, Alanna's story begins as she persuades her brother to switch places with her so she can go to the castle of Prince Jonathan as a new page and knight-in-training. Disguising herself as a boy, Alanna begins an epic adventure that will lead to her ascension as the ultimate warrior in the land. The series includes **Alanna: The First Adventure, In the Hand of the Goddess, The Woman Who Rides Like a Man**, and **Lioness Rampant**. These are grand choices for feminists-in-training.

Pierce has written several other beloved series, connected slightly to the Alanna books. **Trickster's Choice** and **Trickster's Queen** tell the saga of Alanna's daughter, Aly, a spymaster. The Protector of the Small quartet includes **First Test, Page, Squire**, and **Lady Knight**, which together tell the story of Keladry of Mindalen, another girl determined to become a knight. The Immortals quartet, **Wild Magic, Wolf-Speaker, The Emperor Mage**, and **The Realms of the Gods**, is the story of Diane, whose magic powers must be developed to help save Tortall.

Her Circle of Magic (**Sandry's Book, Tris's Book, Daja's Book, Briar's Book**, and **The Will of the Empress**) and The Circle Opens (**Magic Steps, Street Magic, Cold Fire**, and **Shatterglass**) series take place in a different world and may work better for younger readers who might not be quite ready to encounter the emerging sexuality that's found in some of the other books.

SHAPE SHIFTERS

Shape shifting, the ability to become another animal at will, offers lots of opportunities for authors to let their imaginations run wild. What happens if you get stuck in that other body? Is the change for good or ill? Can you change to more than one animal or are you more or less exclusive (e.g., are you an avian shape shifter or can you also become a dog at another time)? However writers approach those questions, the possibilities have made shape shifting a relatively small but popular subgenre in the world of fantasy fiction. You won't want to miss these:

Teenage Owl's ability to shift between being human and being an owl becomes ever more complicated when she falls in love with her (human) biology teacher, Mr. Lindstrom, and discovers a runaway teenager stalking Lindstrom's house in Patrice Kindl's **Owl in Love**.

The fact that Tess can change into whatever animal she chooses has always been her deepest held secret, but when she meets Kevin, who also has the ability to switch bodies, she discovers that the two of them are somehow destined to save the world from ultimate destruction—only there will be a huge cost to pay, in **Switchers** by Kate Thompson.

Others I've enjoyed include Margaret Mahy's **The Changeover**; Jennifer Roberson's **Shapechanger's Song**, the first of the Chronicles of the Cheysuli; **Shapeshifter's Quest** by Dena Landon; and **Hawksong** by Amelia Atwater-Rhodes, followed by **Snakecharm**, **Falcondance**, and **Wolfcry**.

SINK YOUR TEETH INTO THESE

Teenager readers have long been fascinated with the allure of the vampire—all that sensual attractiveness plus the ability to live forever make for an unbeatable combination. "Tall, dark, and handsome" is taken to a whole other level, here. Plus, if you add the angst that teen vampires tend to (understandably) suffer from, you've got some winning reads. Readers who enjoy a gothic atmosphere, a troubled romance, and a subtle undercurrent of menace can quench their thirst with these (dare I say) toothsome novels.

One—if not the first—vampire novel written specifically for teens was Annette Curtis Klause's classic, **The Silver Kiss**. While comforting Zoe, who's grieving for her dying mother, Simon, a vampire, enlists her aid in defeating his evil vampire brother, Christopher.

Twilight by Stephenie Meyer introduces the vampire as a tortured individual who knows that he shouldn't love a human girl but cannot stop himself. The trouble begins when Isabella Swan meets the handsome yet mysterious Edward Cullen at her new high school.

While traveling around Europe to a series of psychic fairs with her mother, a witch, teenage Fran (who has some unusual powers of her own) falls for Benedikt, a motorcycle-riding vampire who beseeches her to find a way to lift the curse that has been bedeviling him for centuries, in Katie Maxwell's **Got Fangs?** Great fun.

In **Vampire Kisses** by Ellen Schreiber, Raven grows up watching *Dracula* on late-night television, idolizing author Anne Rice, and hoping she can become a vampire someday, a wish that just may come true when she meets the strange and very handsome Alexander Sterling. **Kissing Coffins** continues Raven's story.

Author Amelia Atwater-Rhodes is often referred to as the Anne Rice for teen readers. Vampires take center stage in her novels **In the Forests of the Night**, the story of a time-traveling teenage vampire, and **Demon in My View**, in which Jessica (who had a bit part in the former book) realizes that vampires are not just subject matter for her past and future books; they actually exist—and one of them is out to get her.

Cynda falls for the wrong vampire entirely in **Look for Me by Moonlight** by Mary Downing Hahn, when she becomes infatuated with the mad, bad, and dangerous-to-know Vincent Morthanos.

M. T. Anderson, in **Thirsty**, strikes a sadder and more somber note, as Chris struggles to remain human against the inevitable forces that are turning him into a vampire.

Other vampire novels too good to miss include **Companions of the Night** by Vivian Vandé Velde; **Sunshine** by Robin McKinley; **Dangerous Girls** and **The Taste of Night** by R. L. Stine; Scott Westerfeld's **Peeps**; Bram Stoker's **Dracula** (well, duh); **Salem's Lot** by Stephen King; **I Am Legend** by Richard Matheson; and **Vampire High** by Douglas Rees. For a more lighthearted story, try

Gil's All Fright Diner by A. Lee Martinez, in which a vampire and a werewolf join forces to defeat some zombies who are determined to destroy Loretta's diner. (A great choice for fans of Douglas Adams and Terry Pratchett.)

SLOWLY UNRAVELING

Some books reveal all to the reader from the very beginning, while others make us work a little harder, slowly offering pieces of a puzzle to reader and characters alike. Sometimes even the ending is left open, so that the reader is forced to make up his or her mind about what happened. In any case it's a magical sort of ride that leaves the reader reveling in the experience long after the book is finished.

When Clare moves with her mother to a small English town in order to help care for the elderly owner of the Ravensmere Estate, she finds life a bit spooky. Everyone around seems to know Clare and is overjoyed at her arrival; add a gorgeous bad boy into the mix, and it's one puzzling place, in Liz Berry's **The China Garden**.

Anna is odd, unlike anyone that the unnamed teenage narrator in **As Simple as Snow** by Gregory Galloway has ever known before. When she disappears—her dress left beside a hole in the ice shortly before Valentine's Day—he tries to make sense of what happened. But will anyone ever know for sure?

Dead Girls Don't Write Letters by Gail Giles sets up this intriguing plot: Sunny instantly knows that the woman at her door who looks a little like her dead sister and knows everything about her dead sister is really someone pretending to be her dead sister, but why?

Shortly after becoming the hero in a bank robbery, Ed receives the ace of diamonds with a mysterious message and sets out with his smelly dog, the Doorman, to decipher the clue, in the somewhat noirish **I Am the Messenger** by Markus Zusak.

Fifteen-year-old Cait looks back on the events of the previous year, when the arrival of a young drifter on her small, seemingly idyllic island off the coast of England set off a series of events that ended in tragedy, in **Lucas** by Kevin Brooks.

Much to his father's displeasure, Eli decides to take a year off after graduating from high school and go to work for Dr. Quincy Wyatt, a molecular biologist, at Wyatt Transgenics, a company exploring the far reaches of genes and gene-splicing. What he discovers there will change the way he looks at the world, and himself, in Nancy Werlin's gripping **Double Helix**.

SMELLS LIKE TEEN NOSTALGIA

Maybe it simply means that I travel in the wrong circles, but I don't have any friends who want to go back and relive their teenage years. Their twenties, maybe. Their thirties, yes. But those years from thirteen to nineteen are too often filled with enough pangs and pains to preclude ever wanting to go through them again.

Contemporary teenage fiction contrasts sharply with most young adult novels written during the late 1940s through the 1960s. The task of coping with the demands of school, the expectations of one's family, and interpersonal relationships was certainly the subject matter of these older titles, but they had a sweeter certainty that life would turn out fine. In more recent books, this isn't always (or even mostly) the case.

Many of these novels have been brought back in print, and some, like Maureen Daly's **Seventeenth Summer**, have never gone out of print. Forgive me for being self-indulgent, but it gave me enormous pleasure just to write the names of these books down and remember the enjoyment they gave me when I read them.

Betty Cavanna's **Going on Sixteen**, **The Boy Next Door**, **Angel on Skis**, **Paintbox Summer**, **Spurs for Suzanna**, **Accent on April**, **A Girl Can Dream**, **Spring Comes Riding**, and all the rest of her early novels really deserve to be reissued, even knowing that they'll be bought for nostalgia's sake, if at all.

In **Green Eyes** by Jean Nielsen, Jan Marie has to deal with a bratty—and much favored—younger brother, a father who's gone for weeks at a time for his work, and a mother she's convinced doesn't like her. She's also the youngest person in her high school graduating class and she has to deal with fierce competition (in the form of a very cute guy) for the editorship of the school paper.

Madeleine L'Engle's books for middle-grade kids are what made (and make) her beloved among young readers, but these days nobody seems to mention her teenage novel, **And Both Were Young**. Maybe it was never much read, even when it was first published. I've never actually met anyone, except for my daughters and me, who even knows about it, which is a real shame because it's a sensitive, finely written coming-of-age novel set in a boarding school in Switzerland.

Rosamond du Jardin's three series of books, one about Tobey Heydon (**Practically Seventeen**; **Boy Trouble**; **Class Ring**; and more); another about Marcy Howard (**Wait for Marcy**; **Marcy Catches Up**; **A Man for Marcy**; **Senior Prom**); and the third about Pam and Penny Howard (**Double Date**; **Double Feature**;

Showboat Summer; and **Double Wedding**) are perfect exemplars of a world long gone, if it ever existed.

The Beany Malone series by Lenora Mattingly Weber (**Meet the Malones**; **Beany Malone**; **Leave It to Beany!**; **Beany and the Beckoning Road**; and all the rest) gave me enormous pleasure when I was a young teen. The ones I reread most often are **Make a Wish for Me** and **Happy Birthday, Dear Beany**. (And I am far from the only woman of a certain age who remembers them fondly—there's an online discussion group for Beany Malone fans: Weber-l@yahoogroups.com.)

I always enjoyed following Anne Emery's heroine Dinny Gordon through her four years of high school, in the very straightforwardly entitled **Dinny Gordon, Freshman**; **Dinny Gordon, Sophomore**; **Dinny Gordon, Junior**; and **Dinny Gordon, Senior**, but I also found her stand-alone novels like **Tradition** (one of the only—maybe *the* only—teenage novel I know of from the late 1940s that deals with the issue of prejudice against Japanese Americans), and **Married on Wednesday** (teen marriage) to be great fun.

In **Mr. and Mrs. Bo Jo Jones**, Ann Head takes on the subjects of teen pregnancy and marriage, both less prevalent then—in the 1960s when the book first came out—than today.

I know teens are still reading Judy Blume's **Forever**, one of the first teen books to feature a sexually active heroine, and I suspect that it's still giving some parents fits, more than thirty years after it was originally published.

The plots of Gretchen Sprague's **A Question of Harmony** and **White in the Moon** combine classical music and racial prejudice—

and believe me, it works well in these novels, which I often fear nobody but me knows about. I hope that's not true.

I recently met a teenage girl who said Eloise Jarvis McGraw's **Greensleeves** was her favorite book of all time. It's high on my list, too. Very much aimed at the over-sixteen crowd, it takes an unusual summer of pretending to be someone else to make it possible for Shannon Lightley to figure out who she is.

Mary Stolz's terrific stream-of-consciousness novels deal with all sorts of issues that will still resonate with teens today, assuming, of course, that they don't balk at the writing style (many will). Some of my favorites are **In a Mirror**; **Ready or Not**; **Rosemary**; **Because of Madeline**; **To Tell Your Love**; and **The Day and the Way We Met**. If you do decide to introduce a teen reader to Stolz's work, be sure to find books that were published in the 1950s and 1960s—not the later titles, which aren't nearly as good.

TAM LIN

The story of Tam Lin began as a Scottish ballad about a brave maiden named Janet who saves her human lover (who's been kidnapped by fairies) from being sacrificed on Halloween night. That's the bare bones of the tale, but some talented contemporary writers have taken the original ballad (thrilling to read on its own, actually) and adopted and adapted it, producing some impossibly romantic tales that are just perfect for dreamy teenage girls who believe in true love (and what teenage girl doesn't?).

Begin with my absolute favorite, Pamela Dean's **Tam Lin**, which takes place at a college in the Midwest in the 1970s—how Dean winkles the magic elements into what is basically a contemporary novel about relationships is remarkably effective. (It's part of The Fairy Tale Library created by Terri Windling, a series of contemporary novels that retell classic stories; another in the series is Jane Yolen's **Briar Rose**.) There's an excellent chance that readers who enjoy Dean's **Tam Lin** are also likely to adore her **Juniper, Gentian, and Rosemary**, also a magical realist retelling of a Scottish folk tale.

Fire and Hemlock by Diana Wynne Jones, another novel set in the late twentieth century, is a genuinely thrilling story of a young woman whose life gets caught between two sets of very different memories, where the magic and the mundane intertwine and pull her in different directions, although it all seems to have something to do with a cellist named Thomas Lynn.

Elizabeth Marie Pope's **The Perilous Gard** takes place in 1588 during the reign of Queen Mary of England, and the heroine, Kate Sutton, one of Mary's half-sister Elizabeth's ladies-in-waiting, is banished to the Gard, where she finds herself kidnapped by the fairy folk and forced to find a way to save her true (and mortal) love, Christopher.

Janet McNaughton's **An Earthly Knight** is set in twelfth-century Scotland; this story of a love that survives in the face of increasingly difficult tests is romantic enough to satisfy the most demanding teen reader.

Patricia A. McKillip's **Winter Rose** introduces teenage Rois Melior and her older sister, Laurel, who both fall in love with the mysterious Corbet Lynn. Corbet has returned to his ancestral home (now a ruin) in their small town, despite the curse laid upon the family by his vengeful grandfather. How Rois gradually realizes what's going on and ultimately saves Corbet (here's where the Tam

Lin part enters the plot) involves both sacrifice and an understanding of what love is.

There are two illustrated children's books about Tam Lin and the young woman who loved him, and maybe once teen readers are caught up in the magic of the story they'll want to take a look at the versions by Jane Yolen and Charles Mikolaycak, and Susan Cooper and Warwick Hutton, both entitiled, simply, **Tam Lin**.

THIS IS MY LIFE

Sometimes the best young adult novels are those written in the first person, novels in which the narrator comes across as a real person, the emotions are convincing, and the situations are familiar to everyone who's living through, or has lived through, adolescence. The classic novel here is, of course, J. D. Salinger's **The Catcher in the Rye**.

In **Very Far Away from Anywhere Else** by Ursula K. Le Guin, teenage Owen describes his attraction to his classmate Natalie and his confusion over balancing his own desires for his future with what his parents want for him.

Teenage Toby Malone's prematurely gray hair is probably caused by his worry over his older brother Jake's increasing use of illegal drugs; he's finding that despite how much he wants to help Jake, he's powerless to do so, in Patricia McCormick's **My Brother's Keeper**.

In **The First Part Last** by Angela Johnson, Bobby finds that life as a teenage father with full responsibility for his newborn daughter is far different from the old days when school, basketball, and hip-hop took up all his time—but the hardest part is deciding what's best for baby Feather.

A complement to Johnson's book is Margaret Bechard's **Hanging on to Max**, another tale of a teen father and the difficult—impossible, really—choices he faces when he thinks about his son's future.

Laurie Halse Anderson went on to write some other outstanding novels for young adults, including **Catalyst** and **Prom**, but her first, **Speak**, remains one of her very best. It's the realism of Melinda Sordino's voice that will resonate with teen readers, as she suffers through her first year of high school not just because of the normal sort of teen angst, but because something awful happened at an end-of-the-summer party, and Melinda is unable to talk about it, even to defend herself to the girls with whom she used to be close friends. (Anderson has also written picture books and a slew of books for middle readers.)

Another novel in which a teenage girl has trouble articulating what's going on in her life is Patricia McCormick's **Cut**, in which Callie, who's in a residential treatment facility called Sea Pines (although the girls there call it Sick Minds), tries to understand why she cuts herself. The cuts are never deep enough to kill herself, but the pain of cutting herself dispels—for a brief moment, anyway—the greater pain of life.

What if your mother dragged you and your younger brothers and sisters off to a mountaintop to await the end of the world that she and other followers of Reverend Beelson knew would take place on the very day of your birthday? Teenagers Marina and Jed (who comes to Mount Weeupcut with his Believer father) take turns telling the story of what happened during those tumultuous two weeks in Jane Yolen and Bruce Coville's **Armageddon Summer**.

Eleven teenagers from a variety of ethnic groups, genders, and economic levels tell their own stories—in remarkably real voices—of the triumphs and tragedies of adolescence in E. R. Frank's **Life Is Funny**.

The laugh-aloud **Alice, I Think** by Susan Juby begins: "I blame it all on *The Hobbit*. That, and my supportive home life. I grew up in one of those loving families that fail to prepare a person for real life." Its sequel, also a hoot, is **Miss Smithers**, in which Alice, most improbably, enters the local teen pageant and—less improbably—starts a zine.

Tending to Grace by Kimberly Newton Fusco tells the story of fourteen-year-old voracious reader Cornelia, who finally comes to terms with her mother's neglect when she goes to live with a great aunt she never knew existed.

Inexcusable by Chris Lynch is a good choice for an adult/teen book discussion—it's about teenage Chris, who's accused by his old friend and longtime crush, Gigi, of date rape.

In Anne Fine's sensitive **Up on Cloud Nine**, Ian tries to make sense of the accident that put his best friend Stol in the hospital . . . only he's got a sneaking suspicion it wasn't really an accident.

Other outstanding "I" books include David Klass's **You Don't Know Me**, the story of a teenage boy trying to cope with the general trauma of adolescence as well as the abuse (both physical and emotional) his mother's boyfriend metes out; Terry Trueman's riveting **Stuck in Neutral**, in which teenage Shawn, who suffers from cerebral palsy, begins to believe that his father is intending to kill him; K. L. Going's **Fat Kid Rules the World**, a marvelous choice for music fans; and **Funny Little Monkey** by Andrew Auseon, about a pair of feuding twins—four-foot-two Arty, who narrates this darkly humorous novel, and his six-foot-tall brother, Kurt.

UP ALL NIGHT

Well, consider yourself warned. The subject matter of these books is often graphic, they're frequently filled with violence, and they're sometimes downright terrifying. Don't hand these books out to kids on a school night, because they're simply not put-downable, and think twice before giving them to impressionistic, overly sensitive readers who might be too scared ever to sleep again. (I myself had to read most of these books at an emotional arms' length, as I was pretty much unwilling to get involved with them.) With those caveats in mind, it's hard to see how you can miss with recommending these to teens.

And all that being said, Neil Gaiman's **Neverwhere** is one of my all-time favorite books. I recommend it often to both teens and adult readers. It's *Alice in Wonderland* for horror fans. Instead of following a rabbit down a rabbit hole, Richard, who works in the financial district in London, rescues a mysterious young woman who's bleeding to death and follows her into London's underworld, a place of magic, evil, and intrigue. Remember, no good deed ever goes unpunished.

Clive Barker's **The Thief of Always**, the story of a bored kid lured into something totally sinister, is one of the creepiest reads around, yet there's nary a drop of blood in sight.

Unbeknownst to them, five sixteen-year-old orphans become subjects in an eerie experiment in mind control in William Sleator's

House of Stairs, originally published in 1974 and still in print. (When I was at my local library checking this out, the man at the circulation desk—who must have been in his late thirties—commented that this had been one of his favorite books as a teenager.)

Kaye, the human-appearing heroine of **Tithe: A Modern Faerie Tale** by Holly Black, is quite possibly being used as a pawn in an all-out war in the faerie world—and who can she turn to for help? Kaye's adventures—graphic, violent, and scary—continue in **Valiant: A Modern Tale of Faerie**.

In **The Wereling: Wounded** by Stephen Cole, Tom (who's the wereling of the title, someone who's half human, half werewolf) encounters the Folans, a rather strange family who have evidently chosen him to be a mate for their daughter, Kate, who's a werewolf. Can Tom (who's developing a hunger for bloody meat) and Kate escape their fates and still remain together? Fans will want to follow Tom and Kate through the next two books—so offer them **Prey** and **Resurrection**, too.

To say that things get messy with her werewolf pack when the sexy Vivian falls for the sensitive and very human Aiden, a "meat-boy," is an understatement—as you'll discover in **Blood and Chocolate** by Annette Curtis Klause.

Other horrific novels include **Fear Nothing** by Dean Koontz (in fact, Koontz, like Stephen King, is phenomenally popular with horror fans of all ages, but I chose this one because it has a particularly nice dog in it); **Witch Child** and **Sorceress** by Celia Rees (witches in the New World, i.e., Puritan New England); Lois Duncan's **Down a Dark Hall** and **Killing Mr. Griffin**; the Demonata series by Darren Shan, including **Lord Loss** and **Demon Thief**; **The Haunting of Alaizabel Cray** by Chris Wooding (serial killers, evil beings called "wych-kin," a wych hunter named Thaniel, and the key to the power behind the evil, the possessed Alaizabel Cray); Robert Cormier's **Tenderness** (another serial killer); and **Kit's Wilderness** by David Almond, a superior ghost story.

It should go without saying that fans of this category will not want to miss Stephen King's entire œuvre. I'd begin with **Firestarter** (great adventure) or **Christine** (a car possessed).

UTOPIA—NOT!

I think that dystopian fiction is fun to read. It's always interesting to see how writers imagine the unfortunate, often downright frightening, inevitable end to all the "improvements" we've made in contemporary society. Aldous Huxley's **Brave New World** and Ray Bradbury's **Fahrenheit 451**, two classic dystopian novels, are frequently assigned in high school English classes. But check these out, too:

In Uglytown your life changes on your sixteenth birthday—you turn pretty. And Tally can't wait—no more pug-like face, mismatched eyes, or stringy hair. But when she meets Shay, who has decided to run away rather than have the required surgery, Tally begins to rethink her wish to be beautiful. Scott Westerfeld, author of **Uglies**, continues Tally's story in **Pretties** and **Specials**.

You know those annoying pop-up ads that appear unbidden on your computer? Imagine a world, as M. T. Anderson does in the brilliant and cynical **Feed**, where at birth everyone's mind is hardwired into something closely resembling the Internet. Instant messaging, mind to mind, almost takes the place of talking; and there's certainly no need to actually learn anything, since you can simply retrieve it from a Google-like database in your head. And then imagine what happens when the system crashes....

Teens who enjoyed **Feed** are also sure to like two novels generally found in the adult, rather than the young adult, section of bookstores and libraries: **Jennifer Government** by Max Barry (in which people's surnames are indicative of where they work—so, for example, you know immediately what company employs John Nike) and William Gibson's **Pattern Recognition**, whose heroine, Cayce Pollard is a "cool-hunter"—hired by companies to predict the next big thing.

In Gloria Skurzynski's **Virtual War**, fourteen-year-old Corgan was genetically engineered to have faster reflexes than anyone else on Earth, so that he can play the ultimate virtual reality game that will determine who will win the war his federation is engaged in. But along with Sharla and Brig, two other genetically manipulated children, he must decide where his loyalties lie, and who he can trust.

In the world Garth Nix has created in his fast-paced **Shade's Children**, people only live until they're fourteen, at which time their bodies are used to create killing machines for the evil Overlords. But four children—Ella, Drum, Ninde, and Gold-Eye—band together, and, with the help of the mysterious Shade, are determined to bring the rule of the Overlords to an end.

When fifteen-year-old Daisy leaves New York and goes to live with her mother's sister and her children in England, falling in love with her cousin Edmond and losing him when a world war breaks out are the last things on her mind, but she has to try to survive both, in Meg Rosoff's haunting story of life during and after war, **How I Live Now**.

WHAT'D I DO TO DESERVE THIS BIOGRAPHY?

Biographies for teen readers serve a couple of functions, besides being useful for homework assignments. The first is that the best biographies broaden and deepen a reader's awareness of the complexities of well-known people. The second is that biographies are a good way to help less-than-enthusiastic readers discover the joy of books through reading about someone they admire or are curious about. Here are some excellent choices:

In the well-documented and clearly written **The Life and Death of Adolf Hitler**, James Cross Giblin offers an in-depth (but not too long: only 246 pages) biography of one of the most powerful leaders of the nineteenth century.

When she graduated from high school, Valérie Zenatti, like all Israelis, male and female, spent two years in her country's army, from 1988–1990. As she makes clear in **When I Was a Soldier**, she discovers, as others have before her, that "the army changes everything."

Elizabeth Partridge's love for The Beatles (she had a huge crush on George Harrison, originally) comes through on every page of **John Lennon: All I Want Is the Truth**. From his childhood as the son of divorced parents, to the early days with the Beatles, to his marriage to Yoko Ono and the end of the band, John Lennon's life is all here, in great photographs and insightful text.

Partridge also wrote **This Land Was Made for You and Me: The Life and Songs of Woody Guthrie**. Like the Lennon bio, this is filled with an inviting text that places the great folk singer and writer in the context of his times, accompanied by illustrations ranging from vintage photos to concert playbills to reproductions of posters.

Opening **Our Eleanor: A Scrapbook Look at Eleanor Roosevelt's Remarkable Life** by Candace Fleming, readers will be struck by the intimacy of this peek into Roosevelt's life and times; it's filled with quotations, anecdotes, pictures, and all sorts of relevant information that not only makes for quality report fodder, but is also entertaining to read. Fleming's **Ben Franklin's Almanac: Being a True Account of the Good Gentleman's Life** does the same thing for its subject.

Jan Greenberg and Sandra Jordan teamed up to write two excellent biographies that open up the world of art and artists for teens. Take a look at **Andy Warhol: Prince of Pop** and **Runaway Girl**, about sculptor Louise Bourgeois. They both offer insights into the life and work of these two iconoclastic artists in a way that many adult biographies fail to accomplish.

INDEX

A

Abarat, 205
Abel's Island, 151
Abracadabra Kid: A Writer's Life, 96
Abrahams, Peter, 196
Absent Author, The, 156
Absolute Zero, 165
Abuela, 39
Acceleration, 239
Accent on April, 249
Acquainted with the Night, 208
Across Five Aprils, 190
Across the Nightingale Floor, 205
Addams, Charles, 16
Adèle & Simon, 63
Adler, David A., 47
Adopted Jane, 177
Adventures of Blue Avenger, The, 225
Adventures of Captain Underpants, The, 44
Adventures of the Dish and the Spoon, The, 52
Aesop's Fables, 40
Afanas'ev, Aleksandr, 170
Afterlife, The, 208
Agee, Jon, 41, 45
Aiken, Joan, 88, 146, 148
Airball: My Life in Briefs, 143
Airborn, 87
A is for Alibi, 195
Akhenaten Adventure, The, 135
Alan Mendelsohn, the Boy from Mars, 95
Alanna: The First Adventure, 243
Alarcón, Francisco X., 182
Albert, Susan Witting, 195
Al Capone Does My Shirts, 103
Alexander, Anne, 228
Alexander, Lloyd, 95, 164
Alexander and the Terrible, Horrible, No Good, Very Bad Day, 64
Alia's Mission, 48

Alice, I Think, 255
Alice in Wonderland, 98
Alice's Adventures in Wonderland, 21
Aliens in the Family, 189
Aliki, 69, 118
Allard, Harry, 69
Alligator Arrived with Apples, 72
Alligator Pie, 182
All-of-a-Kind Family, 90
All-of-a-Kind Family Downtown, 90
All-of-a-Kind Family Uptown, 90
All Over But the Shoutin', 206
All Rivers Flow to the Sea, 201
All That Remains, 202
Almond, David, 15, 164, 176, 258
Alphabet Under Construction, 73
Alphin, Elaine Marie, 240
Alvin Ailey, 49
Alvin Webster's Surefire Plan for Success (And How It Failed), 137
Amanda Pig, Schoolgirl, 70
Amazing Maurice and His Educated Rodents, The, 151
Amber Spyglass, The, 165, 195
Amelia Bedelia, 19
America, 234
American Heroes, 128
American Indian Myths and Legends, 170
American Indian Trickster Tales, 80
American Plague, An, 119
American Practical Navigator, The, 101
Am I Blue?: Coming Out from the Silence, 196
Among the Brave, 161
Among the Enemy, 161
Among the Hidden, 161
Amulet of Samarkand, The, 98
Amy and Isabelle, 214, 230
Anansi and the Moss-Covered Rock, 79

Anansi the Spider: A Tale from the Ashanti, 78
Anastasia Krupnik, 157
And Both Were Young, 249
Anderson, Hans Christian, 170–71
Anderson, Laurie Halse, 77, 200, 217, 254
Anderson, M. T., 149, 158, 246, 258
Anderson, Susan Carol, 143
And the Dish Ran Away with the Spoon, 52
And Then There Were None, 231
And Then What Happened, Paul Revere?, 48
And to Think That I Saw It on Mulberry Street, 68
Andy and the Lion, 83
Andy Warhol: Prince of Pop, 261
Angel, Cal, 45
Angela and Diabloa, 135
Angelina Ballerina, 6
Angel on Skis, 249
Angels Ride Bikes and Other Fall Poems, 182
Angus, Thongs and Full-Frontal Snogging, 199
Angus and the Cat, 25
Angus and the Ducks, 25
Angus Lost, 25
Animal Family, The, 94
Animalia, 58
An Innocent Soldier, 107
An Island Like You: Stories of the Barrio, 197
Annabel the Actress Starring in Gorilla My Dreams, 20
Anne Frank, 185–86
Anne of Green Gables, 176
Anne of the Island, 177
Annie on My Mind, 211
Anno, Mitsumasa, 27, 57
Anno's Counting Book, 27
Anno's Italy, 57
Anno's Journey, 57
Anno's Spain, 57
Another Heaven, Another Earth, 189
Anshaw, Carol, 212
Anything to Win, 240
Apple Pie 4th of July, 50

ABOUT THE AUTHOR

Nancy Pearl's first job out of library school was as a children's librarian, and since then she has worked as a librarian and bookseller in Detroit, Tulsa, and Seattle. In 1998, she developed the program "If All of Seattle Read the Same Book," which has been replicated in communities around the globe. The former Executive Director of the Washington Center for the Book, Pearl celebrates the written word by speaking at bookstores, community groups, and libraries across the country. She is a regular commentator about books on National Public Radio's "Morning Edition" and NPR affiliate stations KUOW in Seattle and KWGS in Tulsa, and is the model for the Librarian Action Figure. She is the author of *Book Lust* and *More Book Lust*.

In 2004, Pearl became the 50th winner of the Women's National Book Association Award for her extraordinary contribution to the world of books. In the moment when Pearl find herself without a book, she is an avid bicyclist and happy grandmother of two. She lives in Seattle with her husband Joe.